# ASIA & EUROPE
*Beyond Competing Regionalism*

## ORGANISATION FOR ECOMOMIC CO-OPERATION
## AND DEVELOPMENT

Pursuant to Article 1 of the Convention signed in Paris on 14th December 1960, and which came into force on 30th September 1961, the Organisation for Economic Co-operation and Development (OECD) shall promote policies designed:

- to achieve the highest sustainable economic growth and employment and a rising standard of living in Member countries, while maintaining financial stability, and thus to contribute to the development of the world economy;
- to contribute to sound economic expansion in Member as well as non-member countries in the process of economic development; and
- to contribute to the expansion of world trade on a multilateral, non-discriminatory basis in accordance with international obligations.

The original Member countries of the OECD are Austria, Belgium, Canada, Denmark, France, Germany, Greece, Iceland, Ireland, Italy, Luxembourg, the Netherlands, Norway, Portugal, Spain, Sweden, Switzerland, Turkey, the United Kingdom and the United States. The following countries became Members subsequently through accession at the dates indicated hereafter: Japan (28th April 1964), Finland (28th January 1969), Australia (7th June 1971), New Zealand (29th May 1973), Mexico (18th May 1994), the Czech Republic (21st December 1995), Hungary (7th May 1996), Poland (22nd November 1996) and the Republic of Korea (12th December 1996). The Commission of the European Communities takes part in the work of the OECD (Article 13 of the OECD Convention).

*The Development Centre of the Organisation for Economic Co-operation and Development was established by decision of the OECD Council on 23rd October 1962 and comprises twenty-three Member countries of the OECD: Austria, Belgium, Canada, the Czech Republic, Denmark, Finland, France, Germany, Greece, Iceland, Ireland, Italy, Japan, Korea, Luxembourg, Mexico, the Netherlands, Norway, Poland, Portugal, Spain, Sweden and Switzerland, as well as Argentina and Brazil from March 1994. The Commission of the European Communities also takes part in the Centre's Advisory Board.*

*The purpose of the Centre is to bring together the knowledge and experience available in Member countries of both economic development and the formulation and execution of general economic policies; to adapt such knowledge and experience to the actual needs of countries or regions in the process of development and to put the results at the disposal of the countries by appropriate means. The Centre has a special and autonomous position within the OECD which enables it to enjoy scientific independence in the execution of its task. Nevertheless, the Centre can draw upon the experience and knowledge available in the OECD in the development field.*

 THE OPINIONS EXPRESSED AND ARGUMENTS EMPLOYED IN THIS PUBLICATION ARE THE SOLE RESPONSIBILITY OF THE AUTHORS AND DO NOT NECESSARILY REFLECT THOSE OF THE OECD OR OF THE GOVERNMENTS OF ITS MEMBER COUNTRIES.

\*
\* \*

# Asia & Europe
## *Beyond Competing Regionalism*

Edited by

Kiichiro Fukasaku,
Fukunari Kimura *and*
Shujiro Urata

2 4 6 8 10 9 7 5 3 1

*First published 1998 in Great Britain by*
SUSSEX ACADEMIC PRESS
Box 2950
Brighton BN2 5SP

*and in the United States of America by*
SUSSEX ACADEMIC PRESS
c/o International Specialized Book Services, Inc.
5804 N.E. Hassalo St.
Portland, Oregon 97213-3644

*British Library Cataloguing in Publication Data*
A CIP catalogue record for this book is available from the British Library.

*Library of Congress Cataloging-in-Publication Data*
Asia & Europe : beyond competing regionalism / edited by Kiichiro Fukasaku,
Fukunari Kimura, and Shujiro Urata.
p. cm.
"Japan–Europe Symposium 1996"—Pref.
Includes bibliographical references and index.
ISBN 1–898723–99–0 (hc : alk. paper). —ISBN 1–898723–00–1 (pb : alk. paper)
1. Asia—Commercial policy. 2. Europe—Commercial policy.
3. Asia—Foreign economic relations Europe. 4. Europe—Foreign economic
relations Asia. 5. Asia—Economic integration. 6. Europe—Economic integration.
I. Fukasaku, Kiichiro. II. Kimura, Fukunari. III. Urata, Shujiro, 1950– .
IV. Japan–Europe Symposium 1996 (1996 : Paris)
HF1583.A8 1998
337.405—dc21 97–43950
CIP

Typeset by G&G Editorial, Brighton
Printed by Biddles Ltd, Guildford and King's Lynn
This book is printed on acid-free paper

# Contents

# *Preface*

Regionalism in trade policy has been rising in both Asia and Europe during the 1990s. In Asia this is a relatively new phenomenon, reflecting in part the reaction of Asian countries to rising regionalism elsewhere, particularly in OECD countries. Asian regionalism is still at an early stage and limited in terms of both scope and institution building. Yet, it poses an important question by advocating its own approach to trade and investment liberalization based on the notion of 'open regionalism'. Meanwhile, European regionalism has been getting 'deeper and wider' with its supra-national institutions evolving rapidly over the past decade. At the centre of this evolution lies the European Union whose trade policy sees regionalism as a vehicle for establishing deeper economic integration with different groupings of developing countries. As far as its relationship with Asia is concerned, there is no suggestion of taking a specific trade policy option. In its policy paper entitled "Towards a New Asia Strategy" published in July 1994, the European Commission has made it clear that the principal actor of this strategy is the private sector, and the Union's role is to pursue market-opening for both goods and services and to overcome obstacles to European trade and investment by encouraging a favourable regulatory environment for business in Asia.

The development of Asia–European economic relations during the past decade has been largely market-driven, and it is the strategies of Japanese, other Asian and European firms that count most in shaping trade and investment links between the two regions. The papers included in this book suggest that regionalism in Asia and Europe indeed takes distinctive features but that firms are adjusting to it from the global business perspective. In light of the modality for opening markets, the experience of European services industries, such as airline, banking and telecommunication services, provides useful lessons for Asian countries, as they are heading for deeper economic integration in the coming years. Asian countries will have to keep up the momentum of trade and investment liberalization at both regional *and* multilateral levels, if they are to continue to enjoy dynamic growth in the next century.

The *Japan–Europe Symposium 1996* aimed to bring together leading academic and international experts to discuss prominent policy issues related to present Asia–European economic relationships that are changing rapidly in the age of globalization. The first initiative to organize this international meeting came from Keio University in Japan with the generous support of the Japan Foundation in the hope that such an undertaking would help to enhance the mutual understanding of the allegedly weakest link in the Asia–Europe–North America Triad. The Symposium indeed has a wider scope than its name might suggest. It is our hope that this undertaking will generate a great deal of interest and support among policy-makers, business leaders and academic experts in both Asia and Europe.

*Jean Bonvin*                     *Yoko Sazanami*
President                          Professor of Economics
OECD Development Centre            Keio University
Paris                              Tokyo

October 1997

# Acknowledgements

---

This book contains contributions from participants in the *Japan–Europe Symposium 1996* held in Paris on 7–8 October 1996. The Symposium, entitled 'Beyond Regionalism: Asian and European Multinationals in a Globalising Economy', was jointly organized by Keio University in Tokyo and the OECD Development Centre in Paris.

The organizers of this symposium are most grateful to the Japan Foundation and the Paris Office of the Export-Import Bank of Japan for their generous financial support. We owe a huge debt to Professor Yoko Sazanami of Keio University, and Mr. Jean Bonvin, the President of the OECD Development Centre, for their encouragement and kind co-operation. Without their support, this undertaking would not have materialized.

We also take this opportunity to extend our thanks to Ms. Sandra Lloyd, Ms. Mayrose Tucci and Mr. Colm Foy for their able assistance in organizing the symposium and preparing the publication.

*This book is dedicated to*

Professor Yoko Sazanami of Keio University for her long distinguished career as both a teacher and a researcher during which she has given us much intellectual stimulation and continual personal encouragement.

A publication grant from the Keio Economic Society is gratefully acknowledged.

# Participants

| | |
|---|---|
| Luca BARBARITO* | Instituto Universitario Lingue Moderne, Milan |
| Richard BLACKHURST | World Trade Organization |
| Jean BONVIN | OECD Development Centre |
| Vincent CABLE | Shell International |
| CHIA Siow Yue* | Institute of Southeast Asian Studies, Singapore |
| Suthiphand CHIRATHIVAT | Chulalongkorn University |
| Kiichiro FUKASAKU* | OECD Development Centre |
| Ulrich HIEMENZ | OECD Development Centre |
| Fukunari KIMURA* | Keio University |
| Rolf J. LANGHAMMER | Kiel Institute of World Economics |
| David MARTINEAU* | OECD Development Centre |
| Luiz R. de MELLO, Jr. | University of Kent |
| Patrick A. MESSERLIN* | Paris Institute of Political Studies |
| Jean-Louis MUCCHIELLI | University of Paris 1 – Sorbonne |
| Tadihiko NAKAGAWA | Export-Import Bank of Japan |
| Robert F. OWEN | University of Nantes |
| Jacques PELKMANS | European Institute for Asian Studies, Belgium |
| Peter A. PETRI | Brandeis University, USA |
| Frederique SACHWALD | French Institute of International Relations (IFRI) |
| Philippe SAUCIER | University of Orléans |
| Yoko SAZANAMI | Keio University |
| Leo SLEUWAEGEN* | Catholic University, Louvain |
| SUNG Yun-wing* | The Chinese University of Hong Kong |
| Dominique TURQ | McKinsey & Co. Ltd., Belgium |
| Shujiro URATA* | Waseda University |
| Hideki YAMAWAKI* | University of California, Los Angeles |
| Soogil YOUNG | The Korea Transport Institute |

* Contributed a chapter to this volume; attributions are as at the date of the symposium.

# Abbreviations and Acronyms

| | |
|---|---|
| ADB | Asian Development Bank |
| AFTA | ASEAN Free Trade Area |
| AIA | ASEAN Investment Area |
| AIC | ASEAN Industrial Complementation Scheme |
| AICO | ASEAN Industrial Co-operation |
| AIJV | ASEAN Industrial Joint Venture Scheme |
| AIP | ASEAN Industrial Projects |
| APEC | Asia-Pacific Economic Co-operation |
| ASEAN | Association of Southeast Asian Nations |
| ASEM | Asia-Europe Summit Meeting |
| CEA | Chinese Economic Area |
| CEPT | Common Effective Preferential Tariff Scheme |
| CER | Australia-New Zealand Closer Economic Relations Trade Agreement |
| CPI | Consumer Price Index |
| DOT | Direction of Trade Statistics (IMF) |
| EAEC | East Asian Economic Caucus |
| ECAFE | Economic Commission for the Far East (United Nations) |
| ESCAP | Economic and Social Commission for Asia Pacific (United Nations) |
| EC | European Community |
| ECJ | European Court of Justice |
| ECU | European Currency Unit |
| EU | European Union |
| FAJF | Foreign Affiliates of Japanese Firms |
| FDI | Foreign Direct Investment |
| FTA | Free Trade Area |
| GATS | General Agreement on Trade in Services |
| GATT | General Agreement on Tariffs and Trade |
| GDP/GNP | Gross Domestic/National Product |
| GFCF | Gross Fixed Capital Formation |
| GMS | Greater Mekong Subregion |

GSC         Greater South China
GSP         Generalized System of Preferences
HIBOR       Hong Kong Interbank Offered Rate
IFS         International Financial Statistics (IMF)
IMF         International Monetary Fund
JAFF        Japanese Affiliates of Foreign Firms
M&A         Mergers & Acquisitions
MFA         Multifibre Arrangement (formally, Arrangement
            Regarding International Trade in Textiles)
MFN         Most Favoured Nation
MITI        Ministry of International Trade and Industry
MNEs/
MNCs        Multinational Enterprises/Corporations
NAFTA       North American Free Trade Agreement
NEER/
REER        Nominal/Real Effective Exchange Rates
NIEs        Newly Industrializing Economies
OECD        Organisation for Economic Co-operation and
            Development
R&D         Research & Development
RIAs        Regional Integration Agreements
ROW         The Rest of the World
SEZs        Special Economic Zones
SIBOR       Singapore Interbank Rate
SIJORI      Singapore-Johor-Riau Growth Triangle
SMP         Single Market Programme
TNCs        Transnational Corporations
UNCTAD      United Nations Conference for Trade and Development
VERs        Voluntary Export Restraints
WTO         World Trade Organization

# 1

# *Introduction and Overview*

## Kiichiro Fukasaku and Shujiro Urata

The *Japan–Europe Symposium 1996* was organized against the background of new developments during the 1990s in international economic relations, and particularly between Asia and Europe. The world economy was characterized in the mid-1990s by rising regionalism in both OECD and non-OECD areas. Deeper and wider integration in the EU and the formation of NAFTA appear to have inspired regionalism elsewhere. According to the WTO (1995), there were 33 new regional integration agreements (RIAs) notified to the GATT between 1990 and 1994, of which 25 involved Central and East European countries. The appeal of regionalism remains unabated in spite of the successful conclusion of the Uruguay Round trade negotiations and the creation of the WTO. Asia is no exception to that. Arguably, many Asian economies are beginning to embrace regionalism – or what they call 'open regionalism' – as a vehicle to promote trade and investment flows in the region. The move by the ASEAN member countries to establish a free trade area in most products by 2003 is a case in point.[1] Similarly, the APEC initiatives to create "free and open trade and investment" in its region by 2010 for developed members and ten years later for developing ones can be seen as a step towards deeper integration in Asia and the Pacific. Many more RIAs are in place or under preparation in both Europe and Asia.[2]

The main theme of the *Japan–Europe Symposium 1996* was to address the question of how regionalism in Asia and Europe may have affected the global business operations and strategies of Asian and European firms. Is there any convergence of Asian and European approaches to regionalism? Will increased intra-regional dependency lead East Asian economies to create European-type regional institutions? What are the roles of foreign direct investment in the deepening of economic integration in Asia? How are European and non-European multinationals responding to deeper integration in Europe? What role does competition policy play in European economic integration? These are some of main questions we addressed at the Symposium.

Despite the seemingly negative influence of 'distance factors' between the two regions, trade relations between Asia and Europe have become much closer towards the end of the 1990s than they were some ten years ago. Since the beginning of the 1980s the value of Asia-European trade has more than tripled; it reached $350 billion in 1994 and surpassed the value of transatlantic trade ($276 billion).[3] European firms have been taking advantage of trade opportunities created by fast-growing Asian developing economies. Meanwhile, several Asian developing economies have established themselves as major suppliers of manufactured goods in the European market. In 1993 nine out of the ten largest developing exporters (excluding oil exporters) to the EU market were from Asia, despite the fact that these Asian developing economies were – and still are – placed at the bottom of the EU's pyramid of trade preferences.[4] Moreover, the economic recoveries of Central and Eastern Europe will further facilitate trade with and investment from Asia.

European firms' direct investments in Asia have been lagging behind their main competitors from North America and Japan. It has been argued that European firms tend to rely more on direct exports than on direct investment as a means of establishing their own corporate networks in Asia.[5] The transaction costs of European firms investing in Asia may differ considerably across both home and host countries. A relatively high share of British investors in Asia may reflect its closer business and historical relations with Asian countries, which may have made transaction costs lower than for other European investors. Regionalism and its implications for corporate behaviour pose very complex questions which deserve further investigation in the context of present Asia-European economic relationships.[6]

## Asian Regionalism vs. European Regionalism

In comparing Asian and European attitudes towards regionalism, Shujiro Urata (chapter 2) argues that Asian countries are shying away from the (over-)institutionalization of regionalism. ASEAN is the only regional institution in East Asia which provides its member countries with preferential treatment in the form of a free trade area. He stresses, however, that the launching of the ASEAN Free Trade Area (AFTA) was precipitated by the formation of APEC (1989), since ASEAN countries were concerned that the role and standing of ASEAN as a regional institution might be undermined by the creation of APEC, a larger forum involving the United States, Japan and China. In addition, the economic impact of AFTA by itself would be very limited.

Perhaps most interesting from a comparative perspective of regionalism is the notion of *open regionalism* that may characterize the so-called 'Asian way' of thinking; this notion indeed has become a guiding principle of trade policy initiatives under the APEC following the Bogor Declaration by APEC Leaders in November 1994. Open regionalism may be best described as 'concerted voluntarism' as the modality of trade liberalization as opposed to 'reciprocity', which is what regionalism – free trade areas and customs unions – traditionally implies. It is important to recall that this term open regionalism was coined in the late 1980s at a time when there were tremendous uncertainties over the outcome of the Uruguay Round multilateral trade negotiations and Asian policy-makers were fearful that rising regionalism on the part of Europe and North America might lead to a *de facto* Asian trading bloc by default. Urata notes that 'peer pressure', rather than reciprocal negotiation, is believed to promote trade liberalization in Asia and the Pacific, and in theory the commitment to non-discrimination prevents APEC from taking a traditional FTA option based on reciprocity, though this may be difficult to accept for some members of APEC. Open regionalism is thus a novel approach to regional trade liberalization whose success depends crucially on the member countries' voluntarism.

Seen from this perspective, European regionalism is taking a quite different course. Since the early 1980s the European Union has changed drastically its own strategy of regional integration by 'deepening' and 'widening' its integration, while at the same time seeking a rapprochement with its neighbouring countries.[7] On the track record of European economic integration, Vincent Cable argued at the Symposium: 'the idea of *Fortress Europe* is as dead as any idea can be, and for the corporate sector deeper and wider integration in Europe is really part of the globalization process rather than something that is antagonistic towards it'. Nothing is more dramatic in this respect than the recent development of the European telecommunications industry. Several waves of deregulation, liberalization and privatization have been sweeping the European market in telecommunications services, which was once dominated by national giant monopolies. Deeper integration in telecommunications services as part of the EU's Single Market Programme (SMP) is indeed helping European firms to restructure their business operations with a view to facing squarely the *global* competition unleashed by rapid changes in telecommunications and information technologies, privatization and regulatory reforms, in addition to multilateral trade liberalization in services underway at the WTO. Recent episodes of transatlantic corporate alliances and takeover attempts between European and US multinationals in tele-communications services are indicative of the fact that European firms are becoming global in their business strategies.

Another important point Cable stressed at the Symposium is that most multinationals are still 'home-country' biased in terms of the location of their assets, the composition of senior managers and above all, corporate culture, though their production, marketing and procurement activities are becoming global. European regionalism has not yet given birth to 'truly European' multinationals, with some exceptions, such as Royal Dutch Shell, Unilever and Swedish-Swiss ABB as well as those firms that are basically of an inter-governmental character (e.g., Airbus and the Eurofighter). But many non-European multinationals operating in Europe, most of which originate from the United States and Japan, have been able to establish pan-European business networks, taking advantage of the launching of the SMP that set in motion the process of market deregulation and liberalization in Europe. The 15 years' history of Canon Europa N.V. set up in Amsterdam in 1982 – Canon's European headquarters – is a case in point.[8] Thus, for non-European multinationals European economic integration has provided a strong incentive to increase their market presence through direct investments.[9]

## FDI and Economic Integration in East Asia

In light of the increasing importance of FDI in international economic activities in East Asia, Chia Siow Yue (chapter 3) and Sung Yun-wing (chapter 4), respectively, examine FDI in ASEAN and in the Chinese Economic Area (CEA), comprised of China, Chinese Taipei, and Hong Kong (China).

In her analysis of FDI in ASEAN, Chia Siow Yue attributes a substantial inflow of FDI to ASEAN to liberalization of trade and FDI policies and an abundance of qualified labour. However, she observes that ASEAN has been challenged by new emerging players, notably China. As major sources of FDI flows in the ASEAN region shifted from North America and Europe to Japan and the NIEs, the increase of intra-East Asian investment has contributed to the formation of integrated production networks within ASEAN, centred around Japanese and Chinese business concerns. Under these integrated production networks, regional division of labour incorporating the so-called 'flying wild geese pattern' has been developed.

Recognizing the importance of FDI for promoting the region's economic growth, ASEAN has adopted several measures collectively to enhance its attractiveness as a host to FDI. Three growth triangles, which are transnational investment zones with minimal border restrictions to exploit economic complementarity and pooled resources, have been established. The ASEAN Free Trade Area (AFTA) and the ASEAN Investment Area (AIA) have been set up to provide a free and attractive market for foreign investors. The ASEAN Industrial Co-operation (AICO), a new industrial co-operation scheme, was launched not only to attract FDI flows but also to increase intra-ASEAN direct investment. These institutional measures undoubtedly contribute to the expansion of FDI, in particular intra-regional FDI. However, Chia argues that there are other measures that should be implemented to promote FDI inflows. She emphasizes that ASEAN countries individually and collectively will need to improve supply-side conditions, that is, cost competitiveness and productivity, particularly improvements in infrastructure and human resources. Furthermore, noting that ASEAN has not yet produced many large multinationals, Chia asserts that ASEAN needs to nurture home-grown multinationals to enable ASEAN companies to join the mainstream of globalization. In so doing, she proposes, one effective way is to encourage partnerships, joint ventures, strategic alliances and business networking between indigenous ASEAN enterprises and the 'overseas Chinese' enterprises, and between ASEAN and non-ASEAN enterprises.

Turning to the case of the Chinese Economic Area (CEA), Sung Yun-wing observes the deepening of economic integration among the three Chinese economies through the expansion of FDI and trade. The volume of FDI and trade involving the CEA has come to occupy a large share of world FDI and trade flows. He identifies several factors that have promoted FDI and trade in the CEA. First, geographical and cultural proximity are a basic underlying factor. Second, liberalization of FDI and trade policies in China and Chinese Taipei has made a significant contribution to the expansion of FDI and trade flows, while Hong Kong (China) has played a pivotal role as a 'middleman' facilitating the integration of the CEA. He points out that economic integration of the CEA has been promoted without any institutional arrangements, although China has provided favourable treatment to direct investments from Chinese Taipei and Hong Kong (China). Despite uncertainties over the political and economic problems the CEA is facing internally and externally, Sung concludes that the economic fundamentals of this sub-region are strong and that the entry of China and Chinese Taipei into the WTO would further promote the economic integration of the CEA. In this regard, membership of APEC can be seen at best as an imperfect substitute for that of the WTO.

The pattern of Asian economic integration is analysed in depth by Fukunari Kimura (chapter 5) with a focus on the activities of Japanese firms in Asia. His detailed analysis, based on firm survey data, reveals that Japanese firms rely more on direct exports from Japan than sales or production by their affiliates when selling their products in Asia, while they tend to rely more on sales or production by their affiliates when selling to the rest of the world. Based on this finding of limited reliance on foreign affiliates in overseas sales by Japanese firms in Asia, Kimura argues that Asian economic integration is still at an early stage, compared with the pattern of economic integration among OECD countries, and despite recent efforts to liberalize the investment regime, restrictive government policies towards FDI in a number of host countries remain obstacles to the better use of resources. Against the overall pattern of Japanese firms' activities in Asia with their greater reliance on direct exports, he also observes that the affiliates in Hong Kong and Singapore exhibit exceptional patterns in that they play an important role in marketing Japanese products to the world. This observation coincides with those made by Chia Siow Yue on Singapore and Sung Yun-wing on Hong Kong, respectively.

Chapter 6, by Kiichiro Fukasaku and David Martineau, turns attention to the monetary aspects of regional economic integration in East Asia, against the backdrop of increased economic interdependence within the region through intensified FDI and trade flows. More specifically, they examine the following questions: will East Asia need a regional institution or mechanism for monetary policy co-operation as it moves towards deeper economic integration?; what are the economic conditions for effective monetary policy co-operation?; and does East Asia meet such conditions?

Noting that regional monetary co-operation is useful and effective if the economies in the region share a common policy objective, Fukasaku and Martineau argue that regional monetary co-operation in East Asia has achieved this aim, since a common policy objective of maintaining price stability is now a priority in most East Asian economies. They point to the greater presence of financial interdependence among East Asian economies since the late 1980s. Statistical evidence reported in this chapter suggests that money markets in East Asia are highly integrated both regionally and internationally, mainly as a result of financial liberalization during the 1980s and 1990s. Based on their findings of growing interdependence in monetary markets, Fukasaku and Martineau argue that closer co-operation among central banks of the region would be desirable as their economies become more deeply integrated in the coming years, particularly in the case of ASEAN countries. The policy relevance of their analysis has been testified to by currency instability in mid-1997 in several ASEAN countries.

## European Economic Integration and Competition Policy

The EU's Single Market Programme (SMP) is expected to have various impacts on European industries as well as the investment behaviour of non-European multinationals. One potential impact is the changing location of industries in Europe. Hideki Yamawaki, Luca Barbarito and Jean-Marc Thiran (chapter 7) examine the locational decision of US and Japanese firms in the EU by covering 3,528 US affiliates and 450 Japanese affiliates across 45 regions and 12 member states of the EU in the early 1990s. Their econometric analyses find that both US and Japanese multinationals tend to choose the United Kingdom as the prime location for their direct investments, but after the UK their locational choices differ. For US multinationals, the Netherlands, Belgium, and Ireland are popular sites, while for their Japanese counterparts, Germany and France are more attractive. The authors attribute these differences in location to differences in entry modes and industry composition. They argue that US multinationals with a strong preference for acquisitions of local firms over 'greenfield' investments tend to avoid those countries, such as Germany and France, in which the institutional environment concerning corporate governance makes acquisition difficult. With regard to industry composition, which is a factor responsible for the difference in FDI locations between US and Japanese multinationals, they find that their locational patterns become similar, once industry composition is controlled.

In the case of R&D-intensive industries, such as office and data-processing equipment industries, both Japanese and US subsidiaries are highly concentrated in one region, namely, the Southeast region of the United Kingdom. Yamawaki et al. conducted a factor analysis to identify the economic and other characteristics of this region, and found that the region enjoys favourable labour costs and tax rates as well as a relatively high technological capability over other EU member states. Their analysis also points to the importance of agglomeration for industrial activities, especially for R&D-intensive industries. This is because agglomeration or clustering of manufacturing and innovative activities is beneficial for those firms located in the concentrated region due to positive external economies through knowledge spill-over.

The next two chapters, on the EU, discuss the role of competition policy in European economic integration. Leo Sleuwaegen examines the possible anti-competitive impact of cross-border M&A, which has increased its importance in FDI flows in the EU (chapter 8), while Patrick

Messerlin analyses the services liberalization in Europe and its impact on competition (chapter 9).

Leo Sleuwaegen reports a notable increase in FDI flows in the EU since the mid-1980s, which has taken mainly the forms of mergers, acquisitions, and joint ventures within the EU and across Triad regions. A major impetus behind this development is the Single Market Programme which was launched in 1987. FDI has been active especially in the services sector, such as banking and business services, where deregulation and harmonization of policies have been implemented in the EU. While recognizing that active M&A lead to efficiency gains from economies of scale and scope, Sleuwaegen warns about their harmful effect in limiting competition. His primary concern is the changing motives behind M&A from rationalization and diversification to strengthening market position. In this context, Sleuwaegen reviews the US experience of deregulation and finds that it led to restructuring, flexibility being a necessary condition for survival in the first years. This was followed by the period when the weakest firms were driven out of the market, at which time new oligopolies emerged that threatened to become as powerful as the oligopolies that had been destroyed by deregulation!

To deal with the possible anti-competitive measures through M&A, the EU recently implemented the EU Merger Regulation and control system, which is designed to guide European-wide corporate restructuring in the desired direction by prohibiting mergers and joint ventures which could lead to the creation of a dominant market position. However, Sleuwaegen points to the problems of the restrictive criteria and lack of transparency under which the regulation is applied. In order to prevent the harmful impact of anti-competitive behaviour of the firms that increase market power through international M&A, he argues that there is a need for a level playing field by applying a vigilant and coherent competition policy not only at the EU level, but also at the global level. He concludes that in light of declining trade barriers among the Triad, the harmonization of competitive conditions is necessary to realize the gain from greater efficiency.

Patrick Messerlin reviews the European experiences of services liberalization under the Single Market Programme (SMP) and finds that its competition-enhancing impact has been rather limited. He argues that a major reason for this is the regulation-based protection applied in the service sector. According to Messerlin, regulation-based protection provided in services trade, and tariffs applied in goods trade, benefit different groups. Regulation-based protection transfers rent incomes to domestic interests, including domestic firms and workers, while tariffs provide revenues to the government. Since the vested interests often have political power, governments have difficulty liberalizing the sectors under regulation-based protection, such as the services sector. He validates his arguments of difficulty associated with liberalizing services by examining the experiences of the air transport and banking sectors in the EU. He finds that the impact of SMP has been modest in both sectors: In air transport most governments attempted to protect their domestic firms mainly by increasing subsidies, while in banking large banks in most of the EU member states are almost certain to be supported at any cost by their governments.

After examining the experiences in services liberalization in the EU (under SMP) and in the GATT/WTO (under the GATS), Messerlin draws two lessons. First, among the four major options for eliminating the protectionist aspect of regulations and opening markets – no regulation, unconditional mutual recognition of the existing regulations, conditional mutual recognition of these regulations, full harmonization – he argues that unconditional mutual recognition may be the best instrument of service liberalization in the WTO, as it has a large number of diverse countries as its members. Second, within the WTO framework a careful distinction has to be made between regulatory reform and competition policy. Compared with competition policy, regulatory reform is sector-specific and transitory in nature, and thus anti-competitive. Messerlin emphasizes that regulatory reform may be a transitory step towards freer markets, but that the transitory situation of regulatory reform should be clearly distinguished from the targeted final situation of free competition.

The following findings emerge from this book:

• First, a significant rise in intra-regional trade shares among East Asian economies over the period 1980–94 was due to the rapid growth of the region's economies and *not* due to a rise in 'regional bias', as a *declining* trend in intra-regional trade and FDI intensities indicates (Urata, in this volume). A close look at the corporate behaviour of Japanese multinationals suggests that they still rely heavily on direct exports from Japan when selling their products to Asia, while they tend to sell more through their foreign affiliates and produce more abroad when selling to the rest of the world. Such limited diversification of business channels in Asia may be regarded as indicating that economic integration in Asia is still at an early stage, compared with the degree of economic integration among developed countries. The two cases of ASEAN and the Chinese Economic Area indicate that further liberalization and deregulation of foreign trade and investment regimes are required to deepen and widen regional integration in Asia.

- Second, empirical evidence suggests that in the wake of financial liberalization during the 1980s and 1990s money markets in East Asia have become highly integrated both regionally *and* internationally. In particular, Singapore has developed into a key financial centre for the ASEAN region. Given growing interdependence in financial markets, closer co-operation among central banks of the region will be desirable as their economies become more deeply integrated in the coming years. The currency turmoil in several ASEAN countries in mid-1997 should be taken seriously.
- Third, the EU's Single Market Programme has exerted a significant influence over the locational decisions of both European and non-European firms. Some observers even point to the changing paradigm of European business strategies resulting from globalization on the one hand and from regionalism on the other. A regional approach offers a 'test bed' for deeper integration and more advanced rule-making than is often possible globally. However, liberalization in services trade would take more time than initially anticipated, due to the intrinsic nature of services negotiations involved and the political-economy aspects of liberalization in these sectors. A close look at European firms' responses to the EU's Single Market Programme in the areas of air transport and banking indicates that increased competition in global markets is far more important for their business strategies than on EU markets in which competitive pressures remain limited so far.
- Last but not least, mergers and acquisitions and joint ventures account for the most significant share of cross-border direct investment flows within Europe. Economic restructuring, coupled with these investments, is expected to revitalize European industries. At the same time, the restructuring process often leads to increased market power of large firms, and thus an active competition policy is required to prevent anti-competitive behaviours.

## Notes

1   The Association of Southeast Asian Nations (ASEAN) has now come to embrace nine member countries with its membership extended to Vietnam in July 1995 and Laos and Myanmar in July 1997, in addition to Brunei Drussalam, Indonesia, Malaysia, the Philippines, Singapore and Thailand. The three new member countries have been granted a longer 'phase-in' timetable for AFTA (ASEAN Free Trade Area). See Urata (in this volume) for the development of ASEAN.

2   In Europe, RIAs have been used extensively by the European Union as part of bilateral partnership agreements with its neighbouring countries in Central and Eastern Europe and Southern Mediterranean (Pelkmans and Fukasaku 1995). In Asia, too, there have emerged a variety of RIAs. One of

the main characteristics of these regional initiatives in Asia is the emergence of several sub-regional schemes, which are often referred to as 'growth triangles', ranging from the Tumen River Area Development in Northeast Asia to the Singapore–Johor–Riau Growth Triangle (SIJORI) in Southeast Asia (Tang 1995).

3    See Fukasaku and Martineau (1996) table 1.
4    According to the European Commission (1995), these Asian economies are China, Chinese Taipei, Korea, Hong Kong (China), Singapore, Malaysia, India, Thailand and Indonesia in descending order.
5    See the policy report prepared jointly by the European Commission and UNCTAD (1996) for a detailed discussion of European direct investment in Asia.
6    The year 1996 marked a turning point in the light of Asia-European relationships: the first Asia-Europe Summit Meeting (ASEM) was held in Bangkok in March 1996. The start of the ASEM process has enhanced significantly the political standing of the ASEAN as a regional institution, in addition to its increasing importance as an economic grouping over the past decade. While no mention has been made (so far) of taking a RIA option between Asia and Europe, the formation of the ASEM process signifies strong political commitments on the part of government and business leaders of the two regions to strengthen the third leg of the Asia–Europe–North America triad.
7    See, for example, Pelkmans and Fukasaku (1995) for a concise account of European integration.
8    It dates back to 1973 that Canon started plain-paper copier production for the first time in Europe (West Germany). Following the establishment of Canon's European headquarters in Amsterdam in 1982, Canon's business operation in Europe expanded rapidly with the set-up of a personal copier production facility in France (1983), joint venture with Olivetti in Italy (1987), and a new production facility in the UK (1993), as well as two research centres, one in the UK (1989) and the other in France (1992). In 1995 Canon Europa N.V. accounted for 16 per cent of Canon's total workforce (over 72,200 world-wide) and 27 per cent of its consolidated sales ($21 billion), according to the company's report 1996/97.
9    To be sure, European regionalism has a dark side: trade protection against third countries in the forms of VERs and anti-dumping actions targeted mainly against large Asian exporters. A recent incident of government intervention in the 'Thomson-Daewoo' affair provides another reminder that this dark aspect should not be overlooked.

**References**

European Commission (1995) 'Trade Relations between the European Union and the Developing Countries', Document No. DE71, March, Brussels.
European Commission and UNCTAD (1996) 'Investing in Asia's Dynamism: European Union Direct Investment in Asia', Office for Official Publications of the European Communities, Luxembourg.
Fukasaku, Kiichiro and Martineau, David (1996) 'Forging Trade Links between Europe and Asia', Paper prepared for the *Europe, East Asia and APEC* Conference held on 28–29 August 1996 at the Australian National University, Canberra.

Pelkmans, Jacques and Fukasaku, Kiichiro (1995) 'Evolving Trade Links between Europe and Asia: Towards "Open Continentalism?", in K. Fukasaku (ed.), *Regional Co-operation and Integration in Asia*, OECD, Paris.

Tang, Min (1995) 'Asian Economic Co-operation: Opportunities and Challenges', in K. Fukasaku (ed.), *Regional Co-operation and Integration in Asia*, OECD, Paris.

# 2

# Regionalization and the Formation of Regional Institutions in East Asia

## Shujiro Urata

## I   Introduction

East Asia has been an economic growth centre of the world since the end of World War II.[1] In the 1950s and 1960s Japan achieved remarkable economic growth, while in the 1970s and 1980s the four Newly Industrializing Economies (NIEs) consisting of Hong Kong, Korea, Singapore and Taiwan, recorded unprecedentedly high economic growth rates. In the latter half of the 1980s, Indonesia, Malaysia and Thailand, all of which are members of the Association of Southeast Asian Nations (ASEAN), and China started to accelerate their economic growth. From the 1990s onwards, other East Asian economies such as the Philippines, Vietnam and Myanmar joined others in the rapid economic race.

As a result of the rapid economic growth of the East Asian countries in the last four decades, East Asia has become a region whose share of world GDP and trade are comparable to those of the EU and North America. One important factor that contributed to the rapid economic growth of East Asia was the remarkable expansion of exports and inward foreign direct investment (FDI).[2] The recognition of the increasing importance of East Asia in the world economy as well as the increasing intra-regional dependence in East Asia through foreign trade and foreign direct investment has given rise to a strong interest in regionalization in East Asia among researchers as well as policy-makers, not only in the region but also in other parts of the world. Indeed, in light of the growing number of 'closed regions' in the world through preferential regional trading arrangements such as free trade areas (FTA) and common markets, most notably the EU and NAFTA, there is a concern that the regionalization in East Asia may become an added impetus to closed regionalization.

The purpose of this chapter is to discern the emerging pattern of the intra-regional economic relationship among the economies in East Asia. Specifically, we shall ask whether regional integration has been formed through foreign trade and FDI in East Asia. The chapter will also examine the evolution of regional institutions in East Asia, focusing on their objectives and achievements. The analysis is important not only for understanding the economic development in the region but also for formulating regional as well as global policies.

The structure of the chapter is as follows. Section II examines the recent economic development in East Asia, in order to set the stage for the subsequent analyses. Section III addresses the regionalization issue in East Asia by investigating the intra-regional patterns of foreign trade and FDI. Section IV then turns to the regional institutions in East Asia. Finally section V presents some concluding comments.

## II   Rapid Economic Growth in East Asia

East Asia is made up of widely diversified economies. Table 2.1 presents some basic economic indicators for the economies in the region. The size of the population, the size of the economic activities, and the level of economic development vary widely among these economies. China's population, the largest in the world, is more than 400 times greater than that of Singapore, the smallest in the region. Compared to the variations in the size of population, the variations in GNP are significantly smaller, but still quite large. Japan's GNP, the largest in the region, is approximately 80 times greater than that of the Philippines, the smallest in the region. The variations in the level of economic development, measured by per capita GNP, among the economies in the region are also substantial, as Japan's per capita GNP, the largest of the region, is approximately 60 times greater than that of China, the smallest in the region. The observed differences in economic characteristics have important implications for the structure of economic relations and for the formation of regional institutions in East Asia. This will be discussed below.

Despite the sharp differences in their economic characteristics, the economies in East Asia share some common characteristics such as rapid economic growth and rapid structural change, which often take place simultaneously. Section II will first review the economic growth

**Table 2.1**  Main economic indicators for East Asian economies, 1993

| | Population (million) | GNP ($ billion) | GNP per capita ($) | GDP growth rate (%) | | | |
|---|---|---|---|---|---|---|---|
| | | | | 1970–80 | 1980–85 | 1985–90 | 1990–93 |
| Indonesia | 187.2 | 144.7 | 740 | 8.0 | 4.7 | 6.3 | 6.6 |
| Malaysia | 19 | 64.5 | 3140 | 8.0 | 5.1 | 6.8 | 8.3 |
| Philippines | 64.8 | 54.1 | 850 | 6.3 | –1.0 | 4.7 | 0.6 |
| Thailand | 58.1 | 124.9 | 2110 | 6.8 | 5.6 | 10.4 | 8.2 |
| Singapore | 2.8 | 55.2 | 19850 | 9.0 | 6.2 | 8.1 | 7.6 |
| Korea | 44.1 | 330.8 | 7660 | 8.2 | 8.4 | 10.0 | 6.6 |
| Taiwan | 20.8 | 226.2 | 10850 | 9.7 | 9.7 | 9.1 | 6.9 |
| Hong Kong | 5.8 | 90 | 18060 | 9.3 | 5.6 | 7.5 | 5.7 |
| China | 1178.4 | 425.6 | 490 | 5.7 | 10.1 | 5.1 | 13.7 |
| Japan | 124.5 | 4214.2 | 31490 | 4.7 | 4.0 | 4.6 | 1.9 |
| Developing countries | 4689.0 | 4865.0 | 1090 | 5.2 | 3.1 | 4.2 | 4.9 |
| World | 5501.5 | 23112.6 | 4420 | 3.8 | 2.6 | 3.5 | 2.6 |

Sources: ADB, Key Indicators of Developing Asian and Pacific Countries 1995, IMF, International Financial Statistics Yearbook 1995, World Bank, World Development Report 1995.

of the economies in the region and then investigate the mechanism behind this rapid economic growth.

## A Shift from Inward-looking to Outward-looking Policies in the Mid-1980s

After recording favourable economic performance in the 1970s, a number of economies in East Asia experienced an economic slowdown in the early 1980s. The second oil crisis in the late 1970s and its aftermath were major factors behind the slowdown. In addition, inward-looking, import substitution policies coupled with active public investment in the latter part of the 1970s were also a factor leading to the slowdown in the early 1980s.

A sharp rise in oil prices resulted in a world-wide recession as a number of countries pursued tight macroeconomic policies to deal with the inflation triggered by the oil price increase. In particular, industrial economies were hit hard, and their economic growth was negative in 1982. The slowdown in the world economy affected negatively the economic performance of East Asia, mainly by reducing the demand for East Asian products.

In addition to the deterioration in economic environment external to the East Asian economies, several internal problems emerged, contributing to a slowdown in their economic growth. Import substitution policies, which had been pursued for some time in most economies in the region, caused various problems. A protected market behind import substitution policies provided opportunities for local businesses, leading to reasonable economic growth, which was evidenced by the relatively high growth rate of the 1970s. However, prolonged import substitution resulted in a slowdown in economic growth as the possible areas for import substitution became more or less exhausted. Moreover, import substitution policies gave rise to the inefficient use of available resources for three main reasons. First, import substitution policies encouraged non-competitive import substituting production at the expense of competitive export production, resulting in the inefficient use of resources. Second, the absence of competition from foreign sources due to protection under import substitution policies enabled local firms to enjoy a lucrative protected market, thereby retarding technical progress. Third, import substitution policies promoted rent-seeking activities by those who were eager to obtain benefits from protection.

Active public investment, undertaken by a number of East Asian economies in the 1970s, later led to a slowdown in economic growth. Encouraged by favourable economic growth in the 1970s and realizing the underdevelopment of infrastructure, the governments of East Asian economies expanded public investment aggressively in the second half of the 1970s. Coupled with the reduction in government revenue because of the slowdown in economic activities, the expansion in public expenditure resulted in a huge government deficit and a current account deficit. These twin deficits forced the government to reduce expenditure, leading to the economic slowdown.

## Export and FDI-Led Economic Growth since the Mid-1980s

To deal with the serious economic problems of the early 1980s, the economies in distress adopted structural adjustment policies consisting mainly of liberalization in foreign trade and investment and deregulation in domestic economic activities. These policy changes, from inward-looking protection policies to outward-looking liberalization policies, were attributable to the recommendations by the donors of economic assistance such as the World Bank and the IMF, and to the realization on the part of East Asian developing countries that liberalization would promote economic growth as evidenced by the success of Asian NIEs.

The newly adopted market-oriented policies by the East Asian developing economies turned the situation around and prepared the stage for the subsequent expansion of exports and FDI inflow. Trade liberalization shifted the incentives from import-substituting production to export production, and FDI liberalization increased the attractiveness of these economies to foreign investors. The substantial increases of East Asian exports and FDI inflow to East Asia can be seen from tables 2.2 and 2.3. East Asian exports and FDI inflow increased much faster than those of the rest of the world from 1980 to the early 1990s. As a result of these changes, the share of East Asia in world exports and world inward FDI increased over time. For exports the East Asian share increased from 14.35 per cent in 1980 to 26.45 per cent in 1994, while for inward FDI its share increased from 8.31 per cent in 1980 to 13.25 per cent in 1992.

Several important developments took place in the mid-1980s that precipitated the expansion of exports of East Asian developing economies and the expansion of FDI inflow to these economies, which interacted to promote their economic growth. Although the discussions below focus on the developments in the relationship between Japan and its East Asian neighbour economies, the situation is similar for the relationship among other East Asian economies.

One is the substantial realignment of the exchange rates of major currencies, notably the appreciation of the Japanese yen *vis-à-vis* the US

*Shujiro Urata*

**Table 2.2**   Trade performance of East Asian economies

| | Value (US$ million) | | | Shares of world total (%) | |
|---|---|---|---|---|---|
| | 1980 | 1994 | 94/80 | 1980 | 1994 |
| **Exports** | | | | | |
| Indonesia | 21909 | 40054 | 1.83 | 1.16 | 0.95 |
| Malaysia | 12958 | 58756 | 4.53 | 0.68 | 1.40 |
| Philippines | 5741 | 13342 | 2.32 | 0.30 | 0.32 |
| Thailand | 6505 | 45061 | 6.93 | 0.34 | 1.07 |
| Singapore | 19376 | 96826 | 5.00 | 1.02 | 2.30 |
| Korea | 17512 | 96013 | 5.48 | 0.92 | 2.29 |
| Taiwan | 19785 | 92851 | 4.69 | 1.04 | 2.21 |
| Hong Kong | 19752 | 151395 | 7.66 | 1.04 | 3.60 |
| China | 18099 | 119816 | 6.62 | 0.95 | 2.85 |
| Japan | 130441 | 397005 | 3.04 | 6.88 | 9.45 |
| ASEAN4 | 47113 | 157213 | 3.34 | 2.49 | 3.74 |
| NIES | 76425 | 437085 | 5.72 | 4.03 | 10.40 |
| East Asia | 272078 | 1111119 | 4.08 | 14.35 | 26.45 |
| E. Asia ex. Japan | 141637 | 714114 | 5.04 | 7.47 | 17.00 |
| World | 1895600 | 4201300 | 2.22 | 100 | 100 |
| **Imports** | | | | | |
| Indonesia | 10834 | 31985 | 2.95 | 0.55 | 0.74 |
| Malaysia | 10820 | 59581 | 5.51 | 0.54 | 1.38 |
| Philippines | 8295 | 22531 | 2.72 | 0.42 | 0.52 |
| Thailand | 9214 | 54365 | 5.90 | 0.46 | 1.26 |
| Singapore | 24007 | 102670 | 4.28 | 1.21 | 2.37 |
| Korea | 22292 | 102348 | 4.59 | 1.12 | 2.37 |
| Taiwan | 19764 | 85519 | 4.33 | 1.00 | 1.98 |
| Hong Kong | 22447 | 161777 | 7.21 | 1.13 | 3.74 |
| China | 19941 | 114563 | 5.75 | 1.00 | 2.65 |
| Japan | 141296 | 275235 | 1.95 | 7.11 | 6.36 |
| ASEAN4 | 39163 | 168462 | 4.30 | 1.97 | 3.90 |
| NIEs | 88510 | 452314 | 5.11 | 4.46 | 10.46 |
| East Asia | 288910 | 1010574 | 3.50 | 14.55 | 23.37 |
| E. Asia ex. Japan | 147614 | 735339 | 4.98 | 7.43 | 17.00 |
| World | 1986300 | 4324900 | 2.18 | 100 | 100 |

Source: All the figures are taken from IMF, International Financial Statistics Yearbook 1995 except for the figure of Thailand in 1994, which is taken from ADB, Key Indicators of Developing Asian and Pacific Countries.

**Table 2.3**     FDI outflow and inflow of East Asian economies

| | Value of FDI stock (US$ million) | | | Shares of world total (%) | |
|---|---|---|---|---|---|
| | 1980 | 1992 | 92/80 | 1980 | 1992 |
| **FDI Outflow** | | | | | |
| Indonesia | 44 | 2383 | 53.68 | 0.01 | 0.12 |
| Malaysia | 490 | 2104 | 4.30 | 0.10 | 0.10 |
| Philippines | 285 | 874 | 3.07 | 0.06 | 0.04 |
| Thailand | 13 | 705 | 54.67 | 0.00 | 0.03 |
| Singapore | 784 | 10786 | 13.76 | 0.16 | 0.52 |
| Korea | 196 | 5629 | 28.79 | 0.04 | 0.27 |
| Taiwan | 101 | 5620 | 55.48 | 0.02 | 0.27 |
| Hong Kong | 4089 | 42413 | 10.37 | 0.83 | 2.05 |
| China | 99 | 1035 | 10.44 | 0.02 | 0.05 |
| Japan | 36497 | 386530 | 10.59 | 7.42 | 18.69 |
| ASEAN4 | 832 | 6067 | 7.29 | 0.17 | 0.29 |
| NIEs | 5170 | 64448 | 12.47 | 1.05 | 3.12 |
| East Asia | 42598 | 458080 | 10.75 | 8.66 | 22.15 |
| E. Asia ex. Japan | 6101 | 71550 | 11.73 | 1.24 | 3.46 |
| World | 491689 | 2067944 | 4.21 | 100.00 | 100.00 |
| **FDI Inflow** | | | | | |
| Indonesia | 9231 | 63016 | 6.83 | 2.07 | 3.28 |
| Malaysia | 6078 | 22584 | 3.72 | 1.37 | 1.17 |
| Philippines | 1281 | 4011 | 3.13 | 0.29 | 0.21 |
| Thailand | 1205 | 12435 | 10.32 | 0.27 | 0.65 |
| Singapore | 5351 | 34446 | 6.44 | 1.20 | 1.79 |
| Korea | 1296 | 8491 | 6.55 | 0.29 | 0.44 |
| Taiwan | 2718 | 16491 | 6.07 | 0.61 | 0.86 |
| Hong Kong | 5082 | 28506 | 5.61 | 1.14 | 1.48 |
| China | 1767 | 38174 | 21.60 | 0.40 | 1.98 |
| Japan | 2979 | 26855 | 9.01 | 0.67 | 1.40 |
| ASEAN4 | 17795 | 102046 | 5.73 | 4.00 | 5.30 |
| NIEs | 14447 | 87935 | 6.09 | 3.25 | 4.57 |
| East Asia | 36988 | 255010 | 6.89 | 8.31 | 13.25 |
| E. Asia ex. Japan | 34009 | 228155 | 6.71 | 7.64 | 11.86 |
| World | 445174 | 1923881 | 4.32 | 100.00 | 100.00 |

Source: Estimates by Industry Canada.

dollar and other currencies. In September 1985, to correct the imbalances in the current accounts of industrial countries, a huge surplus in Japan and Germany and a contrasting huge deficit in the US, which were a major cause of economic instability, the G-5 countries agreed to realign the exchange rates of their currencies. As a result, the yen and the Deutsche mark appreciated in value *vis-à-vis* the US dollar and other currencies.

The yen appreciation contributed to export expansion of East Asian developing economies and to FDI inflow to these economies through several channels. The yen appreciation increased the prices of Japanese products *vis-à-vis* the prices of the products produced in the economies such as those in East Asia experiencing the currency depreciation. The changes in the relative prices led to the expansion of exports from East Asian developing economies not only to Japan but also to other countries.

The drastic yen appreciation stimulated Japanese FDI to East Asian developing economies in two ways.[3] To cope with the loss in international price competitiveness discussed above, Japanese firms had three choices: They could (a) allocate their productive resources away from the tradable sector to the nontradable sector, (b) they could upgrade their technology and productivity within the tradable sector to increase the proportion of high value-added products, or (c) through FDI, they could move their production base from the home markets to foreign countries where production costs were lower. This was precisely the industrial structural adjustment the Japanese economy went through in the latter half of the 1980s, leading to a rapid expansion in FDI.

Another way in which yen appreciation had a positive impact on Japanese FDI outflows was the 'liquidity' or 'wealth' effect. To the extent that yen appreciation made Japanese firms relatively more 'wealthy' in the sense of increased collateral and liquidity, it enabled them to finance outward FDI relatively more cheaply than their foreign competitors. In addition, liquidity was injected into the economy in the second half of the 1980s, with the objective of reactivating the Japanese economy from a recession caused by a decline in exports, and thus pushing up the prices of shares and land – the emergence of the so-called 'bubble economy'. Such an increase in liquidity and the subsequent asset-price inflation further promoted Japan's FDI. The bubble economy contributed to the expansion of exports from East Asian developing economies as it increased demand for imports.

Japan's trade friction with, and the protectionist sentiment in, industrial countries such as the United States and the European Union discouraged Japan's exports to these regions, giving opportunities to other countries including those in East Asia. It had the effect of promoting Japan's FDI as well. In order to secure their markets in industrial countries, a number of Japanese firms invested not only in those industrial countries but also in other countries, most notably in East Asia, to set up export platforms, which would enable Japanese firms to get around the import barriers in industrial countries.[4]

It should be noted that it was Japan that first contributed to the rapid expansion of exports and FDI in East Asia in the second half of the 1980s, but it was the NIEs that followed Japan in contributing to the rapid expansion of exports and FDI in East Asia in the later period. Facing a similar set of problems such as currency appreciation and the bubble economy, the firms from the NIEs undertook FDI in East Asia, in search of low-cost production. They invested heavily in ASEAN countries, China and other parts of East Asia.

## The Mechanism of Rapid Economic Growth in East Asia: The Emergence of a Virtuous Cycle of Exports and FDI

Exports and FDI inflow in East Asia expanded rapidly in the second half of the 1980s, which resulted in an increase in the importance of exports and FDI inflow in these economies (table 2.4). In East Asia the expansion of exports and FDI interacted with each other to form a virtuous cycle, thereby contributing to the rapid economic growth in East Asia.

By exporting and accepting FDI, the economies obtain foreign exchange, with which they can import foreign items necessary for economic growth such as high-quality foreign investment goods and intermediate goods. In addition, FDI inflow brings with it technologies and managerial know-how, which are in acutely short supply in developing economies. The inflow of these items increases the capacity and capability of productive resources in the economies. FDI inflow exerts competitive pressure on the local firms in the recipient economies. Such pressure is likely to improve the productivity of the local firms. Exporting leads to an increase in productive efficiency as well, as output expansion due to exports enables the firms to exploit scale economies. Furthermore, the exposure to competition in the international market forces the firms to improve productivity. The factors just discussed promote the economic growth of the economies with successful expansion of exports and FDI inflow.

In addition to the supply-side factors examined above, exports and FDI inflow contribute to economic growth by influencing demand-side factors. Export expansion increases overseas demand for domestic products, and FDI inflow is likely to increase demand for domestically produced investment goods, as the funds transferred to the FDI

**Table 2.4** Shares of trade and FDI in GNP in percentages

| | Exports | | Imports | | FDI outflow | | FDI inflow | |
|---|---|---|---|---|---|---|---|---|
| | 1980 | 1994 | 1980 | 1994 | 1980 | 1992 | 1980 | 1992 |
| Indonesia | 30.2 | 23.0 | 14.9 | 18.3 | 0.1 | 1.7 | 12.7 | 45.3 |
| Malaysia | 52.9 | 84.9 | 44.2 | 86.1 | 2.0 | 3.6 | 24.8 | 38.9 |
| Philippines | 17.7 | 20.9 | 25.6 | 35.3 | 0.9 | 1.6 | 3.9 | 7.6 |
| Thailand | 20.1 | 36.1 | 28.5 | 43.5 | 0.0 | 0.6 | 3.7 | 11.1 |
| Singapore | 165.4 | 140.4 | 204.9 | 148.9 | 6.7 | 21.8 | 45.7 | 69.6 |
| Korea | 28.0 | 25.3 | 35.6 | 27.0 | 0.3 | 1.8 | 2.1 | 2.8 |
| Taiwan | 47.8 | 38.5 | 47.7 | 35.5 | 0.2 | 2.6 | 6.6 | 7.8 |
| Hong Kong | 69.3 | 114.8 | 78.8 | 122.7 | 14.4 | 42.4 | 17.8 | 28.5 |
| China | 7.3 | 24.1 | 8.1 | 23.0 | 0.0 | 0.3 | 0.7 | 10.2 |
| Japan | 12.9 | 8.6 | 13.9 | 5.9 | 3.6 | 10.5 | 0.3 | 0.7 |
| ASEAN4 | 29.1 | 36.4 | 24.2 | 39.0 | 0.5 | 1.7 | 11.0 | 28.2 |
| NIEs | 53.0 | 53.2 | 61.4 | 55.1 | 3.6 | 9.6 | 10.0 | 13.1 |
| East Asia | 17.4 | 17.4 | 18.4 | 15.8 | 2.7 | 9.0 | 2.4 | 5.0 |

Sources: ADB, Key Indicators of Developing Asian and Pacific Countries; IMF, International Financial Statistics Yearbook; Estimates by Industry Canada

recipient through FDI are used for investments. The increase in the demand for domestic goods in turn leads to output expansion.

Export expansion and FDI expansion independently promote economic growth as discussed above. But what happened in East Asia is that they interacted with each other to promote economic growth. In response to the increased incentive given to exports by trade liberalization in East Asia, foreign firms set up export platforms in East Asia. As a result, FDI and exports expanded. The economies that were successful in expanding exports attracted FDI by foreign firms, as they were seen to be able to provide an environment conducive to competitive production. In this way, the virtuous cycle of export expansion and FDI expansion was formed in East Asia to promote economic growth.

## III    Regionalization in East Asia

Rapid economic growth in East Asia has been realized mainly by an interaction of foreign trade and foreign direct investment. One interesting question then is whether such outward – oriented economic growth in East Asia resulted in the *regionalization* of economic activities in East Asia. Section III addresses this question. Earlier studies examined this issue by considering only the pattern of foreign trade at the aggregate level. We extend the earlier studies by using disaggregated trade data and by investigating the linkage between trade and FDI, as this linkage has been shown (above) to be an important factor behind the rapid economic growth in East Asia.

*Increasing Intra-regional Dependence in East Asia*

Tables 2.5 and 2.6 respectively, show the regional trade and FDI patterns for East Asian economies along with the NAFTA and the EU. Table 2.5 shows an increase in the importance of intra-regional trade in total trade for the East Asian region. For exports, the share of intra-East Asian exports in total East Asian exports increased from 34.3 per cent in 1980 to 45.8 per cent in 1994, while for imports the corresponding shares increased more sharply from 35.2 per cent to 54.4 per cent. These observations indicate that, relatively speaking, for East Asia the import sources are more regionalized than the export destinations. An increase in intra-regional trade is also observed for NAFTA and the EU. However, the rate of increase in terms of percentage points is in most cases significantly smaller in these regions compared to East Asia.

Although the importance of intra-regional trade increased sharply in East Asia, the level of intra-regional trade in East Asia is still lower in comparison with the EU; the shares of intra-regional exports and

**Table 2.5** Regional trade patterns in percentages

| | | Export destinations | | | | Import sources | | | |
|---|---|---|---|---|---|---|---|---|---|
| | | E. Asia | NAFTA | APEC | EU | E. Asia | NAFTA | APEC | EU |
| Indonesia | 1980 | 66.0 | 19.8 | 87.8 | 6.6 | 56.1 | 15.1 | 75.2 | 16.9 |
| | 1994 | 63.5 | 18.2 | 83.9 | 17.2 | 60.4 | 11.6 | 77.8 | 20.3 |
| Malaysia | 1980 | 53.3 | 16.9 | 72.0 | 17.9 | 56.3 | 13.0 | 74.6 | 15.2 |
| | 1994 | 53.3 | 22.8 | 78.1 | 14.3 | 68.0 | 12.3 | 83.1 | 12.8 |
| Philippines | 1980 | 42.0 | 28.9 | 72.7 | 18.0 | 39.2 | 24.9 | 67.3 | 11.0 |
| | 1994 | 36.0 | 40.3 | 77.5 | 17.5 | 57.6 | 17.3 | 77.5 | 11.5 |
| Thailand | 1980 | 40.2 | 13.0 | 54.4 | 26.5 | 44.9 | 15.8 | 63.0 | 13.3 |
| | 1994 | 43.0 | 24.9 | 69.6 | 16.7 | 60.8 | 10.7 | 73.7 | 15.7 |
| Singapore | 1980 | 45.1 | 13.4 | 64.3 | 13.2 | 44.1 | 12.2 | 58.7 | 10.4 |
| | 1994 | 51.9 | 19.6 | 74.2 | 13.5 | 61.2 | 15.0 | 79.2 | 13.0 |
| Korea | 1980 | 29.7 | 28.8 | 59.9 | 16.8 | 35.6 | 25.7 | 64.1 | 7.3 |
| | 1994 | 43.9 | 24.2 | 69.5 | 11.3 | 45.3 | 22.2 | 72.0 | 14.4 |
| Taiwan | 1980 | 28.0 | 36.8 | 64.8 | 14.9 | 40.6 | 23.9 | 64.6 | 10.6 |
| | 1994 | 47.3 | 28.3 | 77.7 | 12.9 | 46.4 | 22.8 | 72.2 | 15.1 |
| Hong Kong | 1980 | 24.2 | 28.3 | 55.3 | 24.7 | 62.7 | 12.9 | 77.5 | 14.2 |
| | 1994 | 47.2 | 25.2 | 74.0 | 15.1 | 71.8 | 8.6 | 82.0 | 11.8 |

**Table 2.5** (Continued)

| | | Export destinations | | | | Import sources | | | |
|---|---|---|---|---|---|---|---|---|---|
| | | E. Asia | NAFTA | APEC | EU | E. Asia | NAFTA | APEC | EU |
| China | 1980 | 52.9 | 6.3 | 60.6 | 13.7 | 37.2 | 24.2 | 66.5 | 14.4 |
| | 1994 | 55.0 | 19.1 | 75.4 | 12.8 | 66.9 | 9.0 | 77.9 | 13.5 |
| Japan | 1980 | 25.2 | 27.3 | 55.7 | 15.2 | 22.6 | 20.4 | 48.3 | 5.9 |
| | 1994 | 38.9 | 32.6 | 74.1 | 15.5 | 36.2 | 25.1 | 66.8 | 13.6 |
| East Asia | 1980 | 34.3 | 24.4 | 61.2 | 15.5 | 35.2 | 19.3 | 58.5 | 9.3 |
| | 1994 | 45.8 | 26.7 | 74.6 | 14.4 | 54.4 | 16.9 | 74.7 | 13.7 |
| NAFTA | 1980 | 16.8 | 33.6 | 52.2 | 23.9 | 21.1 | 32.6 | 55.0 | 15.9 |
| | 1994 | 21.5 | 47.6 | 70.7 | 16.2 | 33.1 | 39.1 | 72.8 | 16.0 |
| APEC | 1980 | 25.6 | 28.6 | 56.6 | 20.1 | 27.7 | 26.4 | 56.8 | 13.4 |
| | 1994 | 36.7 | 34.2 | 73.1 | 15.1 | 43.8 | 27.5 | 73.6 | 15.0 |
| EU | 1980 | 3.3 | 6.6 | 10.7 | 61.0 | 5.2 | 9.0 | 15.0 | 56.9 |
| | 1994 | 7.9 | 8.9 | 17.7 | 61.7 | 10.4 | 7.7 | 18.5 | 64.1 |
| World | 1980 | 14.0 | 16.5 | 31.7 | 42.6 | 14.4 | 16.0 | 31.8 | 39.8 |
| | 1994 | 22.2 | 21.3 | 44.9 | 36.8 | 26.4 | 17.5 | 45.3 | 38.3 |

Note: The figures are percentage share of total exports or imports of respective countries and regions.
Source: Computed from the data compiled by JETRO. Original sources are IMF, Direction of Trade Statistics, and Republic of China, Foreign Trade Statistics.

**Table 2.6** Regional FDI patterns in percentages

| | | FDI destinations | | | | FDI sources | | | |
|---|---|---|---|---|---|---|---|---|---|
| | | E. Asia | NAFTA | APEC | EU | E. Asia | NAFTA | APEC | EU |
| Indonesia | 1980 | 98.4 | -2.3 | 98.9 | 1.1 | 51.3 | 4.9 | 59.0 | 9.2 |
| | 1992 | 40.8 | 7.0 | 50.8 | 49.2 | 43.7 | 4.4 | 50.1 | 10.7 |
| Malaysia | 1980 | 89.1 | 3.4 | 100.0 | 0.0 | 54.3 | 6.8 | 64.1 | 26.6 |
| | 1992 | 81.9 | 5.1 | 99.7 | 0.3 | 60.3 | 9.5 | 73.7 | 17.9 |
| Philippines | 1980 | 74.1 | 25.6 | 99.7 | 0.3 | 22.2 | 58.5 | 83.2 | 8.9 |
| | 1992 | 89.6 | 7.8 | 97.5 | 2.5 | 31.4 | 48.8 | 81.9 | 10.6 |
| Thailand | 1980 | 50.6 | 45.8 | 96.4 | 2.7 | 46.3 | 35.4 | 82.2 | 15.9 |
| | 1992 | 50.2 | 36.0 | 86.8 | 5.4 | 66.0 | 17.5 | 84.4 | 10.2 |
| Singapore | 1980 | 75.8 | .9 | 81.4 | 3.1 | 31.4 | 22.5 | 56.2 | 33.1 |
| | 1992 | 48.7 | 9.1 | 68.9 | 7.2 | 35.2 | 21.2 | 61.8 | 28.1 |
| Korea | 1980 | 23.3 | 16.8 | 42.3 | 29.7 | 58.2 | 25.5 | 83.8 | 6.6 |
| | 1992 | 33.9 | 37.6 | 75.7 | 6.6 | 45.7 | 26.5 | 72.2 | 20.4 |
| Taiwan | 1980 | 38.7 | 43.4 | 83.0 | 0.1 | 48.8 | 36.8 | 85.7 | 6.4 |
| | 1992 | 35.8 | 33.5 | 69.6 | 1.8 | 48.8 | 27.9 | 77.6 | 8.9 |
| Hong Kong | 1980 | 90.3 | 4.7 | 99.5 | 0.5 | 24.1 | 41.5 | 65.8 | 34.2 |
| | 1992 | 85.0 | 9.0 | 96.9 | 3.2 | 50.2 | 32.9 | 80.5 | 19.5 |

**Table 2.6**  (Continued)

| | | FDI destinations | | | | FDI sources | | | |
|---|---|---|---|---|---|---|---|---|---|
| | | E. Asia | NAFTA | APEC | EU | E. Asia | NAFTA | APEC | EU |
| China | 1980 | 26.9 | 49.0 | 75.9 | 1.9 | 66.1 | 18.7 | 85.6 | 8.4 |
| | 1992 | 72.4 | 16.9 | 89.3 | 10.7 | 79.0 | 9.7 | 89.4 | 4.3 |
| Japan | 1980 | 26.4 | 29.1 | 61.7 | 10.7 | 17.4 | 56.7 | 74.1 | 13.3 |
| | 1992 | 15.3 | 44.4 | 65.4 | 18.3 | 14.2 | 46.3 | 60.5 | 20.1 |
| East Asia | 1980 | 34.6 | 25.9 | 66.5 | 9.4 | 42.0 | 23.5 | 67.3 | 19.2 |
| | 1992 | 23.8 | 39.6 | 68.8 | 16.3 | 48.2 | 19.1 | 68.8 | 14.2 |
| NAFTA | 1980 | 6.1 | 26.9 | 36.7 | 34.7 | 4.1 | 41.5 | 46.0 | 39.5 |
| | 1992 | 11.0 | 22.7 | 37.5 | 38.3 | 19.5 | 23.1 | 44.1 | 44.3 |
| APEC | 1980 | 10.5 | 26.7 | 41.4 | 30.8 | 11.4 | 38.0 | 50.4 | 35.7 |
| | 1992 | 16.3 | 29.9 | 51.4 | 29.0 | 27.5 | 22.6 | 52.2 | 34.7 |
| EU | 1980 | 5.5 | 33.0 | 41.5 | 30.8 | 2.2 | 40.1 | 42.7 | 36.2 |
| | 1992 | 3.7 | 27.6 | 33.6 | 47.7 | 4.4 | 22.6 | 52.2 | 34.7 |
| World | 1980 | 8.7 | 49.4 | 58.6 | 33.5 | 8.3 | 32.7 | 44.5 | 35.7 |
| | 1992 | 22.1 | 28.3 | 52.0 | 38.7 | 13.3 | 29.8 | 47.2 | 37.6 |

Note: The figures are percentage share of total FDI outflows and inflows of respective countries and regions.
Source: Computed from the data prepared by Industry Canada.

imports in their respective total in the EU in 1994 are 61.7 and 64.1 per cent. In comparison with NAFTA, the level of intra-regional trade in East Asia is similar for exports, but substantially higher for imports.

Intra-regional trade in APEC expanded rapidly to result in a sharp increase in the ratio of intra-regional trade to total APEC trade. Indeed, the ratio of intra-regional trade to total regional trade for APEC in 1994 at 73 per cent was approximately 10 percentage points higher than the corresponding ratio for the EU, indicating the importance of trans-Pacific trade.

For all the East Asian economies the dependency on intra-regional trade increased over time. But there are significant variations in the importance of intra-regional trade among these economies. Generally speaking, the level of intra-regional dependency is low for Japan, Korea and Taiwan.

Unlike the patterns observed for international trade, one cannot detect an apparent increase in intra-regional dependency for FDI (table 2.6). For outward FDI from East Asia, the importance of East Asia as a destination region diminished, as the share of East Asia in total outward FDI from East Asia declined from 34.6 per cent in 1980 to 23.8 per cent in 1992. In contrast, for inward FDI in East Asia, the importance of East Asia as a source region increased, as the share of East Asia in total inward FDI into East Asia increased from 42.0 per cent to 48.2 per cent during the same period. The opposite pattern is observed for the EU. That is, in the EU the intra-regional dependency for outward FDI increased while the intra-regional dependency for inward FDI slightly declined. It is interesting to observe that the intra-regional dependency for both outward and inward FDI in NAFTA declined from 1980 to 1992.

A comparison of the level of intra-regional dependency for FDI among different regions in 1992 reveals that intra-regional dependency for inward FDI is high for East Asia at 48.2 per cent, while that for outward FDI is high for the EU at 47.7 per cent. Intra-regional dependency for both outward and inward FDI is low for NAFTA, compared to the other regions.

Among the East Asian economies, there are wide variations in the direction of the changes in intra-regional dependency, that is, their dependency on other East Asian economies, in FDI. As for outward FDI, intra-regional dependency increased in three economies, while it declined in seven economies. As for inward FDI, intra-regional dependency increased in six economies, while it declined in three economies, with one economy showing no change. This finding is in contrast to the pattern observed for international trade, for which intra-regional dependency was shown to have increased over the years for all the East Asian economies. Similar to the finding on international trade, intra-regional dependency regarding FDI is exceptionally low for Japan.

A comparison of intra-regional and extra-regional dependency regarding international trade on the one hand and regarding FDI on the other hand reveals that intra-regional dependency in most cases is higher regarding international trade than that regarding FDI.[5] Three exceptions out of twelve cases (three regions, two periods and two types of inflows and outflows of foreign trade and those of FDI) are observed for 1980 only: exports and FDI destinations; and imports and FDI sources for East Asia in 1980; and imports and FDI sources for NAFTA in 1980. By 1992 these three exceptional relationships had been reversed, as FDI outside of the region expanded rapidly. The fact that intra-regional concentration is lower for FDI in comparison with that for international trade appears to indicate that geographical proximity is not an important factor in determining FDI, compared to the case for international trade. This should be expected since the transfer of investable funds for undertaking FDI does not incur transportation costs, which are partly a function of geographical distance, as is the case for international trade.[6]

We saw that intra-regional dependency in foreign trade and FDI inflow in East Asia increased from 1980 to the early 1990s. This does not mean that globalization of the region receded over the same period. If we define the extent of globalization as the shares of foreign trade and FDI conducted outside of the region in overall economic activities in the region, here measured by GDP, then the globalization of East Asia moved forward (table 2.7). As for foreign trade, the shares of extra-regional exports and imports in the regional GDP increased from 19.1 and 15.7 per cent in 1980 to 19.7 and 17.8 per cent in 1994, respectively. Similarly, the shares of extra-regional outward FDI and inward FDI in the regional GDP increased from 0.3 and 6.4 per cent in 1980 to 1.3 and 14.6 per cent in 1992, respectively.

It is interesting to observe that the globalization concerning FDI intensified for all the economies but the globalization concerning foreign trade did not advance in five out of ten economies. This finding is consistent with the earlier observation that intra-regional dependency increased for all the economies concerning foreign trade, but not concerning FDI.

## Declining Regional Bias in Foreign Trade and FDI in East Asia

Increasing intra-regional dependency in foreign trade and FDI inflow does not necessarily mean that the intra-regional bias increased over time. Increasing intra-regional dependency may be attributable to several factors. The rapid rate of growth in foreign trade and FDI in the

**Table 2.7** Globalization of East Asian economies in percentages

|  | Exports | | Imports | | FDI outflow | | FDI inflow | |
|---|---|---|---|---|---|---|---|---|
|  | 1980 | 1994 | 1980 | 1994 | 1980 | 1992 | 1980 | 1992 |
| Indonesia | 10.3 | 8.4 | 6.6 | 7.3 | 0.0 | 1.0 | 6.2 | 25.5 |
| Malaysia | 24.7 | 39.6 | 19.3 | 27.5 | 0.2 | 0.7 | 11.3 | 15.5 |
| Philippines | 10.3 | 13.4 | 15.5 | 15.0 | 0.2 | 0.2 | 3.1 | 5.2 |
| Thailand | 12.0 | 20.6 | 15.7 | 17.1 | 0.0 | 0.3 | 2.0 | 3.8 |
| Singapore | 90.8 | 67.5 | 114.5 | 57.8 | 1.6 | 11.2 | 31.3 | 45.1 |
| Korea | 19.7 | 14.2 | 22.9 | 14.7 | 0.2 | 1.2 | 0.9 | 1.5 |
| Taiwan | 34.4 | 20.3 | 28.4 | 19.0 | 0.1 | 1.7 | 3.4 | 4.0 |
| Hong Kong | 52.5 | 60.6 | 29.4 | 34.6 | 1.4 | 6.4 | 13.5 | 14.2 |
| China | 3.5 | 10.8 | 5.1 | 7.6 | 0.0 | 0.1 | 0.2 | 2.1 |
| Japan | 9.6 | 5.2 | 10.8 | 3.8 | 2.6 | 8.9 | 0.2 | 0.6 |
| East Asia | 19.1 | 19.7 | 15.7 | 17.8 | 0.3 | 1.3 | 6.4 | 14.6 |

Note: The figures show the proportion of extra-regional trade and FDI to GDP.
Source: Tables 2.4, 2.5, and 2.6.

region, reflecting its rapid economic growth, could lead to an increase in intra-regional dependence. Alternatively, intra-regional preferential arrangements such as free trade areas and customs unions could promote closer economic linkages in the region through foreign trade and FDI. By taking account of the factors resulting from the overall changes in foreign trade and FDI in the region, the trade and FDI intensity measures, or the 'gravity coefficients', are computed to discern the regional bias.[7]

Tables 2.8 and 2.9, respectively, show the computed trade and FDI intensities for various groups of countries and regions. The results on foreign trade indicate that intra-regional biases of East Asian exports as well as imports declined from 1980 to 1994, as the intra-regional export intensities and import intensities for East Asia declined respectively from 2.23 and 2.22 to 1.85 and 1.77 over the same period. Indeed, the export and import intensities among all the groups of countries in East Asia shown in table 2.8, with an exception of the intensity of the NIEs' exports to East Asia, declined between 1980 and 1992, indicating that the trade biases among various groups of countries in East Asia were reduced over the same period. By contrast to the pattern observed for East Asia, the intra-regional biases of exports and imports for NAFTA as well as those for the EU increased in the same period.

The computed FDI intensities shown in table 2.9 reveal similar results to those on foreign trade for East Asia and the EU. The intra-regional bias of East Asian FDI declined in the 1980s, as the intra-regional outward and inward FDI intensities for East Asia declined respectively from 3.94 and 4.62 in 1980 to 1.65 and 2.03 in 1992. It should also be noted that the outward and inward FDI intensities among all the groups of countries in East Asia shown in table 2.9 declined between 1980 and 1992. By contrast, the intra-regional bias of outward and inward FDI for the EU increased over the same period. Somewhat different from the finding on foreign trade, the intra-regional bias of NAFTA FDI declined between 1980 and 1992.

These findings indicate that the increasing intra-regional dependency in East Asia observed for foreign trade and inward FDI is attributable to the expansion of foreign trade and FDI in the region. Indeed, the decline in the intra-regional bias in East Asia is attributable to trade and FDI liberalization, which was pursued by governments in the region. By contrast, the increasing intra-regional dependency in the EU observed for foreign trade and outward FDI is attributable to the increase in the regional bias, which appears to have resulted largely from the preferential regional arrangement.

It is important to note that despite the decline in the intra-regional bias for foreign trade and FDI in East Asia the extent of the bias in the

**Table 2.8** Trade intensity among various regions

| | | Export intensity East Asia | | | | | | | Import intensity East Asia | | | | | | |
|---|---|---|---|---|---|---|---|---|---|---|---|---|---|---|---|
| | | ASEAN5 | NIEs3 | East Asia | (ex.Japan) | NAFTA | APEC | EU | ASEAN5 | NIEs3 | East Asia | (ex.Japan) | NAFTA | APEC | EU |
| ASEAN5 | 1980 | 5.09 | 2.23 | 3.68 | 3.40 | 1.10 | 2.25 | 0.31 | 5.09 | 2.41 | 3.23 | 3.60 | 0.95 | 2.01 | 0.31 |
| | 1994 | 3.62 | 1.58 | 2.22 | 2.19 | 1.06 | 1.61 | 0.39 | 3.62 | 1.50 | 2.25 | 2.13 | 0.79 | 1.66 | 0.35 |
| NIEs3 | 1980 | 2.42 | 1.86 | 1.90 | 2.15 | 1.97 | 1.84 | 0.43 | 2.23 | 1.85 | 3.22 | 2.80 | 1.29 | 2.12 | 0.27 |
| | 1994 | 1.47 | 1.37 | 1.94 | 2.10 | 1.20 | 1.53 | 0.34 | 1.53 | 1.36 | 2.02 | 1.86 | 0.93 | 1.57 | 0.32 |
| East Asia | 1980 | 3.02 | 3.01 | 2.23 | 2.93 | 1.41 | 1.75 | 0.33 | 3.43 | 1.77 | 2.22 | 2.76 | 1.13 | 1.66 | 0.21 |
| | 1994 | 2.12 | 1.96 | 1.85 | 2.07 | 1.19 | 1.49 | 0.35 | 1.99 | 1.78 | 1.77 | 1.91 | 0.89 | 1.41 | 0.31 |
| East Asia (ex.Japan) | 1980 | 3.49 | 2.72 | 2.87 | 2.89 | 1.32 | 1.97 | 0.35 | 3.29 | 2.09 | 3.03 | 2.88 | 1.13 | 1.99 | 0.29 |
| | 1994 | 2.01 | 1.80 | 2.01 | 2.04 | 1.05 | 1.50 | 0.34 | 2.05 | 2.01 | 2.06 | 2.03 | 0.77 | 1.53 | 0.32 |
| NAFTA | 1980 | 0.87 | 1.17 | 1.10 | 1.06 | 1.53 | 1.43 | 0.51 | 1.00 | 1.80 | 1.38 | 1.24 | 1.53 | 1.49 | 0.36 |
| | 1994 | 0.71 | 0.86 | 0.89 | 0.74 | 1.62 | 1.33 | 0.40 | 1.00 | 1.15 | 1.19 | 1.05 | 1.69 | 1.43 | 0.38 |
| APEC | 1980 | 1.78 | 1.88 | 1.58 | 1.83 | 1.44 | 1.54 | 0.41 | 1.99 | 1.63 | 1.66 | 1.80 | 1.39 | 1.54 | 0.29 |
| | 1994 | 1.53 | 1.49 | 1.45 | 1.51 | 1.40 | 1.43 | 0.36 | 1.49 | 1.44 | 1.46 | 1.46 | 1.35 | 1.43 | 0.35 |
| EU | 1980 | 0.26 | 0.22 | 0.19 | 0.25 | 0.33 | 0.27 | 1.17 | 0.27 | 0.37 | 0.31 | 0.31 | 0.48 | 0.40 | 1.21 |
| | 1994 | 0.38 | 0.30 | 0.31 | 0.31 | 0.37 | 0.34 | 1.45 | 0.35 | 0.31 | 0.33 | 0.32 | 0.40 | 0.35 | 1.43 |

Note: The export (import) intensity of region i and region j is computed as tij=A/B where A=Xij/Xi, B=X.j/(X..-X.i+Xij), where Xij is i's exports to (imports from) j and "." indicates the summation over n (the total number of regions).

**Table 2.9**  FDI intensity among various regions

| | | Outward FDI intensity East Asia | | | | | | | Inward FDI intensity East Asia | | | | | | |
|---|---|---|---|---|---|---|---|---|---|---|---|---|---|---|---|
| | | ASEAN5 | NIES3 | East Asia | (ex.Japan) | NAFTA | APEC | EU | ASEAN5 | NIES3 | East Asia | (ex.Japan) | NAFTA | APEC | EU |
| ASEAN5 | 1980 | 10.81 | 9.58 | 9.14 | 9.94 | 0.21 | 1.94 | 0.04 | 29.66 | 18.46 | 23.25 | 25.29 | 0.41 | 4.73 | 0.00 |
| | 1992 | 4.38 | 6.19 | 3.79 | 4.21 | 0.31 | 1.43 | 0.30 | 7.18 | 7.89 | 5.84 | 6.50 | 0.32 | 2.04 | 0.05 |
| NIEs3 | 1980 | 10.60 | 4.08 | 10.17 | 10.83 | 0.19 | 2.13 | 0.05 | 11.70 | 4.56 | 11.29 | 11.98 | 0.09 | 2.26 | 0.07 |
| | 1992 | 3.47 | 1.33 | 5.47 | 6.00 | 0.51 | 1.89 | 0.09 | 6.30 | 1.44 | 7.44 | 8.20 | 0.41 | 2.39 | 0.10 |
| East Asia | 1980 | 4.46 | 3.62 | 3.94 | 4.26 | 0.74 | 1.41 | 0.25 | 5.01 | 3.99 | 4.62 | 4.85 | 0.44 | 1.25 | 0.24 |
| | 1992 | 1.54 | 1.83 | 1.65 | 1.83 | 1.29 | 1.34 | 0.40 | 1.93 | 2.06 | 2.03 | 2.19 | 0.86 | 1.16 | 0.18 |
| East Asia (ex.Japan) | 1980 | 10.07 | 5.44 | 9.39 | 10.06 | 0.21 | 1.99 | 0.05 | 15.79 | 8.15 | 13.88 | 14.89 | 0.17 | 2.80 | 0.05 |
| | 1992 | 3.46 | 2.58 | 4.75 | 5.23 | 0.43 | 1.67 | 0.13 | 6.14 | 3.10 | 6.67 | 7.37 | 0.37 | 2.18 | 0.08 |
| NAFTA | 1980 | 0.35 | 0.52 | 0.60 | 0.38 | 0.64 | 0.67 | 0.79 | 0.23 | 0.62 | 0.39 | 0.34 | 0.65 | 0.62 | 0.66 |
| | 1992 | 0.37 | 0.74 | 0.65 | 0.40 | 0.56 | 0.62 | 0.79 | 0.33 | 0.84 | 0.53 | 0.44 | 0.55 | 0.62 | 0.69 |
| APEC | 1980 | 0.88 | 0.89 | 1.01 | 0.86 | 0.63 | 0.74 | 0.69 | 0.83 | 0.99 | 0.89 | 0.89 | 0.59 | 0.67 | 0.57 |
| | 1992 | 0.80 | 1.06 | 0.98 | 0.91 | 0.81 | 0.87 | 0.61 | 0.91 | 1.16 | 1.02 | 1.04 | 0.63 | 0.78 | 0.47 |
| EU | 1980 | 0.51 | 0.40 | 0.49 | 0.46 | 0.79 | 0.73 | 0.67 | 0.45 | 0.51 | 0.44 | 0.45 | 0.94 | 0.82 | 0.83 |
| | 1992 | 0.18 | 0.24 | 0.22 | 0.17 | 0.79 | 0.58 | 1.02 | 0.31 | 0.34 | 0.30 | 0.28 | 0.96 | 0.72 | 1.01 |

Note: The outward (inward) FDI intensity of region i and region j is computed as tij=A/B where A=Xij/Xi, B=X.j/(X..−X.i+Xii), where Xij is i's outward FDI to (inward FDI from) j and "." indicates the summation over n (the total number of regions).
Source: Computed from the data prepared by Industry Canada.

early 1990s is still significantly greater than that observed either in the
EU or in NAFTA. Geographical proximity, presence of a production
network, cultural similarity and other regional elements are behind the
high intra-regional bias in East Asia. The continuation of trade and FDI
liberalization policies on the MFN basis is likely to contribute to a
further reduction in the intra-regional bias.[8]

An examination of the intra-regional trade intensities for disaggregated product categories reveals that the regional bias in East Asia
declined in all the product categories (table 2.10). For NAFTA trade, a
decline in the intra-regional bias is also observed notably in machines
and transport equipment. In both East Asia and NAFTA, the intra-
regional bias is small in machines and transport equipment. This may
reflect the fact that inter-regional obstacles to trade such as high transportation costs and differences in tastes are low for machines and
transport equipment.

## IV   Regional Institutions in Asia

East Asia is often characterized as an underinstitutionalized area,
compared to the situation in other parts of the world such as Western
Europe.[9] ASEAN (the Association of Southeast Asian Nations) is the
only regional economic institution in East Asia that provides its
members with preferential treatment in the form of a free trade area.
However, membership is limited to certain East Asian economies.
APEC (Asia Pacific Economic Co-operation) was created to promote
foreign trade and FDI in the Asia Pacific region, and as such its membership extends beyond East Asia. EAEC (the East Asian Economic
Caucus), whose membership is limited to East Asian economies, has
been proposed to promote economic co-operation among its members.
EAEC has faced significant opposition from North America and
Australia, which are excluded from the membership, and moreover,
some member countries such as Japan have taken a cautious attitude
towards the idea. Therefore, EAEC has not made much progress. In
addition to these regional institutions, various subregional groups –
without any formal commitment by the governments concerned – have
been developed. Some of them are the Growth Triangle, centred on
Singapore and including Johor state in Malaysia and Batam Island in
Indonesia, and the Greater South China Economic Zone, centred on
Hong Kong and including China's Guangdong and Fujian provinces,
and Taiwan (see chapters 3 and 4).

These regional and subregional institutions have been established or
proposed to promote further economic growth of the region. These
institutions are generally in the early stages of development. Section IV

**Table 2.10**     Intra-regional trade intensities for disaggregated product categories

|  | Exports | | Imports | |
|---|---|---|---|---|
|  | 1980 | 1993 | 1980 | 1993 |
| **East Asia** | | | | |
| Food and live animals(0) | 4.44 | 2.56 | 4.72 | 2.80 |
| Beverage and tobacco(1) | 4.39 | 3.43 | 4.63 | 3.71 |
| Crude materials excl. fuels(2) | 2.18 | 1.34 | 2.52 | 1.76 |
| Mineral fuels etc.(3) | 3.79 | 2.36 | 4.38 | 2.86 |
| Animal and vegetable oil & fats(4) | 2.59 | 2.34 | 2.13 | 1.93 |
| Chemicals(5) | 5.02 | 2.71 | 5.22 | 2.89 |
| Basic manufactures(6) | 4.38 | 2.44 | 4.08 | 2.40 |
| Machines, transport equipment(7) | 2.82 | 1.68 | 2.52 | 1.42 |
| Electric machinery(75,76,77) | 1.91 | 1.35 | 1.59 | 1.02 |
| Misc. manufactured goods (8) | 2.06 | 1.43 | 1.62 | 1.13 |
| Manufactured goods, total | 3.21 | 1.81 | 2.91 | 1.61 |
| **East Asia excluding Japan** | | | | |
| Food and live animals(0) | 6.80 | 2.84 | 6.76 | 2.75 |
| Beverage and tobacco(1) | 7.90 | 4.96 | 8.07 | 4.96 |
| Crude materials excl. fuels(2) | 3.85 | 1.84 | 3.73 | 1.99 |
| Mineral fuels etc.(3) | 5.04 | 3.12 | 5.06 | 3.25 |
| Animal and vegetable oil & fats(4) | 2.85 | 2.53 | 2.30 | 2.02 |
| Chemicals(5) | 6.67 | 3.52 | 6.99 | 3.79 |
| Basic manufactures(6) | 5.60 | 2.45 | 5.59 | 2.48 |
| Machines, transport equipment(7) | 4.20 | 1.88 | 4.31 | 1.92 |
| Electric machinery(75,76,77) | 2.23 | 1.30 | 2.21 | 1.21 |
| Misc. manufactured goods (8) | 1.94 | 1.24 | 1.66 | 0.98 |
| Manufactured goods, total | 3.77 | 1.87 | 3.77 | 1.83 |
| **North America** | | | | |
| Food and live animals(0) | 0.67 | 1.91 | 0.61 | 1.83 |
| Beverage and tobacco(1) | 0.65 | 1.04 | 0.65 | 1.00 |
| Crude materials excl. fuels(2) | 1.77 | 2.02 | 1.44 | 1.72 |
| Mineral fuels etc.(3) | 2.78 | 2.57 | 3.24 | 2.92 |
| Animal and vegetable oil & fats(4) | 0.37 | 2.25 | 0.31 | 2.15 |
| Chemicals(5) | 1.66 | 2.06 | 1.49 | 1.97 |
| Basic manufactures(6) | 2.70 | 3.34 | 2.74 | 3.49 |
| Machines, transport equipment(7) | 1.62 | 1.36 | 1.56 | 1.43 |
| Electric machinery(75,76,77) | 0.82 | 0.73 | 0.79 | 0.82 |
| Misc. manufactured goods (8) | 0.78 | 0.81 | 0.88 | 0.95 |
| Manufactured goods, total | 1.70 | 1.52 | 1.68 | 1.60 |

Note: The numbers in parentheses are SITC classfication. Total manufactured goods are those products under the classification of SITC 5 through 8 except 68.
The trade intensity of region i and region j is computed as $t_{ij}=A/B$, where $A=X_{ij}/X_i$ and $B=X_{.j}/(X_{..}-X_{.i}+X_{ii})$, where $X_{ij}$ is i's exports to j and "." means the summation over n (the total number of regions).
Source: Computed from the trade data compiled by the Institute of Developing Economies in Tokyo.

takes up the two most important regional economic institutions in East Asia so far, that is ASEAN and APEC, and examines their history and achievements.[10]

## ASEAN

The ASEAN was established in 1967 to deal mainly with the political fear arising from instability in Indochina and in China.[11] As such, most joint efforts were made in the political sphere. It was in the latter half of the 1970s when economic co-operation was put into action through such programs as the ASEAN industrial projects (AIP) in 1976, the ASEAN industrial complementation scheme (AIC) in 1981, and the ASEAN industrial joint venture scheme (AIJV) in 1983. However, joint economic co-operation did not produce the expected results. Indeed, it was independent efforts by the member countries, rather than joint efforts, that resulted in the successful economic growth of the members. One important reason that joint economic co-operation was not successful was its orientation towards inward-looking development strategies behind strong government involvement, which reflected the import-substitution bias of most of the members. Joint efforts, led by government bureaucracy, limited the scope and functioning of market mechanisms, resulting in inefficiency.

On the foreign trade front, the Agreement on ASEAN Preferential Trading Arrangements (PTA) was signed in 1977 with the aim of promoting economic growth by encouraging greater intra-regional trade. The main feature of the agreement was granting preferential tariff treatment to ASEAN members. The impact of PTA was small, mainly because the scope of preference offered by ASEAN members in terms of commodity coverage and the extent of concession were very limited. The idea of an ASEAN Free Trade Area (AFTA) was revived in 1991. It gained official endorsement in January 1992. Several external and internal factors accounted for the renewed interest in AFTA.

As for the external factors, the moves towards regionalization in Europe and North America towards the end of the 1980s, which later materialized as the Single European Market and the North American Free Trade Agreement (NAFTA), played a key role in the formation of AFTA. The deepening and widening of the trading blocs in Europe and North America was considered a possible threat to ASEAN's economic success, because it might divert FDI from ASEAN and because it might reduce export opportunities for ASEAN exports. In addition, the protracted Uruguay Round negotiations, coupled with increasing use of non-tariff barriers by developed countries, aroused a fear among ASEAN that their export opportunities might be reduced.

The emergence of China, India, and Vietnam from statism to capitalism was seen as a threat to ASEAN, contributing to the creation of AFTA. These countries, with their abundant low-cost labour, could attract labour-intensive FDI away from ASEAN. Furthermore, rapidly expanding local markets in populous China, India and Vietnam, resulting from rapid economic growth, were another possible factor diverting FDI from ASEAN to these countries.

Finally, the formation of APEC in 1989 precipitated the formation of AFTA. ASEAN leaders were concerned that the formation of a larger forum, which encompassed ASEAN, might diminish the role and position of ASEAN in the regional as well as the global politico-economic arena. To deal with such a possibility, they speeded up the formation of AFTA.

In addition to these external factors, several internal factors also contributed to the creation of AFTA. The successive trade and FDI liberalization efforts by the ASEAN members in the 1980s brought rapid economic growth by expanding exports and attracting foreign direct investment. The favourable impact of trade and FDI liberalization on their economic growth created a favourable attitude towards trade liberalization among ASEAN members. Liberalization in external economic policies by ASEAN members was accompanied and supported by economic reforms in their domestic market in the forms of privatization and deregulation.

The completion of AFTA was targeted within 15 years, from 1 January 1993, by using the Common Effective Preferential Tariff Scheme (CEPT).[12] Under the CEPT, ASEAN member countries would reduce intra-regional tariffs on all manufactured items, including capital goods and processed agricultural products, to 0.5 per cent. All quantitative restrictions and other non-tariff barriers restraining intra-regional trade would also be removed. Exclusions on some specific products are allowed on a temporary basis. As the momentum for trade liberalization was gathering in other parts of the world, namely global liberalization under the GATT and regional liberalization under APEC, in September 1994 the ASEAN member countries decided to shorten the implementation period to 10 years, and extend the product coverage to include all agricultural products. They also agreed to phase out the Exclusion List within five years, starting 1 January 1996.

The effect of ASEAN on the economic growth of its members has been limited so far. However, it should be stressed that ASEAN contributed to the economic growth of ASEAN members by providing a stable political environment, under which economic activities were promoted. Moreover, numerous meetings among officials of ASEAN members at various levels increased mutual understanding of the issues and problems, contributing to the formation of common strategies for internal as well as external issues.

Several studies have dealt with estimates of the likely impact of integration of ASEAN.[13] Their results show that the impacts would be small. For example, Imada et al. (1991) found by using a partial equilibrium model that the impact of AFTA on intra-ASEAN trade as a percentage of total trade would be an increase to 2.31 per cent for imports and 3.40 per cent for exports.

ASEAN is widening its membership. In July 1995, Vietnam became a member. Cambodia, Laos and Myanmar will possibly join ASEAN to form an 'ASEAN-10' in the future.[14] Despite the widening of its membership, ASEAN is likely to be outward-looking by reducing trade barriers involving not only intra-regional trade but also extra-regional trade. Unless an outward-looking strategy is adopted, it will be difficult for ASEAN to maintain the growth momentum based on FDI and export expansion. In addition to unilateral trade and FDI liberalization by individual members, ASEAN has started informal consultation with other regional institutions such as the Closer Economic Relations (CER) of Australia and New Zealand in order to establish closer linkages.

## APEC

The Asia-Pacific Economic Co-operation (APEC) forum was formed in 1989 as the first broad regional institution for intergovernmental dialogue on economic policy issues.[15] APEC started with twelve countries, the then six ASEAN nations (Brunei, Indonesia, Malaysia, Philippines, Singapore and Thailand), the five developed nations (Australia, Canada, Japan, New Zealand and the United States), and South Korea, and it started without a clear mandate.

Several factors account for the formation of APEC. One important factor was the fear of losing export opportunities on the part of the Asian as well as US firms. Recognizing the rapid economic growth in Asia and its likely continuation for the next several decades, the US was eager to maintain and expand its business position in Asia. The US was concerned that its opportunities in Asia might be foreclosed by intensifying intra-Asia trade and FDI relations, where exclusionary production and information networks have been created, in the eyes of US businesses, by *keiretsu*-driven Japanese and family-connected Chinese firms.

A similar fear on the part of Asians was the motivation behind establishing APEC. The US has been a large and important export market for most Asian economies. However, in the 1980s the Asians perceived protectionist sentiments growing in the US, which were reflected in intensifying trade frictions and an increase in the use of non-tariff measures such as anti-dumping tariffs against Asian exports. Further-more, the moves towards regionalization in North America also raised a concern among the Asians, since it would not only reduce their export market but also divert FDI away from Asia.

In order to deal with these fears, the member economies thought that a regional forum such as APEC could become a means to ensure their export opportunities in the markets of other member economies.

Regionalization in Europe also played a role in the creation of APEC on at least two accounts. First, the emergence of 'fortress Europe' under an expanded EC meant limited export opportunities for outsiders such as the US and Asian countries. Faced with this situation, it was natural that the countries in North America and Asia looked to each other for their export market. Second, the creation of Asia-Pacific co-operation was considered important in order to gain bargaining power against the EC in multilateral trade negotiations, particularly when the Uruguay Round negotiations were under way.

Finally, the end of the Cold War removed a barrier to Asia-Pacific co-operation.[16] During the Cold War era, any regional arrangements involving the US, but not the Soviet Union, even if exclusively confined to economic co-operation, would have been seen as a form of alignment and would have been heavily criticized domestically in some Asian countries. The end of the Cold War removed this barrier. At the same time, in the post-Cold War era, Asia-Pacific co-operation was seen as a means to maintain political stability in Asia, where destabilizing elements still exist.

APEC was widened, heightened and deepened over time. APEC was widened by accepting new members: China, Taiwan and Hong Kong, all in 1991; Mexico and Papua New Guinea in 1993; and Chile in 1994.[17] As can be seen from the list of member economies, APEC is character-ized by a rich diversity in the level of economic development, culture, economic systems etc.

Although a number of countries – Vietnam, India, Russia and others – have indicated their desire to join, APEC members have become more reluctant to continue expanding the membership, fearing that it was becoming unwieldy.[18]

APEC hosted annual ministerial meetings until 1993, when President Clinton heightened APEC by adding an annual leaders' meeting. Although the leaders' meeting started as an ad hoc event, the hosts of the subsequent meetings followed suit except for the top leaders of Hong Kong and Taiwan. The leaders' meetings provided an opportu-nity to exchange views on economic and other issues, and they also increased the significance of APEC.

Through a series of annual meetings, APEC members deepened their mutual understanding through dialogue, and they reached an agreement on the objectives of APEC:[19] to attain sustainable growth, equitable development and national stability.[20] To achieve this objective three main goals were set in 1994: (1) free and open trade and investment in the Asia-Pacific by no later than 2010 in the case of industrialized economies and by 2020 in the case of developing economies; (2) expansion and acceleration of trade and investment facilitation programmes; and (3) intensified development co-operation. In 1995, in Osaka, a set of fundamental principles to guide the achievement of trade and investment liberalization was agreed on.

Two unique features of APEC liberalization should be noted, both concerning reciprocity: one for the members and the other for non-members. To achieve the goal of free and open trade and investment, the APEC leaders encourage concerted, voluntary liberalization.[21] Under this framework, the member economies prepare individual action plans and carry them out according to their own schedule. 'Peer pressure' rather than negotiations on a reciprocal basis is believed to promote liberalization. At the Osaka APEC meeting, initial action plans for liberalization were delivered by members, and it was agreed that substantive action plans for liberalization would be submitted to the 1996 Ministerial Meeting in the Philippines and that the implementation of the action plans would begin in January 1997.

Another unique feature of APEC is its adherence to GATT/WTO consistency. 'Open regional co-operation', or open regionalism, under which liberalization is applied without discrimination to non-members on a multilateral basis *à la* WTO, is a basic principle of APEC. The pursuance of open regionalism on the basis of non-reciprocity is believed to contribute to the promotion of global free trade. Indeed, the early implementation of the WTO agreements is explicitly stated as a means to pursue APEC liberalization. In some countries, especially in the US, political pressure makes it difficult to accept non-discrimination, as the latter condones a free ride by non-members.

Although the content and the procedures of the APEC trade and investment liberalization are not yet clear, several studies have examined its likely impact by making assumptions on the methods and procedures of APEC liberalization. Dee et al. (1996) estimated the impact of MFN trade liberalization of APEC members and found that trade and welfare would increase significantly. Specifically, the increase in exports (imports) for individual members ranges between 66.0 (63.8) per cent for Indonesia and 8.5 (10.1) per cent for Singapore; the increase in real GDP ranges between 6.9 per cent for Singapore and 0.7 per cent for NAFTA. These estimates are consistent with the expectation that the trade expansion from the liberalization would be large for highly protected economies and its benefits would be large for highly trade-dependent economies.

Lewis et al. (1995) showed that the formation of a free trade area consisting of the US, Japan, Asian NIEs, China and ASEAN-4 would lead to an increase in total exports: 3 per cent in the US; 6–7 per cent in China, Japan and Asian NIEs; 11 per cent in ASEAN-4. They also showed that real GDP growth ranges from near zero in the US, 1–2 per cent in China and Japan, to 3–5 per cent in Asian NIEs and ASEAN-4. These estimates are significantly larger than the estimates obtained from unilateral liberalization or regional liberalization on a smaller scale such as ASEAN.

Recognition of the diversity in the level of economic development among members has led to the introduction of economic and technical co-operation, in order to attain growth and equitable development in the Asia-Pacific region. Economic and technical co-operation is expected to promote the growth of trade and investment in the region.[22] Some specific areas chosen for economic and technical co-operation are human resource development, industrial science and technology, small and medium enterprises, and economic infrastructure.

## Conclusions

Intra-regional interdependency through foreign trade and foreign direct investment has increased in East Asia, North America and Western Europe in recent years. Although regionalization has been intensified in these three regions, the causal factors behind regionalization in East Asia on the one hand and those in North America and Western Europe on the other hand appear to be different. For the regionalization in Western Europe and in North America, the formal preferential regional economic institutions, giving preferential treatment to the members and discriminatory treatment against non-members, namely the EU in Western Europe and NAFTA in North America, played an important role, while in East Asia market forces have been a major factor intensifying regionalization. Indeed, unilateral trade and FDI liberalization on an MFN basis has been an important policy measure in the East Asian economies and has promoted economic growth.

In recent years, however, regional institution building has become active in East Asia. ASEAN, whose members include seven East Asian countries, formed a free trade area, and APEC, whose members include not only East Asian economies but also those in North and South America and Oceania, has agreed to promote trade and FDI liberalization. In addition to these trade and FDI measures, both the ASEAN and

APEC have been active in promoting economic co-operation among their members.

There is a concern that APEC will turn inward-looking by becoming a free trade area, and that only the members will be treated preferentially. Since the intra-APEC trade is substantial for the APEC members, the trade diversion effect is likely to be small. As such, the members would gain from the formation of an FTA. However, its impact on non-members may be quite substantial, as their trade and FDI opportunities in the APEC economies would be greatly reduced. The APEC FTA may harm the world trading system.

East Asian countries should rigorously carry out trade and FDI liberalization not only to benefit themselves but also their trading partners and foreign investors. Moreover, further trade and FDI liberalization would contribute to the world economy, by promoting global free trade and FDI. This is important at a time when inward-looking regionalism is on the rise. As the scope for easy liberalization has been diminished for East Asian economies, regional as well as multilateral frameworks such as the ASEAN, APEC and the WTO should be effectively utilized.

**Notes**

The author wishes to thank Akie Iriyama for his research assistance.

1  In this chapter the term East Asia is used to include the following ten economies: China, Hong Kong, Indonesia, Japan, Korea, Malaysia, Philippines, Singapore, Taiwan and Thailand.
2  In addition to external factors such as rapid expansion of exports and FDI, the World Bank (1993) attributes the rapid economic growth of East Asia to such internal factors as sound macroeconomic policies and the accumulation of human and physical capital.
3  See Kawai and Urata (forthcoming) for a detailed discussion.
4  Kawai and Urata (1996) present evidence of such behaviour by Japanese firms.
5  Kawai and Urata (forthcoming) and Urata (1993) found in their studies that foreign trade and FDI are closely related.
6  In their study on Japan's foreign trade and FDI, Kawai and Urata (forthcoming) find that distance has a negative effect on Japan's bilateral trade flows, while it has a positive effect on its outward FDI.
7  Petri (1995) discusses the measurement and the interpretation of the gravity coefficients and presents the computed gravity coefficients for East Asia, North America, Western Europe, and the Pacific region.
8  It is worth noting that Urata (1996) finds that the inter-country linkages, measured by intensity indicators, in foreign trade and those in FDI are closely related, suggesting that foreign trade and FDI are complements. A similar observation is reported in Kawai and Urata (forthcoming) by applying the gravity model in their investigation of the determinants of the bilateral trade and FDI relationship.

9    For example, see Buzan (1995).
10   Other inter-governmental economic organizations established in the region include the Economic and Social Commission for Asia Pacific (ESCAP), established in 1947 as the UN Economic Commission for the Far East (ECAFE) and mainly noted for statistical compilations, and the Asian Development Bank, created in 1967 to facilitate development capital investment (Morrison 1996).
11   Tan (1995) and Plummer (1996) present concise discussions of the evolution and accomplishments of ASEAN.
12   See Tantraporn (1996) for a detailed description of the AFTA scheme.
13   See Tan (1995) for a description of these studies.
14   In July 1997, Laos and Myanmar became new members of ASEAN simultaneousy.
15   Morrison (1996) presents an overview of APEC.
16   Morrison (1996).
17   Today, APEC includes all the major economies of the region and the most dynamic, fastest growing economies in the world. APEC's 18 current member economies have a combined share of approximately one half of world GNP and world trade.
18   Morrison (1996).
19   It was the 1991 Seoul APEC Declaration that stated the objectives explicitly. At the first APEC leaders' meeting at Blake Island near Seattle in 1993, the vision of a community of Asia-Pacific economies was established. And then at Bogor in Indonesia in 1994, the leaders endorsed the Bogor Declaration with the explicit objectives and goals of APEC.
20   APEC Secretariat (1995).
21   The Osaka Declaration. APEC Secretariat (1995).
22   APEC Secretariat (1995).

**References**

APEC Secretariat (1995) Selected APEC Documents, Singapore.
Buzan, Barry (1995) 'The Post-Cold War Asia-Pacific Security Order: Conflict or Cooperation?' in Andrew Mack and John Ravenhill (eds), *Pacific Cooperation: Building Economic and Security Regimes in the Asia-Pacific Region*, Boulder CO: Westview Press.
Dee, Philippa, Chris Geisler, and Greg Watts (1996) 'The Impact of APEC's Free Trade Commitment', *Staff Information Paper*, Industry Commission.
Imada, Pearl, Manuel Montes, and Seiji Naya (1991) *A Free Trade Area*, Institute of Southeast Asian Studies, Singapore.
Kawai, Masahiro and Shujiro Urata (1996) 'Trade Imbalances and Japanese Foreign Direct Investment: Bilateral and Triangular Issues', *Discussion Paper Series* no. F-52, The Institute of Social Sciences, University of Tokyo.
—— (forthcoming) 'Are Trade and Direct Investment Substitutes or Complements?: An Empirical Analysis of Japanese Manufacturing Industries', in H. Lee and D. W. Roland-Holst (eds), *Economic Development and Cooperation in the Pacific Basin: Trade, Investment, and Environmental Issues*, Cambridge: Cambridge University Press.
Lewis, Jeffrey D., Sherman Robinson and Zhi Wang (1995) 'Beyond the Uruguay Round: The Implications of an Asian Free Trade Area', mimeo.
Morrison, Charles E. (1996) 'APEC: The Evolution of an Institution'. Paper

presented at the second workshop on APEC and Regime Creation, Seattle, Washington, 13–15August.

Petri, Peter A. (1995) 'The Interdependence of Trade and Investment in the Pacific', in E. K. Y. Chen and P. Drysdale (eds), *Corporate Links and Foreign Direct Investment in Asia and the Pacific*, Harper International, Australia.

Plummer, Michael G. (1996) 'ASEAN and Institutional Nesting in the Asia-Pacific: Leading from Behind in APEC'. Paper presented at the workshop on APEC and Regime Creation in Asia and the Pacific, East-West Centre, Hawaii, 11–13 January.

Tan, Kong Yam (1995) 'Regionalism in the Pacific Basin: Stumbling or Building Blocks for Global Free Trade'. Paper presented at the International Conference on Economic Development and Cooperation in the Pacific Basin, University of California, Berkeley, 30 June–1 July.

Tantraporn, Apiradi (1996) 'ASEAN and Regional Economic Cooperation', in OECD, *Regionalism and Its Place in the Multilateral Trading System*.

Urata, Shujiro (1993) 'Japanese Foreign Direct Investment and Its Effect on Foreign Trade in Asia', in T. Ito and A. O. Krueger (eds), *Trade and Protectionism*, The University of Chicago Press for NBER.

—— (1996) 'The Determinants of Intra-regional Economic Relationships in East Asia', mimeo.

World Bank (1993) *The East Asian Miracle: Economic Growth and Public Policy*, Oxford: Oxford University Press.

—————— *3* ——————

# Foreign and Intra-regional Direct Investments in ASEAN and Emerging ASEAN Multinationals

## Chia Siow Yue

## I Introduction

The focus of this chapter is on foreign and intra-regional direct investment flows into ASEAN countries and emerging ASEAN multinationals. The treatment of emerging ASEAN multinationals is necessarily brief in the absence of readily available data and the difficulty of generating case studies. Section II examines the trends and patterns of foreign direct investment (FDI) inflows in the ASEAN countries and the respective roles played by investors from the Triad, Asian NIEs and ASEAN, the vertical and horizontal regional division of labour, and the existence of business and production networks. Section III examines the investment environment in ASEAN, focusing on the growing investment competition that faces ASEAN countries and various measures and initiatives aimed at improving ASEAN's investment competitiveness. Section IV is a case study of Singapore's regionalization drive and its contribution to ASEAN economic integration and three emerging Singapore multinationals. Section V concludes.

## II Foreign Direct Investment in ASEAN Countries

*Trends in Inward FDI Stocks and Flows*

The lack of comprehensive, consistent, accurate and comparable data severely limits the analysis of trends and patterns of FDI in the ASEAN region as well as data aggregations and intercountry comparisons. National FDI data are usually drawn from balance of payments statistics and from investment boards' approval or commitment statistics. Balance of payments data do not provide country and sectoral breakdowns. Investment board data differ with respect to the definition and measurement of FDI and comprehensiveness of coverage; approvals/commitments also overstate the actual or realized investments.[1]

At the macro-level, FDI takes place in response to home country push factors and host country pull factors. The former includes the push to secure natural resources, surplus capital seeking higher returns, land and labour constraints, and rising costs and appreciating currencies. The latter includes attractive investment climates arising from large and rapidly growing markets, abundance of natural resources and low-wage labour, economic liberalization programmes and pro-investment policy regimes. At the micro level, Dunning's (1981) eclectic theory identified three sets of determinants of FDI flows. First, the investing firm must have an ownership advantage over competitors in the host country, usually in management skills, technology (patents, copyrights, production processes), marketing networks and financial resources. Second, the host country must possess some locational advantage to attract investments, usually availability of specific resources, market size and potential, and lower operating costs. Third, there must be an internalization advantage that induces the investing firm to choose the direct investment option over other arrangements for market penetration and technology transfer.

The ASEAN region's locational attractions lie in rich natural resource endowments, abundant labour supply, political and social stability, buoyant economies with rapidly growing markets, sound macroeconomic management policies and an FDI-friendly policy environment (particularly following economic reforms in Indonesia, Malaysia, Philippines, and Thailand since the mid-1980s). Table 3.1 shows four ASEAN countries (Malaysia, Singapore, Indonesia, Thailand) ranked among the top ten developing country recipients of FDI flows in the 1991–5 period.

Motivations of foreign investors in ASEAN countries have undergone significant changes. In the 1960s and 1970s the major motivations were to gain access to the abundant natural resources and protected domestic markets of ASEAN-4 countries (Indonesia, Malaysia, Philippines, Thailand), while using Singapore as an export platform. In the 1980s, investors were increasingly attracted to ASEAN as a manufacturing base and export platform, capitalizing on the abundant labour and low operating costs. Since the mid-1980s, ASEAN-4 countries have benefited from the surge in outward investments by Japan and the Asian newly

**Table 3.1**  Ten largest developing country recipients of FDI flows, 1991–95

| Rank | 1991 | | 1992 | | 1993 | | 1994 | | 1995 | | 1991–95 ann. aver. | |
|---|---|---|---|---|---|---|---|---|---|---|---|---|
| | Country | US$m. | Country | US$m. | Country | US$m. | Country | US$m. | Country | US$m. | Country | US$m. |
| 1 | Singapore | 4879 | China | 11156 | China | 27515 | China | 33787 | China | 37500 | China | 22865 |
| 2 | Mexico | 4742 | Malaysia | 5183 | Argentina | 6305 | Mexico | 7978 | Mexico | 6984 | Mexico | 5697 |
| 3 | China | 4366 | Mexico | 4393 | Singapore | 5016 | Singapore | 5588 | Malaysia | 5800 | Malaysia | 4867 |
| 4 | Malaysia | 3998 | Argentina | 4179 | Malaysia | 5006 | Malaysia | 4348 | Singapore | 5302 | Singapore | 4627 |
| 5 | Bermuda | 2489 | Bermuda | 3321 | Mexico | 4389 | Brazil | 3072 | Brazil | 4859 | Argentina | 3605 |
| 6 | Argentina | 2439 | Singapore | 2351 | Bermuda | 2960 | Bermuda | 2923 | Indonesia | 4500 | Bermuda | 2919 |
| 7 | Thailand | 2014 | Thailand | 2116 | Hungary | 2350 | Chile | 2518 | Argentina | 3900 | Brazil | 2477 |
| 8 | Venezuela | 1916 | Brazil | 2061 | Indonesia | 2004 | Peru | 2326 | Hungary | 3500 | Indonesia | 2374 |
| 9 | Indonesia | 1482 | Hong Kong | 2051 | Thailand | 1726 | Indonesia | 2109 | Chile | 3021 | Hungary | 1987 |
| 10 | Hungary | 1462 | Indonesia | 1777 | Poland | 1777 | Hong Kong | 2000 | Bermuda | 2900 | Thailand | 1759 |

Source: UNCTAD FDI database as reported in Odle (1996).

industrialized economies of Hong Kong, South Korea and Taiwan in response to currency appreciation, rising labour and land costs, growing labour shortage, and the globalization drive. The locational attractions of ASEAN-4 improved following economic reforms and FDI policy liberalization. The 1980s and 1990s witnessed a growing recognition of ASEAN's dynamic market potential, particularly in the larger ASEAN economies. The 1990s is also witnessing growing interest among multinational corporations (MNCs) in regional production networks, value chains and strategic alliances.

Inward FDI stock in the ASEAN-7 (including Vietnam) rose rapidly from US $24.8 billion in 1980 to US $168.8 billion in 1995 (table 3.2), while inflows rose from an annual average of US $4.4 billion in the period 1984–89 to US $19.6 billion by 1995 (table 3.3). The inward FDI stocks and flows were, however, very unevenly spread among the ASEAN countries. The major FDI recipients were Singapore, Indonesia and Malaysia; Singapore had the largest FDI stock of US $55.5 billion by 1995 but Malaysia had the largest inflow in 1995, followed by Singapore and Indonesia. The small inward FDI of Brunei reflects the smallness of the economy, while the small inward FDI of Vietnam reflects its restrictive FDI regime up to 1990. Up to 1995 FDI flows to the Philippines failed to grow in pace with those of its more dynamic neighbours; sharp increases in FDI were reported in 1996 as the political environment improved.

That ASEAN had become highly attractive to foreign investors is evident from the region's large share of FDI. By 1990, the ASEAN-7 accounted for 35.6 per cent of FDI flows to the developing world. However, the investment share declined in subsequent years as China experienced a phenomenal surge in inward investments. By 1994, ASEAN's investment share had declined to 16.4 per cent while China's share surged to 38.8 per cent. The following year showed faster growth of FDI flows to ASEAN than to China. This reversal may be temporary as China's huge and dynamic economy remains a strong magnet for global investment capital. Among the ASEAN countries, Singapore experienced the sharpest fall in investment share during the 1990–95 period, from 16.5 per cent in 1990 to 5.3 per cent in 1995. The Singapore experience is echoed in the other Asian NIEs of Hong Kong, South Korea and Taiwan, reflecting a 'switch' in investment destinations from the NIEs to the ASEAN-4 and from the ASEAN-4 to China. Falling investment shares are to be expected as new players enter the global investment market. Host countries should not be unduly concerned with falling investment shares as long as they continue to enjoy a growing volume of inward investment.

Sectoral and industrial distribution of inward FDI in ASEAN

**Table 3.2**   ASEAN – inward FDI stock, 1980–95

|  | 1980 | 1985 | 1990 | 1994 | 1995 |
|---|---|---|---|---|---|
| US$million: | | | | | |
| ASEAN: | 24787 | 49869 | 95529 | 149226 | 168785 |
| Brunei | 19 | 33 | 30 | 55 | 62 |
| Indonesia | 10274 | 24971 | 38883 | 46255 | 50755 |
| Malaysia | 6078 | 8510 | 14117 | 32653 | 38453 |
| Philippines | 1225 | 1302 | 2098 | 5352 | 6852 |
| Singapore | 6203 | 13016 | 32355 | 50189 | 55491 |
| Thailand | 981 | 1999 | 7980 | 14475 | 16775 |
| Vietnam | 7 | 38 | 66 | 247 | 397 |
| China | – | 3444 | 14135 | 90959 | 128959 |
| India | 1177 | 1075 | 1593 | 2778 | 4528 |
| Percentage share of developing countries: | | | | | |
| ASEAN: | 22.9 | 25.3 | 28.0 | 25.1 | 24.3 |
| Brunei | 0.0 | 0.0 | 0.0 | 0.0 | 0.0 |
| Indonesia | 9.5 | 12.7 | 11.4 | 7.8 | 7.3 |
| Malaysia | 5.6 | 4.3 | 4.1 | 5.5 | 5.5 |
| Philippines | 1.1 | 0.7 | 0.6 | 0.9 | 1.0 |
| Singapore | 5.7 | 6.6 | 9.5 | 8.5 | 8.0 |
| Thailand | 0.9 | 1.0 | 2.3 | 2.4 | 2.4 |
| Vietnam | 0.0 | 0.0 | 0.0 | 0.0 | 0.1 |
| China | 0.0 | 1.8 | 4.1 | 15.3 | 18.6 |
| India | 1.1 | 0.5 | 0.5 | 0.5 | 0.7 |
| S,E,SE Asia | 29.8 | 32.7 | 42.8 | 49.7 | 52.0 |
| Developing | 100.0 | 100.0 | 100.0 | 100.0 | 100.0 |

Source: UNCTAD, World Investment Report 1996, Annex Table 3.

countries reflects not only underlying comparative advantage but also biases created by selective industrial and FDI policies, and statistical biases due to incomplete statistical coverage. Every ASEAN country has pursued selective sectoral policies, and FDI has been actively promoted in some sectors and restricted or prohibited in others. In Singapore, FDI has been welcomed into almost all areas of economic activity, with restrictions imposed only on investments in the mass media, defence industries and financial institutions serving the domestic market. However, in accordance with the country's changing comparative advantage, FDI increasingly focuses on high-tech and high value-added industries and services, and the more sophisticated segments of the value chain.

The ASEAN-4 are resource-rich developing economies, with some-what different patterns of FDI inflows from that of Singapore. FDI is important in the resource sector, in plantations and minerals in the colonial period and in forestry and oil in the post-independence period. In

**Table 3.3** ASEAN – inward FDI flows, 1984–95

| | 1984-89 ann. av. | 1990 | 1991 | 1992 | 1993 | 1994 | 1995 |
|---|---|---|---|---|---|---|---|
| US$ million: | | | | | | | |
| ASEAN: | 4447 | 11994 | 12950 | 11683 | 14816 | 14248 | 19559 |
| Brunei | - | 3 | 1 | 4 | 14 | 6 | 7 |
| Indonesia | 406 | 1093 | 1482 | 1777 | 2004 | 2109 | 4500 |
| Malaysia | 798 | 2333 | 3998 | 5183 | 5006 | 4348 | 5800 |
| Philippines | 326 | 530 | 544 | 228 | 1025 | 1457 | 1500 |
| Singapore | 2239 | 5575 | 4879 | 2351 | 5016 | 5588 | 5302 |
| Thailand | 676 | 2444 | 2014 | 2116 | 1726 | 640 | 2300 |
| Vietnam | 2 | 16 | 32 | 24 | 25 | 100 | 150 |
| China | 2282 | 3487 | 4366 | 11156 | 27515 | 33787 | 37500 |
| India | 133 | 162 | 141 | 151 | 273 | 620 | 1750 |
| S,E,SE Asia | 9852 | 19803 | 20775 | 27174 | 46481 | 53619 | 65033 |
| Developing | 22195 | 33735 | 41324 | 50376 | 73135 | 87024 | 99670 |
| Percentage share of developing countries: | | | | | | | |
| ASEAN: | 20.0 | 35.6 | 31.3 | 23.2 | 20.3 | 16.4 | 19.6 |
| Brunei | 0.0 | 0.0 | 0.0 | 0.0 | 0.0 | 0.0 | 0.0 |
| Indonesia | 1.8 | 3.2 | 3.6 | 3.5 | 2.7 | 2.4 | 4.5 |
| Malaysia | 3.6 | 6.9 | 9.7 | 10.3 | 6.8 | 5.0 | 5.8 |
| Philippines | 1.5 | 1.6 | 1.3 | 0.5 | 1.4 | 1.7 | 1.5 |
| Singapore | 10.1 | 16.5 | 11.8 | 4.7 | 6.9 | 6.4 | 5.3 |
| Thailand | 3.0 | 7.2 | 4.9 | 4.2 | 2.4 | 0.7 | 2.3 |
| Vietnam | 0.0 | 0.0 | 0.1 | 0.0 | 0.0 | 0.1 | 0.2 |
| China | 10.3 | 10.3 | 10.6 | 22.1 | 37.6 | 38.8 | 37.6 |
| India | 0.6 | 0.5 | 0.3 | 0.3 | 0.4 | 0.7 | 1.8 |
| S,E,SE Asia | 44.4 | 58.7 | 50.3 | 53.9 | 63.6 | 61.6 | 65.2 |
| Developing | 100.0 | 100.0 | 100.0 | 100.0 | 100.0 | 100.0 | 100.0 |

Source: UNCTAD, World Investment Report 1996, Annex Table 1.

manufacturing, the focus of post-independence FDI up to the 1970s was on import substitution industries aimed at the domestic markets. Since then, FDI in manufacturing is increasingly in labour intensive and light manufactures for export. In recent years, FDI in electronics has grown rapidly in Malaysia and Thailand, while FDI in textiles and garments for export has grown rapidly in Indonesia and the Philippines. In Vietnam, FDI inflows have dominated four sectors, namely oil and gas, hotels and tourism, telecommunications, and light industries such as textiles and garments. Infrastructure-related investments are increasingly sought by ASEAN countries except Singapore to help overcome severe infrastructure bottlenecks and prepare for the future. New forms of foreign participation in infrastructure development have emerged, including build-operate-transfer (BOT) schemes.

*Sourcing of FDI*

Global investment flows reached US $315 billion in 1995 (UNCTAD 1996). FDI is spearheading globalization, as 39,000 parent firms invested US $2.7 trillion in 270,000 affiliates. The Triad (US, EU, Japan) are the major sources of the world's FDI stocks and flows, although the Asian NIEs (Hong Kong, Singapore, South Korea and Taiwan) are rapidly emerging as significant foreign investors within East Asia. FDI in developing countries is concentrated in East Asia, and more particularly in a limited number of countries.

Since the mid-1980s, intra-East Asian investments have been growing rapidly in volume and gaining investment share over FDI inflows from the US and EU. The major intra-regional flows are from Japan to Asian NIEs and ASEAN and from the Asian NIEs to China, ASEAN and Indochina. Smaller flows are from China to Hong Kong, among Asian NIEs, and among ASEAN members. The rapid growth of intra-East Asian investment flows reflects several developments. First, the past decade has witnessed the surge in Japanese outward FDI and the emergence of Asian NIEs as major regional investors. Second, the sluggish economic performance of western economies in the 1980s and their preoccupation with North American and West European economic integration have diverted the investment interest of western MNCs. Third, East Asian developing countries have become highly attractive investment locations in the 1980s. They have attractive factor endowments and cost competitiveness and their investment environments have improved with domestic political and social stability, trade and investment liberalization measures, and the rapid growth of domestic markets. Fourth, the geographical proximity of East Asian economies has facilitated intra-regional investments as they reduce information and transaction costs. Fifth, the resource diversity and different developmental stages among countries of the region facilitated a regional division of labour based on economic complementarities and differences in comparative advantages.

Table 3.4 shows Triad investments in ASEAN. Up to the mid-1980s, FDI flowing into the ASEAN region was mostly from the EC (mainly UK, Germany, Netherlands, France) and the US. Investing foreign firms have ownership advantages of capital, technology, managerial and marketing knowhow. Since then, FDI from the EC has grown in volume but declined in relative terms, except in Singapore. FDI from the US declined sharply in the Philippines but grew rapidly in the other ASEAN countries in the 1970s, with some levelling off in the 1980s, except in Singapore. In the 1980s FDI from Japan grew rapidly, particularly in the post-1986 period when Japanese outward investments

**Table 3.4** ASEAN – inward FDI from the Triad, 1980–93

|  | Inward Stock | | | Inward Flow | |
|  | 1980 | 1985 | 1993 | 1985–87 | 1990–93 |
|---|---|---|---|---|---|
| Indonesia (US$m) | 10274 | 15353 | 67625 | 1047 | 8999 |
| Percentage distribution: | | | | | |
| EU | 8.3 | 17.4 | 14.7 | 25.7 | 13.4 |
| Japan | 33.7 | 32.6 | 20.6 | 31.4 | 15.3 |
| US | 4.3 | 6.3 | 5.5 | 11.7 | 5.0 |
| Triad | 46.2 | 56.4 | 40.8 | 68.9 | 33.7 |
| Others | 53.8 | 43.6 | 59.2 | 31.1 | 66.3 |
| Malaysia (US$m) | 6462 | 8510 | 34091 | 818 | 5508 |
| Percentage distribution: | | | | | |
| EU | 26.6 | 26.6 | 17.1 | 10.3 | 15.2 |
| Japan | 17.6 | 18.8 | 21.8 | 34.7 | 20.7 |
| US | 6.4 | 7.1 | 10.5 | 7.9 | 12.9 |
| Triad | 50.6 | 52.5 | 49.5 | 52.9 | 48.8 |
| Others | 49.4 | 47.5 | 50.5 | 47.1 | 51.2 |
| Philippines (US$m) | 1225 | 2589 | 4389 | 121 | 329 |
| Percentage distribution: | | | | | |
| EU | 9.3 | 13.5 | 17.0 | 12.4 | 21.6 |
| Japan | 16.8 | 14.0 | 20.3 | 9.9 | 33.7 |
| US | 54.6 | 75.7 | 44.1 | 65.3 | 16.7 |
| Triad | 80.7 | 103.2 | 81.5 | 87.6 | 72.0 |
| Others | 19.3 | -3.2 | 18.5 | 12.4 | 28.0 |
| Singapore (US$m) | 3387 | 6708 | 19581 | 894 | 2098 |
| Percentage distribution: | | | | | |
| EU | 39.6 | 30.4 | 26.9 | 16.4 | 16.3 |
| Japan | 16.7 | 23.9 | 31.5 | 39.7 | 23.3 |
| US | 29.6 | 36.4 | 35.0 | 30.0 | 27.3 |
| Triad | 85.9 | 90.6 | 93.4 | 86.1 | 66.9 |
| Others | 14.1 | 9.4 | 6.6 | 13.9 | 33.1 |
| Thailand (US$m) | 981 | 2221 | 13918 | 259 | 2050 |
| Percentage distribution: | | | | | |
| EU | 15.9 | 15.8 | 10.7 | 9.3 | 10.2 |
| Japan | 29.1 | 28.0 | 32.9 | 38.6 | 29.4 |
| US | 32.8 | 32.5 | 17.3 | 26.6 | 15.2 |
| Triad | 77.8 | 76.2 | 60.9 | 74.5 | 54.8 |
| Others | 22.2 | 23.8 | 39.1 | 25.5 | 45.2 |

Source: UNCTAD, World Investment Report 1995. Singapore figures are revised and from Odle (1996).

surged after the sharp yen appreciation. ASEAN's share of Japanese outward FDI rose from 3.8 per cent in 1986 to 12.0 per cent by 1994. Japan's outward FDI worldwide peaked in 1989 and fell sharply in subsequent years, but investments in ASEAN experienced a less sharp decline in 1990–91 and grew absolutely in 1992.

Among the ASEAN countries only Singapore's FDI inflows into manufacturing continue to be dominated by the Triad. In the ASEAN-4 since the mid-1980s and in Vietnam more recently, FDI has been increasingly dominated by Japan and Asian NIEs. Investments from the Asian NIEs became pronounced after 1987 as investors were pushed into outward investment by cost factors and the exchange rate. Investments in ASEAN-4 (and China) capitalize on lower production costs, gain access to natural resources, and take advantage of textile quotas under the MFA (Multifibre Arrangement) and tariff preferences under the GSP (Generalized System of Preferences). These investors are also able to exploit firm-specific advantages such as lower managerial costs, appropriate technology and better understanding of host countries' business environment and consumer preferences than Western investors. Geographical proximity and infrastructure facilities in host countries have enabled these investors, most of whom are medium-sized enterprises, to locate their overseas operations near home headquarters so as to minimize transportation and transaction costs. Geographical proximity has been enhanced by ethnic and cultural affinity with the Chinese communities in the ASEAN countries. NIE investments in ASEAN-4 jumped three-fold in 1988 and overtook Japan by 1990.

In Vietnam, European investors dominated inflows in the early years of the open-door policy, largely in offshore oil and gas exploration. In the 1990s Asian investors have become the most prominent, with Hong Kong and Taiwan leading. Entry of US investors was restricted until the full lifting of the US embargo in early 1994 and subsequent normalization of diplomatic relations between the two countries. Japanese firms were initially constrained by the US embargo but have moved into Vietnam rapidly in recent years and are expected to increase rapidly their presence over the coming years. A 1995 survey of the Export-Import Bank of Japan shows that Japanese investors rate Vietnam the most attractive place to invest in the next ten years, after China and ahead of earlier favourites such as Malaysia and Singapore (Tejima 1995).

## Intra-ASEAN Investments

Official statistics show that intra-ASEAN investments account for only a small share of ASEAN's total inward FDI. Singapore is the main investor and Malaysia the main recipient. However, it is suspected that large amounts of intra-regional investments are not captured by the official statistics, including large cross-investments in real estate, mergers and acquisitions (some of which are reported in the Singapore press) and interlocking shareholdings of 'overseas Chinese' businesses. The establishment of the ASEAN Free Trade Area (AFTA) and growth triangles, and impending adoption of the ASEAN Investment Area (AIA), are expected to spur intra-regional investments.

As shown in table 3.5, the combined stock of inward and outward intra-ASEAN investments rose from US $3.3 billion in 1980 to US $14.2 billion in 1992, showing an annual growth rate of 12.9 per cent. However, with the faster growth of extra-ASEAN investments, the intra-ASEAN share (excluding Brunei and Vietnam for lack of data) fell from 13.4 per cent in 1980 to 9.2 per cent in 1992. This is much smaller than the intra-regional shares in the case of NAFTA (22.9%) and the EU (48.1%). Malaysia and Singapore dominate intra-ASEAN investments. In 1980, Malaysia accounted for 62.2 per cent of intra-ASEAN investments, followed by Singapore (26.6%) and Indonesia (7.3%); in 1992 Malaysia's share fell to 34.0 per cent, while the shares rose sharply for Singapore (33.3%) and Indonesia (22.4%).

The intra-ASEAN investment share is lower for inward investments and higher for outward investments. For inward FDI stock, the intra-ASEAN investment share fell from 10.2 per cent in 1980 to 6.3 per cent by 1992 even though the value of such investments grew from US $2.4 billion to US $8.6 billion (table 3.6); in contrast, the investment share of NIEs-3 rose from 10.6 to 16.8 per cent. The Triad's investment share remained dominant although it fell from 58.0 to 48.5 per cent. The low intra-ASEAN share of inward investments reflects the development level of ASEAN economies and their external orientation, since the major sources of capital and technology (and markets) are outside the region. While Singapore is a net capital exporter, the other ASEAN countries are still dependent on foreign capital inflows to cover the savings-investment gap and all ASEAN countries are heavily dependent on the advanced industrial countries (and to a lesser extent the Asian NIEs) for technology transfer. The bulk of intra-ASEAN investments is represented by Singapore investments in Malaysia, Indonesia and Thailand, and by Malaysian counter-investments in Singapore.

Although ASEAN's outward investment stock has grown rapidly, in 1992 it amounted to only 12 per cent of the region's inward FDI. And while the intra-ASEAN investment share of ASEAN's outward investment stock is high, it is declining, from 59.1 per cent in 1980 to 33.3 per cent in 1992 (table 3.7). The bulk of outward investments are concentrated in East Asia, indicating the strong regional orientation of ASEAN investors. Internationalization is growing, however, with the East Asian share falling from 79.9 per cent in 1980 to 53.9 per cent in 1992. The bulk of outward investments is accounted for by Singapore, with smaller shares by Malaysia and Indonesia.

**Table 3.5** ASEAN – distribution of inward and outward direct investment stock, 1980 and 1992

| | | World | Indon-esia | Malay-sia | Philip-pines | Singa-pore | Thai-land | ASEAN-5 | NIEs-3 | Japan | United States | European Union | Rest of world |
|---|---|---|---|---|---|---|---|---|---|---|---|---|---|
| **Amount in US$million:** | | | | | | | | | | | | | |
| Indonesia | 1980 | 9275.0 | – | 27.8 | 40.8 | 168.8 | 6.5 | 243.9 | 1067.6 | 3461.4 | 435.9 | 851.4 | 3214.7 |
| | 1992 | 65399.1 | – | 954.8 | 13.1 | 2099.3 | 111.2 | 3178.4 | 12196.9 | 13079.8 | 2818.7 | 7906.8 | 26218.5 |
| Malaysia | 1980 | 6567.8 | 27.6 | – | 0.7 | 2009.1 | 26.9 | 2064.3 | 601.0 | 1067.9 | 403.9 | 1618.3 | 812.4 |
| | 1992 | 24688.4 | 953.0 | – | 56.8 | 3698.3 | 111.1 | 4819.2 | 5500.6 | 4871.0 | 2115.8 | 4058.8 | 3323.1 |
| Philippines | 1980 | 1565.7 | 40.4 | 0.8 | – | 10.6 | 3.3 | 55.1 | 222.5 | 215.1 | 772.4 | 114.9 | 185.7 |
| | 1992 | 4885.1 | 14.7 | 56.2 | – | 129.9 | 6.8 | 207.6 | 946.7 | 843.7 | 1969.7 | 444.1 | 473.4 |
| Singapore | 1980 | 6134.7 | 52.1 | 798.1 | 14.1 | – | 17.8 | 882.2 | 762.5 | 626.4 | 1216.5 | 1795.6 | 851.5 |
| | 1992 | 45232.0 | 235.2 | 3731.6 | 153.8 | – | 592.5 | 4713.2 | 4351.3 | 7969.9 | 6830.0 | 8729.8 | 12637.8 |
| Thailand | 1980 | 1218.1 | 0.5 | 12.9 | 3.3 | 58.3 | – | 75.0 | 142.0 | 347.8 | 435.0 | 192.0 | 26.3 |
| | 1992 | 13140.0 | 38.1 | 53.9 | 6.6 | 1147.1 | – | 1245.7 | 3034.0 | 4233.7 | 2399.4 | 1311.4 | 915.9 |
| **ASEAN-5** | **1980** | **24761.3** | **120.6** | **839.6** | **58.9** | **2246.9** | **54.5** | **3320.5** | **2795.6** | **5718.6** | **3263.7** | **4572.3** | **5090.7** |
| | **1992** | **153344.6** | **1240.9** | **4796.5** | **230.2** | **7074.7** | **821.7** | **14164.0** | **26029.6** | **30998.1** | **16133.6** | **22450.7** | **43568.6** |
| **Percentage distribution:** | | | | | | | | | | | | | |
| Indonesia | 1980 | 100.0 | – | 0.3 | 0.4 | 1.8 | 0.1 | 2.6 | 11.5 | 37.3 | 4.7 | 9.2 | 34.7 |
| | 1992 | 100.0 | – | 1.5 | 0.0 | 3.2 | 0.2 | 4.9 | 18.7 | 20.0 | 4.3 | 12.1 | 40.1 |
| Malaysia | 1980 | 100.0 | 0.4 | – | 0.0 | 30.6 | 0.4 | 31.4 | 9.2 | 16.3 | 6.2 | 24.6 | 12.4 |
| | 1992 | 100.0 | 3.9 | – | 0.2 | 15.0 | 0.5 | 19.5 | 22.3 | 19.7 | 8.6 | 16.4 | 13.5 |
| Philippines | 1980 | 100.0 | 2.6 | 0.1 | – | 0.7 | 0.2 | 3.5 | 14.2 | 13.7 | 49.3 | 7.3 | 11.9 |
| | 1992 | 100.0 | 0.3 | 1.2 | – | 2.7 | 0.1 | 4.3 | 19.4 | 17.3 | 40.3 | 9.1 | 9.7 |
| Singapore | 1980 | 100.0 | 0.9 | 13.0 | 0.2 | – | 0.3 | 14.4 | 12.4 | 10.2 | 19.8 | 29.3 | 13.9 |
| | 1992 | 100.0 | 0.5 | 8.3 | 0.3 | – | 1.3 | 10.4 | 9.6 | 17.6 | 15.1 | 19.3 | 27.9 |
| Thailand | 1980 | 100.0 | 0.0 | 1.1 | 0.3 | 4.8 | – | 6.2 | 11.7 | 28.6 | 35.7 | 15.8 | 2.2 |
| | 1992 | 100.0 | 0.3 | 0.4 | 0.1 | 8.7 | – | 9.5 | 23.1 | 32.2 | 18.3 | 10.0 | 7.0 |
| **ASEAN-5** | **1980** | **100.0** | **0.5** | **3.4** | **0.2** | **9.1** | **0.2** | **13.4** | **11.3** | **23.1** | **13.2** | **18.5** | **20.6** |
| | **1992** | **100.0** | **0.8** | **3.1** | **0.2** | **4.6** | **0.5** | **9.2** | **17.0** | **20.2** | **10.5** | **14.6** | **28.4** |

Source: APEC, Foreign Direct Investment and APEC Economic Integration, 1995.

**Table 3.6** ASEAN – distribution of inward foreign direct investment stock, 1980 and 1992

| To | From | World | Indon-esia | Malay-sia | Philip-pines | Singa-pore | Thai-land | ASEAN-5 | NIEs-3 | Japan | United States | European Union | Rest of world |
|---|---|---|---|---|---|---|---|---|---|---|---|---|---|
| **Amount in US$million:** | | | | | | | | | | | | | |
| Indonesia | 1980 | 9230.6 | — | 25.8 | 40.6 | 134.8 | 6.5 | **206.8** | 1061.5 | 3461.5 | 437.5 | 851.1 | 3212.2 |
| | 1992 | 63015.8 | — | 132.3 | 12.6 | 2060.6 | 94.5 | **2300.1** | 12136.8 | 13069.5 | 2716.0 | 6736.4 | 26057.0 |
| Malaysia | 1980 | 6078.0 | 2.4 | — | 0.6 | 1682.4 | 14.0 | **1698.8** | 531.2 | 1067.3 | 388.4 | 1618.0 | 774.3 |
| | 1992 | 22584.0 | 822.1 | — | 45.2 | 2348.7 | 65.5 | **3281.5** | 5345.6 | 4871.4 | 2041.6 | 4051.6 | 2992.4 |
| Philippines | 1980 | 1280.9 | 0.0 | 0.4 | — | 5.3 | 0.0 | **5.6** | 63.8 | 215.1 | 699.4 | 114.1 | 182.9 |
| | 1992 | 4011.2 | 0.0 | 11.6 | — | 38.1 | 0.0 | **49.7** | 364.6 | 844.0 | 1901.7 | 422.4 | 428.8 |
| Singapore | 1980 | 5350.7 | 34.2 | 326.9 | 5.4 | — | 12.8 | **378.8** | 672.0 | 626.6 | 1201.7 | 1772.2 | 699.3 |
| | 1992 | 34446.4 | 37.9 | 1350.3 | 93.0 | — | 313.5 | **1794.7** | 2249.3 | 8015.7 | 5866.2 | 7953.7 | 8566.8 |
| Thailand | 1980 | 1205.2 | 0.5 | 12.9 | 3.3 | 57.7 | 0.0 | **74.5** | 136.1 | 347.8 | 429.1 | 191.6 | 26.2 |
| | 1992 | 12434.8 | 17.4 | 46.0 | 7.5 | 1057.0 | 0.0 | **1126.6** | 2822.7 | 4230.3 | 2150.0 | 1273.3 | 831.9 |
| **ASEAN-5** | **1980** | **23145.4** | **37.2** | **366.1** | **49.8** | **1880.1** | **33.3** | **2364.5** | **2464.6** | **5718.2** | **3156.1** | **4546.9** | **4895.0** |
| | **1992** | **136492.2** | **877.4** | **1540.3** | **158.2** | **5504.4** | **473.5** | **8552.5** | **22919.1** | **31030.8** | **14675.5** | **20437.3** | **38876.9** |
| **Percentsage distribution:** | | | | | | | | | | | | | |
| Indonesia | 1980 | 100.0 | — | 0.3 | 0.4 | 1.5 | 0.1 | **2.2** | 11.5 | 37.5 | 4.7 | 9.2 | 34.8 |
| | 1992 | 100.0 | — | 0.2 | 0.0 | 3.3 | 0.2 | **3.7** | 19.3 | 20.7 | 4.3 | 10.7 | 41.4 |
| Malaysia | 1980 | 100.0 | 0.0 | — | 0.0 | 27.7 | 0.2 | **28.0** | 8.7 | 17.6 | 6.4 | 26.6 | 12.7 |
| | 1992 | 100.0 | 3.6 | — | 0.2 | 10.4 | 0.3 | **14.5** | 23.7 | 21.6 | 9.0 | 17.9 | 13.3 |
| Philippines | 1980 | 100.0 | 0.0 | 0.0 | — | 0.4 | 0.0 | **0.4** | 5.0 | 16.8 | 54.6 | 8.9 | 14.3 |
| | 1992 | 100.0 | 0.0 | 0.3 | — | 1.0 | .. | **1.2** | 9.1 | 21.0 | 47.4 | 10.5 | 10.7 |
| Singapore | 1980 | 100.0 | 0.6 | 6.1 | 0.1 | — | 0.2 | **7.1** | 12.6 | 11.7 | 22.5 | 33.1 | 13.1 |
| | 1992 | 100.0 | 0.1 | 3.9 | 0.3 | — | 0.9 | **5.2** | 6.5 | 23.3 | 17.0 | 23.1 | 24.9 |
| Thailand | 1980 | 100.0 | 0.0 | 1.1 | 0.3 | 4.8 | — | **6.2** | 11.3 | 28.9 | 35.6 | 15.9 | 2.2 |
| | 1992 | 100.0 | 0.1 | 0.4 | 0.1 | 8.5 | — | **9.1** | 22.7 | 34.0 | 17.3 | 10.2 | 6.7 |
| **ASEAN-5** | **1980** | **100.0** | **0.2** | **1.6** | **0.2** | **8.1** | **0.1** | **10.2** | **10.6** | **24.7** | **13.6** | **19.6** | **21.1** |
| | **1992** | **100.0** | **0.6** | **1.1** | **0.1** | **4.0** | **0.3** | **6.3** | **16.8** | **22.7** | **10.8** | **15.0** | **28.5** |

Source: APEC, Foreign Direct Investment and APEC Economic Integration, 1995.

**Table 3.7**  ASEAN economies – distribution of outward direct investment stock, 1980 and 1992

| From | To | World | Indon-esia | Malay-sia | Philip-pines | Singa-pore | Thai-land | ASEAN-5 | NIEs-3 | Japan | United States | European Union | Rest of world |
|---|---|---|---|---|---|---|---|---|---|---|---|---|---|
| **Amount in US$million:** | | | | | | | | | | | | | |
| Indonesia | 1980 | 44.4 | – | 2.2 | 0.0 | 34.0 | 0.5 | 36.7 | 6.9 | 0.0 | -1.0 | 0.5 | 1.3 |
| | 1992 | 2383.3 | – | 822.7 | 0.0 | 37.4 | 16.7 | 876.8 | 61.5 | 9.1 | 101.1 | 1173.1 | 161.8 |
| Malaysia | 1980 | 489.8 | 25.5 | – | 0.4 | 326.9 | 12.9 | 365.7 | 70.7 | 0.0 | 16.0 | 0.0 | 37.4 |
| | 1992 | 2104.4 | 130.5 | – | 11.8 | 1350.2 | 46.3 | 1538.7 | 154.3 | 0.0 | 73.0 | 6.9 | 331.4 |
| Philippines | 1980 | 284.8 | 40.4 | 0.5 | – | 5.4 | 3.3 | 49.6 | 158.6 | 0.0 | 73.0 | 0.8 | 2.8 |
| | 1992 | 873.9 | 14.8 | 44.3 | – | 91.4 | 7.0 | 157.5 | 581.7 | 0.0 | 68.0 | 21.8 | 45.0 |
| Singapore | 1980 | 784.0 | 18.0 | 471.0 | 9.0 | – | 5.0 | 503.0 | 89.5 | 0.0 | 15.0 | 24.0 | 152.6 |
| | 1992 | 10785.6 | 199.5 | 2381.5 | 64.7 | – | 278.3 | 2922.9 | 2107.5 | 46.4 | 966.4 | 777.6 | 3964.8 |
| Thailand | 1980 | 12.9 | 0.0 | 0.0 | 0.0 | 0.6 | – | 0.6 | 5.9 | 0.0 | 5.9 | 0.3 | 0.1 |
| | 1992 | 705.2 | 21.3 | 7.8 | 0.1 | 90.5 | – | 119.7 | 209.5 | 4.0 | 249.1 | 37.9 | 85.0 |
| **ASEAN-5** | **1980** | **1615.9** | **84.0** | **473.7** | **9.4** | **367.0** | **21.7** | **955.7** | **331.5** | **0.0** | **108.9** | **25.6** | **194.2** |
| | **1992** | **16852.4** | **366.1** | **3256.3** | **76.6** | **1569.5** | **348.2** | **5615.6** | **3114.4** | **59.5** | **1457.5** | **2017.3** | **4588.1** |
| **Percentage distribution:** | | | | | | | | | | | | | |
| Indonesia | 1980 | 100.0 | – | 5.0 | : | 76.6 | 1.1 | 82.7 | 15.5 | : | -2.3 | 1.1 | 2.9 |
| | 1992 | 100.0 | – | 34.5 | – | 1.6 | 0.7 | 36.8 | 2.6 | 0.4 | 4.2 | 49.2 | 6.8 |
| Malaysia | 1980 | 100.0 | 5.2 | – | 0.1 | 66.7 | 2.6 | 74.7 | 14.4 | : | 3.3 | :: | 7.6 |
| | 1992 | 100.0 | 6.2 | – | 0.6 | 64.2 | 2.2 | 73.1 | 7.3 | : | 3.5 | 0.3 | 15.8 |
| Philippines | 1980 | 100.0 | 14.2 | 0.2 | – | 1.9 | 1.2 | 17.4 | 55.7 | : | 25.6 | 0.3 | 1.0 |
| | 1992 | 100.0 | 1.7 | 5.1 | – | 10.5 | 0.8 | 18.0 | 66.6 | : | 7.8 | 2.5 | 5.2 |
| Singapore | 1980 | 100.0 | 2.3 | 60.1 | 1.2 | – | 0.6 | 64.2 | 11.4 | : | 1.9 | 3.1 | 19.5 |
| | 1992 | 100.0 | 1.9 | 22.1 | 0.6 | – | 2.6 | 27.1 | 19.5 | 0.4 | 9.0 | 7.2 | 36.8 |
| Thailand | 1980 | 100.0 | : | : | 0.0 | 5.0 | – | 5.0 | 45.6 | : | 45.8 | 2.7 | 0.9 |
| | 1992 | 100.0 | 3.0 | 1.1 | 0.0 | 12.8 | – | 17.0 | 29.7 | 0.6 | 35.3 | 5.4 | 12.1 |
| **ASEAN-5** | **1980** | **100.0** | **5.2** | **29.3** | **0.6** | **22.7** | **1.3** | **59.1** | **20.5** | **0.0** | **6.7** | **1.6** | **12.0** |
| | **1992** | **100.0** | **2.2** | **19.3** | **0.5** | **9.3** | **2.1** | **33.3** | **18.5** | **0.4** | **8.6** | **12.0** | **27.2** |

Source: APEC, Foreign Direct Investment and APEC Economic Integration, 1995.

Table 3.8 Malaysia: cumulative investments in manufacturing from ASEAN countries, 1993

| Manufacturing industry | World | Brunei | Indonesia | Philippines | Singapore | Thailand | ASEAN | ASEAN % distribution | ASEAN share of world (%) |
|---|---|---|---|---|---|---|---|---|---|
| | | | | Paid-up capital in RM million | | | | | |
| Food manufacturing | 1,251.03 | 0.37 | 5.31 | 0.33 | 545.66 | 2.41 | 554.08 | 18.4 | 44.3 |
| Beverages & tobacco | 471.60 | 0.00 | 3.74 | 0.00 | 270.40 | 0.03 | 274.18 | 9.1 | 58.1 |
| Textiles & textile products | 825.45 | 3.01 | 0.57 | 0.00 | 206.82 | 3.00 | 213.40 | 7.1 | 25.9 |
| Leather & leather products | 34.94 | 0.00 | 0.00 | 0.00 | 4.74 | 0.00 | 4.74 | 0.2 | 13.6 |
| Wood & wood products | 468.87 | 0.04 | 5.93 | 0.00 | 54.69 | 0.08 | 60.74 | 2.0 | 13.0 |
| Furniture & fixtures | 94.59 | 0.00 | 0.00 | 0.00 | 16.49 | 0.00 | 16.50 | 0.5 | 17.4 |
| Paper, printing, publishing | 130.96 | 0.01 | 0.00 | 0.00 | 51.46 | 0.00 | 51.47 | 1.7 | 39.3 |
| Chemical & chemical products | 885.45 | 0.01 | 42.45 | 28.50 | 163.56 | 39.03 | 273.55 | 9.1 | 30.9 |
| Petroleum & coal | 883.15 | 0.11 | 0.00 | 0.00 | 39.12 | 0.00 | 39.23 | 1.3 | 4.4 |
| Rubber products | 454.98 | 0.08 | 0.57 | 0.00 | 119.44 | 0.56 | 120.64 | 4.0 | 26.5 |
| Plastic products | 432.85 | 0.00 | 0.00 | 0.00 | 65.85 | 0.58 | 66.43 | 2.2 | 15.3 |
| Non-metallic minerals | 738.16 | 0.00 | 0.01 | 0.01 | 296.34 | 0.28 | 296.65 | 9.8 | 40.2 |
| Base metal products | 659.67 | 0.01 | 7.17 | 0.00 | 219.66 | 0.00 | 226.83 | 7.5 | 34.4 |
| Fabricated metal products | 634.79 | 0.00 | 0.34 | 0.00 | 178.10 | 0.13 | 178.57 | 5.9 | 28.1 |
| Machinery | 389.72 | 0.43 | 0.38 | 0.00 | 110.19 | 0.42 | 111.46 | 3.7 | 28.6 |
| Electrical & electronics | 4,207.22 | 0.00 | 0.00 | 0.00 | 358.06 | 0.34 | 358.40 | 11.9 | 8.5 |
| Transport equipment | 539.38 | 0.00 | 0.03 | 1.00 | 113.72 | 2.78 | 117.53 | 3.9 | 21.8 |
| Scientific instruments | 254.98 | 0.00 | 0.00 | 0.00 | 31.50 | 0.00 | 31.50 | 1.0 | 12.4 |
| Miscellaneous | 141.75 | 0.00 | 1.10 | 0.00 | 22.31 | 0.53 | 23.94 | 0.8 | 16.9 |
| Total manufacturing | 13,499.50 | 1.12 | 67.50 | 29.85 | 2,868.08 | 50.21 | 3,016.76 | 100.0 | 22.3 |

Source: Malaysian Industrial Development Authority, Statistics on the Manufacturing Sector 1990–1994.

**Table 3.9**  Vietnam: inward foreign investment as of mid-August 1996

| Source Country | Inward Investment US$ million | % distribution |
|---|---|---|
| **ASEAN:** | **4464** | **20.48** |
| Brunei | 10 | 0.05 |
| Indonesia | 240 | 1.10 |
| Malaysia | 931 | 4.27 |
| Philippines | 217 | 1.00 |
| Singapore | 2400 | 11.01 |
| Thailand | 666 | 3.06 |
| Cambodia | 1.6 | 0.01 |
| Laos | 11 | 0.05 |
| **Asian NIEs):** | **8300** | **38.07** |
| Hong Kong | 2300 | 10.55 |
| South Korea | 2000 | 9.17 |
| Taiwan | 4200 | 18.35 |
| **Triad:** | **6126** | **28.10** |
| EU | 2426 | 11.13 |
| Japan | 2400 | 11.01 |
| United States | 1300 | 5.96 |
| Eastern Europe | 253 | 1.16 |
| Australia | 620 | 2.84 |
| Rest of World | 2024 | 9.28 |
| | | |
| Total | 21800 | 100.00 |

Source: Vietnam Economic Times, September 1996 reporting data from Ministry of Planning and Investment.

Table 3.8 shows the industrial breakdown of cumulative ASEAN investments in Malaysia's manufacturing sector in 1993. ASEAN investments constituted less than a quarter of the total and are concentrated in food manufacturing, electrical and electronics, non-metallic mineral products, beverages and tobacco, basic metal products and textiles and textile products. Singapore is the main regional investor. Table 3.9 shows that ASEAN accounts for a significant quarter share of Vietnam's FDI up to mid-August 1996, with Singapore the largest investor from ASEAN and the third largest after Taiwan and Japan.

## Regional Division of Labour and Production and Business Networks

Intra-East Asian investment is integrating production in East Asia (and ASEAN) and giving rise to a regional division of labour incorporating the flying geese (product cycle), value chain and production networks.

A vertical division of labour is emerging in East Asia among countries

at different tiers of economic development and stages of industrializa-
tion. Industries, production processes and technologies are transmitted
from a higher tier to a lower tier country as comparative advantage
changes and according to different stages of the product cycle, first from
Japan to Asian NIEs and then to ASEAN, China and Vietnam. Outward
intra-regional investments have facilitated the industrial restructuring
of the more advanced economies, while inward intra-regional investments have created new industrial capability in the next tier of
economies. In the 1980s the Asian NIEs were engaged in industrial
restructuring in response to land and labour scarcities and rising costs
following a sustained period of high economic and industrial growth;
they progressively relocated their labour intensive operations to neighbouring countries. By the early 1990s, the second tier NIEs, such as
Malaysia, were also experiencing labour shortages and rising
wages and the need for industrial restructuring. China, Vietnam,
Indonesia and the Philippines with low wages and abundant labour
supplies form the next tier.

A regional horizontal division of labour has also been evolving in East
Asia in response to the rapid development of new technologies,
shortened product life-cycles and increasing globalization and regionalization of production. It is no longer always true that an industry/
product is first established/produced in an advanced country and then
passed on to the next tier with the maturing product cycle. Increasingly,
countries specialize in different parts of the value chain and product
niches, and a new pattern of division of labour takes place. In the electronics industry, for example, Singapore became a global producer and
supplier of hard-disk drives and Malaysia of semiconductors, while
South Korea leads in the production of chips and Taiwan of personal
computers. Similarly, Hong Kong and Singapore increasingly function
as regional operational headquarters and procurement centres while
manufacturing functions are undertaken by other countries. International companies locate different parts of the value chain in different
host countries according to the comparative and competitive advantages of each location.

The dynamic industrial restructuring, emerging regional division of
labour and growth in intra-industry trade can be illustrated by
Singapore's trade in electronics (Chia 1996). In 1995, Singapore's total
trade in electronics reached S$153.5 billion, with imports of S$65.8
billion, domestic exports (that is, exports of domestic production) of
S$58.4 billion and re-exports of S$29.3 billion. Imports (for domestic use
and re-export) comprised 54.5 per cent electronic components, 30.6 per
cent industrial electronics and 14.9 per cent consumer electronics.
Domestic exports comprised 58.6 per cent industrial electronics, 28.6 per

cent electronic components and 13.3 per cent consumer electronics. Domestic exports have shifted increasingly from consumer electronics to industrial electronics, reflecting the restructuring of the Singapore electronics industry out of lower-end components and consumer electronics towards higher-end industrial electronics.

By 1995 Singapore's electronics trade with ASEAN reached S$41.3 billion, with imports of S$22.2 billion, domestic exports of S$9.6 billion and re-exports of S$9.5 billion, accounting respectively for 33.7, 16.5 and 32.4 per cent of Singapore's global electronics trade. The main trading partners in ASEAN are Malaysia and Thailand. Malaysia accounted for 22.4, 12.5 and 24.1 per cent respectively of Singapore's global trade while Thailand respectively accounted for 9.6, 3.2 and 6.4 per cent. The import, domestic export and re-export trade with Malaysia and Thailand is dominated by electronics parts and components, more particularly ICs, parts of data processing machines and peripherals, parts of TV/radio and telecommunications equipment, and parts of video sound recorders and reproducers. Imports of electronic components (including ICs), parts of data processing machines and peripherals, parts of TV/radio and telecommunications equipment and parts of video sound recorders and reproducers accounted for 68.9 per cent of electronics imports from Malaysia and 74.4 per cent from Thailand. Domestic exports of these electronic components and parts accounted for 94.0 per cent of domestic electronics exports to Malaysia and 77.6 per cent to Thailand. Re-exports of these electronic components and parts accounted for 86.7 per cent of electronics re-exports to Malaysia and 70.9 per cent to Thailand. The intra-industry trade (IIT) index for electronic components was 0.97 for Thailand and 0.87 for Malaysia; IIT for ICs was 0.91 for Malaysia and 0.95 for Thailand, for parts of data processing machines and peripherals it was 0.95 and 0.33, for parts of TV/radio and telecommunications equipment it was 0.67 and 0.32 and for parts of video sound recorders and reproducers it was 0.87 and 0.58. The high IIT index for some categories of electronics between Singapore on the one hand and Malaysia and Thailand on the other reflects in part the restructuring of lower-end production out of Singapore and its relocation to neighbouring countries. For example, Hewlett Packard in Singapore relocated its labour intensive production of disk drives and semiconductors to Malaysia and Thailand respectively; these are then shipped back to Singapore for testing, assembly and packaging, and the finished goods are then shipped to the parent company in the US.

There has been considerable interest in East Asian (and ASEAN) de facto integration by Japanese and 'overseas Chinese' business and production networks. Japanese manufacturers increasingly treat the East Asian region as an integrated unit, relocating plants to service regional and global markets and promoting a regional division of labour according to production costs, technology and target markets. Since the mid-1980s, Japan has invested heavily in the manufacturing sectors of Asian NIEs initially and ASEAN subsequently, relocating production which was no longer competitive in Japan. There has been upgrading of production processes and products in the Asian NIEs, transfer of mature production processes and products to locations with lower manufacturing costs, and concentration of production of single products to achieve economies of scale and improve cost competitiveness (JETRO 1995). Overseas affiliates are linked with parents and affiliates in Japan through management control and sourcing of capital goods and parts and components.

In a different way, the 'overseas Chinese' businesses in East Asia have been linking with each other to form webs of business networks. This process has accelerated in the past decade as the overseas Chinese investors gained in financial and technological strength, and as China and the Southeast Asian countries became more open to foreign investments. The best example of the Chinese business and production network is that taking place in the Chinese economic zone encompassing Hong Kong-Macau, Taiwan and south China's coastal provinces of Guangdong and Fujian. However, business networking between the overseas Chinese of Hong Kong and Taiwan and those of Southeast Asia, and among the ASEAN countries, is also increasingly evident. Many studies have shown the role of 'quanxi', or relationships and networks in the organization of Chinese business. Yeung's (1995) study of Hong Kong TNCs in ASEAN noted the interaction of regulatory regimes, social organization and network relationships at three distinct levels. First, at the macro extra-firm level, regulatory barriers, in particular the suspicion of some host ASEAN countries towards foreign capital, including that from overseas Chinese, induce Hong Kong investors to enter into various extra-firm political relationships. Second, at the micro level, co-ordination and control within the Chinese business networks are best achieved through trusted family members and associates. Third, at the intermediate inter-firm level are the friendship and partnership networks. The Chinese business system has traditionally been built upon interpersonal trust relations and family and business networks. And Chinese businesses develop a complex shareholding to overcome equity ownership regulations in several ASEAN countries. Cross-border investments may involve multiple partners from several countries; ethnic and cultural ties reduce transaction costs.

## III   Improving the ASEAN Investment Environment

*Unilateral Investment Liberalization and Facilitation*

The ASEAN region has been highly successful in attracting FDI. However, there is growing concern among ASEAN countries over their ability to maintain their positions as favoured locations. First, investment competitiveness in some economies has been eroded by rising costs and emerging shortages of labour, skills and infrastructure after a period of sustained high economic growth. Second, the ASEAN region is facing increased competition for FDI from many directions, particularly integration movements and economic liberalization and reforms in various parts of the world.

The investment competitiveness of ASEAN can be examined from three perspectives, namely policy competitiveness, cost competitiveness and market competitiveness (Chia 1996). First, there is a need for policy reforms to deregulate and 'marketize' their economies, and for greater policy coherence in the use of investment incentives and disincentives. Second, there is a need to accelerate the development of physical infrastructure and human resources, which have become serious bottlenecks to FDI in some ASEAN countries, and to adopt further measures to raise productivity levels. Third, there is a need to improve the market attraction of ASEAN and improve cost competitiveness through accelerating the pace of trade liberalization under the ASEAN Free Trade Area (AFTA) and through development of growth triangles. Given the limited market size of AFTA, it is critical for ASEAN to remain outward looking and to seek strategic trade and investment alliances with other regional groupings, countries and firms. Section III focuses on policy competitiveness.

Until the mid-1980s, ASEAN countries showed wide diversities in policies and attitudes towards FDI, which reflected different historical experiences and national priorities. Singapore has always maintained a highly open economy with free trade and capital flows. The government pursues a strongly pro-active policy with aggressive investment promotion efforts by the Economic Development Board; liberal use of investment incentives; and, to overcome the limitations posed by lack of natural resources and market, more stringent labour and environmental regulations, and relatively high land and labour costs, performance requirements are minimal. Singapore also has locational advantages in the form of political stability, sound macroeconomic policies, and efficient administration and infrastructure.

Until the mid-1980s, the ASEAN-4 (Indonesia, Malaysia, Philippines, Thailand) had fairly restrictive FDI policies. For some countries, constitutional provisions and economic nationalism prohibited or severely restricted foreign ownership of land, natural resources and corporate equity. The desire to nurture infant industries, protect domestic entrepreneurs and small and medium enterprises, and maintain control of the financial sector, led to import substitution in manufacturing and restrictions on foreign ownership and participation in manufacturing, distributive trades and financial services. Restrictive FDI regimes in these countries have been facilitated by ready access to other forms of external financing (official flows and commercial borrowing) and by the oil and commodity booms.

By the mid-1980s the ASEAN-4 economies were confronted with problems – the international debt crisis and drying up of commercial bank lending; the domestic economic slowdown; falling oil and commodity prices, which impacted adversely on export earnings, balance of payments, government revenue and development finance; and the heavy fiscal burden of non-performing state-owned enterprises. There was growing recognition that FDI could contribute positively to economic growth and employment generation, industrial upgrading and the creation of internationally competitive industries. FDI brings not only capital, but also technology, management skills, modern industrial organization and marketing networks. There was also growing recognition of the linkage between trade and FDI. Trade liberalization efforts in ASEAN have to be complemented by investment liberalization to reap maximum benefits. Growth in FDI arises from reductions in trade barriers as well as reductions in investment barriers. Finally, the formation of trading blocs in North America and Western Europe, and the economic reforms and liberalization sweeping across the socialist economies in Eastern Europe and East Asia, led to fears of investment diversion and pressured ASEAN governments towards 'competitive liberalization'.

Governments embarked on unilateral liberalization, deregulation and privatization. FDI policy liberalization is characterized by the following (Chia 1995): First, the general policy environment becomes more friendly towards private enterprise, as governments seek to limit their intervention in the economy through deregulation and privatization. Second, the administration of FDI is streamlined towards simpler, speedier and less restrictive investment approval procedures, greater transparency and consistency in applying investment incentives and performance requirements, and better co-ordination between government agencies in policy formulation and implementation, resulting in reduced administrative costs and speedier and more effective policy delivery. One stop investment centres eased the administrative hassle facing foreign investors. Decentralized investment approvals for geographically dispersed areas help speed up the approval and implementation process.

Third, the FDI incentive–disincentive package has shifted towards positive incentives and away from restrictions and performance requirements, in recognition that it is net incentives that matter. Existing FDI legislations have been amended or more liberal interpretations of their restrictive elements allowed. Incentives are also more geared towards promoting competitive industries and activities, with less reliance on protective measures such as tariffs and restrictive licensing. Investment incentives include tax holidays, accelerated depreciation allowances, import duty exemptions and concessions, and subsidised credit and infrastructural facilities. Performance requirements and restrictions generally pertain to land and equity ownership, restricted sectors and industries, local content, local employment and manpower training, technology transfer, and export performance.

Fourth, the liberalization trend is also towards greater equality in policy treatment of foreign and domestic investors. National treatment is likely to become more acceptable as domestic enterprises gain competence and two-way investments become more commonplace, with individual countries having interests as both investor and recipient.

Fifth, in an effort to create favourable operating conditions for foreign investors, host countries have established industrial estates and export processing zones to provide easier access to land and infrastructural facilities and services. In land-scarce Singapore, such estates have enabled the quick start-up of commercial production, an important consideration for investors in electronics, an industry characterized by rapid technological changes and ever-shortening product life-cycles. In other ASEAN countries, export processing zones provide a production environment with minimal trade restrictions, allowing for the imports of capital goods and intermediate products at competitive world prices, in addition to tax holidays, and provision of infrastructure and industrial facilities. The existence of these zones, however, raises questions regarding the subsidies to infrastructure and industrial facilities provided, and the extent of linkages and spillover effects with the rest of the economy.

FDI inflows into various ASEAN countries surged after 1986, except in the Philippines, where political uncertainties continued to deter investors. The relaxation of performance requirements and restrictive regulations and the generous offer of investment incentives led to a convergence of FDI policies among ASEAN countries. This convergence has meant that host countries have to pay greater attention to other factors to maintain or secure a competitive edge, such as improvements in bureaucratic efficiency, greater emphasis on human resource development and provision of physical infrastructure and industrial facilities. Countries are also exploring investment co-operation to improve their locational attractions.

## Regional Co-operation Initiatives

### Industrial co-operation schemes
As part of ASEAN's efforts to promote trade and investment flows and industrial development, three industrial co-operation schemes were introduced in the late 1970s and early 1980s. However, the ASEAN Industrial Projects (AIP), ASEAN Industrial Complementation (AIC) and ASEAN Industrial Joint Venture (AIJV) schemes produced limited results in regional industrial co-operation and intra-ASEAN industrial investments. The lack of success indicates that these efforts are second-best solutions to generalized trade and investment liberalization.

Nonetheless, a new ASEAN Industrial Co-operation (AICO) scheme was launched in April 1996. AICO aims not only to attract more investments to the ASEAN region but also to increase intra-ASEAN investments by providing an institutional framework for private sector collaboration. AICO is an improvement on earlier industrial co-operation schemes and AICO projects enjoy better benefits than AFTA. The approval process is simpler and speedier; applications will be processed within 60 days of submission. And while AFTA products will enjoy 0–5 per cent tariffs only by year 2003, or at best by year 2000, AICO products enjoy 0–5 per cent tariffs immediately upon approval. To qualify for AICO, a project has to involve at least two ASEAN countries and at least one company from each; the company must be incorporated in an ASEAN country with at least 30 per cent national equity (with waiver on a case-by-case basis).

Hopefully AICO will overcome the problems faced by earlier industrial co-operation schemes. To succeed, the emphasis should not be on market-sharing but on production networking and regional specialization to realize the benefits of clustering and economies of scale in order to achieve international competitiveness. An early beneficiary of the new scheme could be the ASEAN automotive industry, given the nature of its production process. For example, an 'ASEAN car' could be produced with parts and components produced in different ASEAN countries. Such a car could be the joint product of indigenous ASEAN car producers, the joint product of affiliates of Triad car producers located in various ASEAN countries, or the joint effort of indigenous ASEAN and foreign investors. A Singapore newspaper (*Business Times*, 1 May 1996) reporting on the finalization of the AICO scheme in late April, noted that Singapore and the Philippines were already considering at least 20 joint industrial projects to take advantage of the AICO scheme.

*ASEAN growth triangles*
The ASEAN growth triangle is an innovative form of subregional co-operation aimed at promoting intra-ASEAN and foreign investments. It is a transnational investment zone offering in a contiguous area minimal border restrictions to exploit economic complementarity and pooled resources. It combines the competitive strengths of its constituent areas – integrating the capital, technology and human resources of its more advanced areas with the land, natural resources and labour of its less advanced areas. Three ASEAN growth triangles (GTs) are now established.

The southern IMS (Indonesia–Malaysia–Singapore) growth triangle was launched in 1989 and encompasses the Indonesian Riau islands, Johor state in south Malaysia and Singapore. This growth triangle is characterized by strong government support (particularly Indonesia and Singapore), economic complementarity of the participating areas, geographical proximity and a well established facilitating infrastructure. Government support ensures speedy project approval and implementation. Economic complementarity improves the locational advantage of the investment zone – pooling of resources, exploiting differences in comparative advantage and cost structures. Geographical proximity and developed transportation and telecommunications links minimize transaction and information costs, allow for exploitation of economies of agglomeration and scale and the rationalization of production. Foreign MNCs and local enterprises in Singapore relocate manufacturing functions to the lower-cost areas of IMS while retaining in Singapore the less labour-intensive and land-intensive functions. However, the growth of IMS is increasingly constrained by labour shortages in Johor and Batam, as well as a lack of free trade between its constituent parts.

The northern IMT (Indonesia–Malaysia–Thailand) growth triangle encompasses provinces and states in western Indonesia, northern Malaysia and southern Thailand. The BIMP–EAGA (Brunei–Indonesia–Malaysia–Philippines East ASEAN growth area) encompasses Brunei, eastern Indonesia, southern Philippines and eastern Malaysia. Both growth triangles are much larger in area and more geographically dispersed than the southern GT and lack interlinking transportation networks, so that extensive infrastructural development would be crucial to their success. Prospects for industrial co-operation through relocation of industrial activities from the more advanced to the less advanced areas are less favourable than those in the southern GT. However, both GTs are rich in natural resources and there are good prospects for investment co-operation to develop natural resources, tourism facilities and infrastructure. Private sector participation would depend crucially on commercial viability.

The Greater Mekong Subregion (GMS) encompasses the Mekong River and riparian parts of Cambodia, Laos, Myanmar, Thailand, Vietnam and Yunnan province in southwest China. These areas cover over 2 million sq km, have a population of over 220 million, and form a natural economic territory with shared resources as well as ethnic and cultural links. However, development is severely constrained by short-ages of financial and technical resources and poor infrastructure. Investment requirements for infrastructure alone are estimated at US $40 billion over the next 25 years. Multilateral institutions like the World Bank and Asian Development Bank are expected to invest about US $20 billion. As countries in the GMS (except for Yunnan in China) are members and potential members of ASEAN, the present ASEAN membership has collectively and separately expressed great interest in co-operating to develop the subregion and in mobilizing other countries to provide financial and technical resources. ASEAN endorsed its commitment to the development of the Greater Mekong at its 5th Summit in December 1995.

*ASEAN Free Trade Area (AFTA)*
Agreement to establish the ASEAN Free Trade Area (AFTA) was reached in January 1992. The process of dismantling intra-regional trade barriers should be completed by year 2003 when tariffs would reach the 0–5 per cent level. The market integration initiative is aimed at improving the ASEAN region's investment competitiveness and enhancing investment flows in a number a ways – it induces intra-ASEAN investments through rationalization and regional special-ization; it attracts defensive FDI as foreign suppliers seek to maintain market share through investments; and it induces other foreign investors to gain an early foothold in a larger and rapidly expanding market.

With an integrated market and pooled resources, ASEAN would be more attractive to foreign and regional investors, and production in the region could be rationalized to reflect comparative advantage and scale economies, which could be exploited to improve international competitiveness. A number of studies are currently under way to examine foreign investor responses to the establishment of AFTA – are investors attracted by AFTA as a market and production base? would there be regional division of labour? what are the competitive strengths and locational advantages of each ASEAN country? The attraction of AFTA as a market will depend on the size of the integrated market and its pace of integration, while its attraction as an export production base will depend on its cost level and structure. In 1995 the ASEAN-7 had a combined market of 420 million people and purchasing power of around US $500 billion growing at 6–8 per cent a year. In market size, AFTA is much smaller than the EU or NAFTA; while the differences in population size are not too large, ASEAN's effective market size as determined by its GNP is only a fraction of those of the EU or NAFTA; this would be true even if AFTA membership is eventually extended to include the whole of Southeast Asia. In cost levels, AFTA is on average more cost competitive than the EU or NAFTA. However, cost levels of some NAFTA and EU members such as Mexico and Portugal are not out of line with that of the more advanced ASEAN countries. More importantly, the cost levels in ASEAN countries, with the exception of Vietnam, are perceived to be higher than in China and India.

The ASEAN Free Trade Area attempts to achieve market integration through removing all border and non-border impediments to trade flows. However, reduction in trade barriers alone may not be enough to maintain ASEAN's investment competitiveness for foreign and regional investors. ASEAN countries need to further liberalize their investment regimes and engage in joint efforts at investment promotion.

*ASEAN Investment Area (AIA)*
In response to the growing concern regarding ASEAN's competitiveness as an investment location, the 5th ASEAN Summit in December 1995 agreed to establish an ASEAN Investment Area (AIA) to attract foreign investment into ASEAN and promote intra-ASEAN investment. ASEAN governments are studying the feasiblity of realizing AIA by year 2010.

The AFTA Agreement contains no specific investment provisions. Investment matters in the ASEAN grouping are governed by the 1987 Agreement for the Promotion and Protection of Investments — all intra-ASEAN investments are to be governed by the laws and regulations of the host country; right of establishment and national treatment are bilateral matters and there are no general provisions on an ASEAN-wide basis; there are no provisions on investment incentives and performance requirements; investors are protected from expropriation and nationalization, except for public purpose or interest, in which case there should be due process of law, non-discrimination, and prompt and adequate compensation; repatriation of capital and earnings should be permitted without unreasonable delay and in convertible currencies; taxation matters are governed by domestic laws and bilateral investment agreements; investment disputes should as far as possible be settled between the disputing parties, failing which the ASEAN economic ministers would arbitrate, failing which the dispute can be submitted for international arbitration by either disputing party. These investment provisions are limited in comparison to NAFTA's investment provisions or with the APEC Nonbinding Investment Principles.

The NAFTA Agreement includes a far-reaching investment agreement providing for the elimination of investment barriers, basic guarantees for investors, and a dispute settlement mechanism. Investors are accorded national treatment. Performance requirements are disallowed, except for public sector procurement, export incentive programmes and international aid activities; also disallowed is the lowering of domestic standards on the environment to attract investment. National treatment is extended to the protection of intellectual property. Member economies determine their liberalization commitments and exceptions to national treatment and performance requirements; for example, Mexico liberalized its investment regulations for both partner economies and extended this liberalization to others on a most-favoured-nation (MFN) basis. Expropriation is prohibited except for reasons of public welfare and on a non-discriminatory basis, and with fair and timely compensation.

The APEC Nonbinding Investment Principles agreed upon at the Bogor Summit in November 1994, call for, *inter alia*, transparency of investment laws and regulations, non-discrimination between source economies, national treatment except as provided for in domestic laws, and minimization of performance requirements. The Principles should reduce informational and transaction costs facing investors, improve the welfare effects of foreign investments, avoid zero-sum competition among host countries, and balance the interests of home and host governments and investing firms. However, as a non-binding agreement, accession would depend on the convergence of national and regional interests. ASEAN countries are not in common agreement on APEC's investment principles, more particularly in multilateralizing national treatment.

Instead ASEAN governments are considering the establishment of an ASEAN Investment Area (AIA) to promote intra-ASEAN and international investments. The proposed AIA raises a number of issues regarding investment co-operation and investment rules. First, there is an urgent need for standardizing the collection and compilation of investment data and providing adequate, transparent and timely information on the ASEAN countries' investment laws, policies, regulations, administrative procedures and guidelines. The APEC Informal Group on Regional Trade Liberalization (November 1993) and the APEC Economic Committee (June 1995) have, respectively, taken the first steps in compiling information on foreign investment regimes and constructing matrices on inward and outward FDI stocks of APEC countries. Such efforts need follow-up action in ASEAN countries. Adequate, reliable and timely information would improve official policy making, business decision making and economic analysis. Transparency and common simplified rules and procedures would reduce uncertainty and information and transaction costs, particularly for investors operating in more than one ASEAN country.

Second, co-operation in investment promotion would be more effective than investment competition in maximizing the investment flows to the ASEAN region, particularly in attracting MNCs that are looking at alternative investment locations in NAFTA, Latin America, Eastern and Central Europe, China and India. Investment boards could map out common strategies and mount joint investment promotion missions. Competition between member states to influence investment location through the competitive offer of investment incentives lowers the regional benefits that FDI provides. Unfortunately, investment promotion efforts are still very much viewed as zero-sum games by national investment boards.

Third, ASEAN governments have pro-active industrial policy and make widespread use of investment incentives and performance requirements to promote FDI inflows, channel them into priority sectors, activities and locations, and improve their contributions to the economy. The use of investment incentives, particularly fiscal incentives such as the tax holiday, to influence investment decisions have come under criticism by economists who are concerned over their distortionary effects on investment and production. They question their efficacy when linked to performance requirements as they can cancel out. It is preferable for ASEAN governments to remove restrictions and performance requirements rather than offset their negative effects by the offer of generous investment incentives. Many restrictions and performance requirements have been liberalized in recent years. ASEAN countries have already achieved a high level of uniformity in incentive packages through unilateral reforms. Closer co-operation on policies on incentives and performance requirements would facilitate cross-border investments among ASEAN countries as this would minimize information and transaction costs – businesses would then face an almost common policy regime and make their investment decisions based on economic fundamentals.

Fourth, there is the issue of right of establishment, national treatment and MFN, treatment. All countries impose some restrictions on right of establishment, prohibiting or limiting inward FDI in certain sectors and activities – this includes screening of FDI, restrictions on land and equity ownership, and prohibition or restriction on entry into 'strategic' sectors. Governments justify such restrictions on grounds of national sovereignty and public interest, including public security, cultural preservation, and development and protection of local enterprise. However, non-transparency and the high degree of discretionary power could lead to abuse.

Measures violating national treatment include restrictions on ownership and performance requirements which do not apply equally to domestic enterprises, as well as differential access to investment incentives, government assistance, and subsidies and procurement contracts. Should ASEAN governments accord national treatment (including right of establishment) to investments from other ASEAN countries to promote intra-ASEAN investments? A priori, when foreign investments yield similar economic benefits as domestic investments, restrictions on right of establishment and performance requirements cannot be justified on economic grounds. The 1987 Investment Agreement only provides national treatment for ASEAN investors through bilateral negotiations, not extendable to other ASEAN countries on an MFN basis. The APEC Nonbinding Investment Principles provide for national treatment, but allow for exceptions as provided for in domestic laws, regulations and policies. There is a strong case for the national treatment principle to be adopted ASEAN-wide; it promotes intra-regional investments and is consistent with the provisions in other regional trading arrangements such as NAFTA and with GATT/WTO principles (Chia 1996). Highly selective exceptions to national treatment can be made on grounds of 'public interest' and for measures aimed more specifically at promoting and upgrading domestic enterprise rather than at restricting FDI. In all ASEAN countries, there is need to develop robust domestic private sectors, and the infant industry argument can be advanced to justify preferential treatment for domestic industries and small and medium enterprises. However, both exceptions should be clearly identified, transparent and time-bound. As ASEAN countries increasingly are both host and home to cross-border investments, 'public interest' would increasingly converge with the national treatment principle. However, ASEAN governments may not be ready to adopt the national treatment principle alongside an unconditional MFN principle.

The MFN principle is enshrined in the GATT/WTO and is embodied in the APEC Nonbinding Investment Principles and the multilateral investment codes being proposed by the OECD and the European

Commission. The fundamental economic argument in its favour is that discrimination distorts investment decisions and encourages less efficient production. Should ASEAN investors be accorded preferential treatment over investors from non-ASEAN sources? A case for preferential treatment of ASEAN investors is hard to justify on economic grounds, unless ASEAN investors confer unique and special advantages on host economies. ASEAN investing firms are unlike Triad multinationals – they are less globalized, are smaller in size and have weaker ownership advantages in terms of financial, technological and managerial resources and procurement and marketing networks. Some studies, however, have noted that TNCs from developing countries (including ASEAN) have different ownership-specific advantages – they are more amenable to joint ventures with local partners (reflecting weaker ownership advantages), thus providing stronger local linkages and integrating more effectively with the host economy; they bring with them more appropriate and compatible technologies, management styles and products. A case can also be made for preferential treatment if it promotes the growth of indigenous ASEAN multinationals; ASEAN needs more indigenous multinationals to compete in the global economy. The exclusionary impact would be reduced when non-ASEAN investors enter into partnership with ASEAN investors and receive national treatment.

Fifth, there is the issue of protection of foreign investments. In the 1987 Investment Agreement, ASEAN investors are protected from expropriation and nationalization, except for public purpose or interest, in which case there should be due process of law, non-discrimination, and prompt and adequate compensation. Repatriation of capital and earnings is permitted without unreasonable delay and in convertible currencies. On taxation, separate bilateral agreements provide for avoidance of double taxation. Both the Investment Agreement and the AFTA Agreement made no provisions for a dispute settlement mechanism, reflecting the general reluctance in ASEAN to resort to legalistic procedures to resolve conflicts. To simplify legal and administrative procedures, ASEAN should have a region-wide agreement guaranteeing investors protection from expropriation and the right to repatriation of capital and earnings and avoidance of double taxation. It is also time that ASEAN move towards a formal settlement mechanism for the resolution of trade and investment disputes; such disputes could become increasingly common as trade and investment linkages grow and would put an undue strain on the ASEAN economic ministers.

## IV　Singapore's Regionalization Drive and Emerging TNCs

Singapore's direct investment abroad has expanded rapidly in recent years, with the stock reaching S$46.2 billion (US $32.6 billion) by 1995 (table 3.10) and the number of overseas affiliates exceeding 5000. Investments were concentrated in finance (50.1%), manufacturing (24.6%), commerce (9.8%) and real estate and construction (8.4%). Firms with foreign-equity capital spearheaded the outward investment drive – wholly Singaporean firms accounted for only 24.0 per cent of the outward investments, while foreign-controlled firms (wholly and majority foreign-owned) accounted for 47.5 per cent and majority local-owned firms accounted for 28.4 per cent.

The outward investment, particularly in manufacturing, reflects the maturing of the Singapore economy after three decades of sustained economic growth. Domestic factor supply constraints, specifically land and labour shortages, pose limits to continuing high and non-inflationary economic growth. Industrial upgrading, productivity improvement and outward investment are necessary to help overcome resource constraints and maintain international competitiveness. The outward push has also responded to the strong Singapore dollar, improvements in the investment climate in the ASEAN region and new investment opportunities in the liberalizing economies of Indochina and China.

The largest destination countries were Malaysia (dominated by manufacturing, finance and commerce), Hong Kong (dominated by finance), and Indonesia (dominated by manufacturing). The ASEAN region absorbed S$16.1 billion (US $11.4 billion) or 34.8 per cent of Singapore's global direct investments. Manufacturing dominates investments in ASEAN, unlike investments in other regions, to account for half of the investments in ASEAN and 70.4 per cent of total manufacturing investments abroad.

A pioneering study by Lee (1993) examined motivations for outward investment, factors in the choice of location and problems encountered based on sample interviews with 14 firms. The most common motivations for overseas investments were cost push and market pull. The push was from escalating wage and/or property costs in Singapore and difficulty in labour recruitment which constrained future expansion; the cost push factor was less important for production where labour cost accounted for less than 10 per cent. The market-pull factor had two dimensions – first, the market opportunities in the host country and second, subcontractors in the electronics industry followed their MNC clients when the latter shifted their manufacturing operations to

**Table 3.10** Singapore: direct investment stock in ASEAN countries by activity in host country, 1995

| Host country | Total | Manufacturing | Construction | Commerce | Transport | Financial | Real estate | Business serv. | Others |
|---|---|---|---|---|---|---|---|---|---|
| **Amount in S$million:** | | | | | | | | | |
| ASEAN | 16,088.2 | 8,024.8 | 295.0 | 2,076.3 | 275.8 | 3,771.6 | 944.1 | 339.9 | 360.8 |
| Brunei | 92.0 | 4.0 | 33.0 | 15.4 | 0.3 | 3.1 | 0.0 | 4.9 | 31.3 |
| Indonesia | 4,030.9 | 3,002.9 | 94.0 | 147.2 | 96.1 | 243.1 | 345.6 | 36.5 | 65.6 |
| Malaysia | 9,715.9 | 4,045.0 | 46.9 | 1,512.7 | 130.9 | 3,182.4 | 475.7 | 117.0 | 205.4 |
| Philippines | 625.1 | 162.4 | 86.2 | 29.3 | 6.2 | 153.7 | 18.6 | 138.4 | 30.3 |
| Thailand | 1,252.8 | 629.5 | 32.8 | 367.0 | 38.6 | 64.7 | 73.6 | 26.5 | 20.1 |
| Vietnam | 371.3 | 180.9 | 2.1 | 4.7 | 3.7 | 124.6 | 30.5 | 16.6 | 8.2 |
| Asia | 27,101.2 | 10,636.8 | 477.6 | 3,921.0 | 568.4 | 7,913.6 | 2,433.5 | 678.5 | 471.6 |
| World | 46,240.2 | 11,396.6 | 504.7 | 4,528.3 | 1,353.5 | 23,171.8 | 3,379.6 | 1,317.5 | 588.2 |
| ASEAN's % share | 34.8 | 70.4 | 58.5 | 45.9 | 20.4 | 16.3 | 27.9 | 25.8 | 61.3 |
| **Percentage distribution:** | | | | | | | | | |
| ASEAN | 100.0 | 100.0 | 100.0 | 100.0 | 100.0 | 100.0 | 100.0 | 100.0 | 100.0 |
| Brunei | 0.6 | 0.1 | 11.2 | 0.7 | 0.1 | 0.1 | 0.0 | 1.5 | 8.7 |
| Indonesia | 25.1 | 37.4 | 31.9 | 7.1 | 34.9 | 6.4 | 36.6 | 10.7 | 18.2 |
| Malaysia | 60.4 | 50.4 | 15.9 | 72.9 | 47.5 | 84.4 | 50.4 | 34.4 | 56.9 |
| Philippines | 3.9 | 2.0 | 29.2 | 1.4 | 2.2 | 4.1 | 2.0 | 40.7 | 8.4 |
| Thailand | 7.8 | 7.8 | 11.1 | 17.7 | 14.0 | 1.7 | 7.8 | 7.8 | 5.6 |
| Vietnam | 2.3 | 2.3 | 0.7 | 0.2 | 1.3 | 3.3 | 3.2 | 4.9 | 2.3 |
| **Percentage distribution:** | | | | | | | | | |
| ASEAN | 100.0 | 49.9 | 1.8 | 12.9 | 1.7 | 23.4 | 5.9 | 2.1 | 2.2 |
| Brunei | 100.0 | 4.4 | 35.8 | 16.8 | 0.3 | 3.4 | 0.0 | 5.4 | 34.0 |
| Indonesia | 100.0 | 74.5 | 2.3 | 3.7 | 2.4 | 6.0 | 8.6 | 0.9 | 1.6 |
| Malaysia | 100.0 | 41.6 | 0.5 | 15.6 | 1.3 | 32.8 | 4.9 | 1.2 | 2.1 |
| Philippines | 100.0 | 26.0 | 13.8 | 4.7 | 1.0 | 24.6 | 3.0 | 22.1 | 4.8 |
| Thailand | 100.0 | 50.2 | 2.6 | 29.3 | 3.1 | 5.2 | 5.9 | 2.1 | 1.6 |
| Vietnam | 100.0 | 48.7 | 0.6 | 1.3 | 1.0 | 33.6 | 8.2 | 4.5 | 2.2 |

Source: Singapore Department of Statistics, Foreign Direct Investment Activities of Singapore Companies, 1995.

Malaysia and Thailand. As companies established overseas manufacturing plants, typically the Singapore operations became the corporate headquarters. And as overseas investments require sizeable capital resources, some companies were able to make this move only after public listing on the stock exchange. Choice of investment location was determined by market and cost considerations; proximity to Singapore was a key factor for some, as it facilitated procurement of inputs and shipments of output, and provided ready access to engineering support staff based in Singapore. A commonly cited problem in overseas investment was the quality and availability of production and management staff in the host location and the need to provide training to improve labour productivity. Transferring Singaporean managerial and professional staff abroad had its problems, as Singaporeans were reluctant to work abroad and as the investing firms did not have managerial resources to spare for overseas assignments. A second problem was the hassles and delays in starting operations abroad, as Singaporean investors faced bureaucratic delays and inadequate industrial facilities and infrastructure.

In early 1993 the Singapore government launched the regionalization strategy, actively encouraging Singapore private enterprises to invest in Asia. Several factors motivated the regional emphasis. First, a maturing Singapore economy needs to develop 'an external wing' to sustain its high growth performance, particularly as it faces severe land and labour constraints and rising costs; the emphasis would increasingly be on the growth of GNP rather than GDP. Second, to take advantage of the economic boom in East Asia. The region offers abundant natural resources, low cost labour and rapidly expanding markets, with investment opportunities for Singapore in manufacturing, services and infrastructural projects. Singapore can also share with the regional economies its expertise in economic management, development and management of townships, infrastructure, industrial parks and tourist facilities, manpower training, and technology adaptation. Third, domestic enterprises with limited outward investment experience will find it easier to regionalize than go global. Geographical proximity, cultural and linguistic familiarity help reduce information and transaction costs. For small and medium enterprises with limited managerial resources, investments in geographically proximate areas facilitate management supervision from the home base. Additionally, the Singapore government and its various agencies have developed close relations and extensive networks with governments and businesses in the region, and its regional projects, information networks and contacts can facilitate investments by the Singapore private sector.

The Economic Development Board has identified some integrating roles which Singapore is playing or could play. First, partnership with other countries to develop infrastructure, co-invest in each other's country or co-invest in third countries. The advantage arises from partners' pooling their complementary strengths. Investments in infrastructure projects in Batam and Bintan in Indonesia, Song Be in Vietnam, Bangalore in India, and Suzhou in China reflect this strategy. Second, partnership with foreign MNCs to help develop regional economies. MNCs from developed countries have played a crucial role in Singapore's economic development and this successful and mutually beneficial partnership experience could be extended to third countries. Singapore could provide these foreign MNCs with an efficient and competitive base of operations and a strategic location to expand into the dynamic Asian region, facilitating their allocation of value chain segments among countries according to their comparative advantage. They could also enter into joint ventures with Singaporean companies to co-invest in other countries, particularly China, pooling corporate resources and utilizing their respective corporate strengths.

Singapore government agencies and government-linked enterprises are facilitating many outward investment projects by identifying investment opportunities, supporting feasibility studies, arranging business consortia, as well as directly investing in and implementing overseas development projects. The projects undertaken by government agencies in partnership with private enterprises include the Batam Industrial Park, Bintan Industrial Estate and Bintan Beach International Resort in the Indonesia–Malaysia–Singapore growth triangle, the Suzhou township project in China, the Bangalore Information Technology Park in India, and the Vietnam–Singapore Industrial Park.

The *World Investment Report 1996* (UNCTAD) identified the top 50 TNCs from developing countries, of which 9 are from ASEAN, including 4 from Singapore (table 3.11). Singapore's Keppel Group ranked 12th in foreign assets and 23rd in transnationality index, the Fraser and Neave Group ranked 20th in foreign assets and 2nd in transnationality index, Singapore Telecommunications ranked 21st in foreign assets and 39th in transnationality index and Creative Technology ranked 36th in foreign assets but 1st in transnationality index. Three of these indigenous Singapore TNCs are examined below.

*Keppel Corporation*
Keppel Corporation is a conglomerate with its core business in shipbuilding and ship repair. When the British military base in Singapore closed down in the early 1970s, the naval dockyards were converted into commercial use and the spinoffs were Keppel Shipyard and Sembawang Shipyard. Keppel was initially a state enterprise but

**Table 3.11** The top 50 TNCs based in developing economies, 1994

| Source country | Foreign assets ranking | Transnationality Ranking | Index | Company | Industry | Assets (US$m) Foreign | Total | Sales (US$m) Foreign | Total | Employment (no.) Foreign | Total |
|---|---|---|---|---|---|---|---|---|---|---|---|
| China | 5 | – | na | China State Construction | Construction | 2189 | na | 1010 | na | na | na |
| | 6 | – | na | China Chemicals Imports & Exports | Trading | 1915 | na | 7914 | na | na | na |
| | 17 | – | na | China Metals & Minerals | Trading | 710 | – | 2270 | na | na | na |
| | 22 | – | na | China Harbours Engineering | Construction | 559 | na | 409 | na | na | na |
| | 25 | – | na | China Shougang Group | Metals | 446 | na | 980 | na | na | na |
| | 26 | – | na | China Cereals, Oil, Foodstuff Import Export | Trading | 440 | na | 6200 | na | na | na |
| | 38 | – | na | China Iron & Steel Industrial & Trading Group | Metals | 188 | na | 257 | na | na | na |
| Hong Kong | 2 | 10 | 34.4 | Hutchison Whampoa | Diversified | na | 52192 | 12500 | 30168 | 15086 | 26855 |
| | 4 | 5 | 43.4 | Jardine Matheson Holdings | Construction | 2539 | 6350 | 6463 | 9559 | 50000 | 220000 |
| | 19 | 30 | 12.1 | New World Development | Diversified | 624 | 6944 | 316 | 1721 | 2520 | 28000 |
| | 24 | 21 | 18.4 | Wing On International (Holdings) | Diversified | 491 | 1499 | 62 | 393 | 188 | 2792 |
| | 34 | 16 | 27.0 | Hong Kong & Shanghai Hotels Ltd | Hotel | 292 | 2628 | 47 | 230 | 2756 | 5540 |
| South Korea | 1 | 11 | 33.0 | Daewoo | Electronics | na | 33000 | 16000 | 40000 | 100000 | 200000 |
| | 7 | 20 | 19.5 | Samsung Co. Ltd | Electronics | na | 38000 | 21440 | 67000 | 42235 | 195429 |
| | 8 | 17 | 25.1 | LG Group | Electronics | na | 25000 | 8600 | 43000 | 29061 | 59200 |
| | 10 | 34 | 9.2 | Hyundai | Diversified | 1293 | 9657 | 1610 | 13081 | 814 | 44835 |
| | 15 | 7 | 40.0 | Dong Ah Construction | Construction | 734 | 3431 | 1134 | 2547 | 6828 | 12630 |
| | 40 | 33 | 10.4 | Sam Yang Co. Ltd | Diversified | 170 | 1964 | 115 | 1487 | 864 | 5795 |
| | 42 | 4 | 43.9 | Hyosung Corporation | Trading | 117 | 553 | 2206 | 2812 | 470 | 1460 |
| | 45 | 40 | 5.3 | Tong Yang Cement | Cement | 91 | 1733 | 39 | 736 | 116 | 2208 |
| Taiwan | 14 | 14 | 29.5 | Tatung Co. Ltd | Electrical equip. | 805 | 3983 | 1200 | 3621 | 9777 | 27769 |
| | 18 | 3 | 46.7 | Acer | Electronics | 665 | 2033 | 2079 | 3172 | 4164 | 9981 |
| | 28 | 42 | 1.3 | Chinese Petroleum | Petroleum | 349 | 14148 | 157 | 10748 | 19 | 21231 |
| | 29 | 31 | 11.5 | Formosa Plastic | Chemicals | 327 | 1906 | 233 | 1491 | 60 | 3645 |
| | 41 | 37 | 7.3 | China Steel Corporation | Metals | 170 | 5737 | 467 | 2492 | 6 | 9561 |
| | 43 | 38 | 7.0 | Evergreen Marine | Transport | 117 | 1678 | 80 | 1152 | 91 | 1298 |

| Source country | Foreign assets ranking | Transnationality Ranking | Transnationality Index | Company | Industry | Assets (US$m) Foreign | Total | Sales (US$m) Foreign | Total | Employment (no.) Foreign | Total |
|---|---|---|---|---|---|---|---|---|---|---|---|
| Malaysia | 23 | 6 | 43.0 | Sime Darby | Food | 557 | 1189 | 1857 | 3159 | 7500 | 32000 |
| | 37 | 24 | 16.5 | Amsteel Corporation | Diversified | 209 | 1459 | 80 | 1066 | 7800 | 28200 |
| | 47 | 12 | 32.8 | Malaysia International Shipping | Transport | 72 | 172 | 406 | 885 | 321 | 3004 |
| Philippines | 13 | 25 | 15.3 | San Miguel Corporation | Food | 806 | 2939 | 252 | 2599 | 2702 | 30965 |
| Singapore | 12 | 23 | 16.8 | Keppel Corporation | Diversified | 817 | 9118 | 248 | 1377 | 2847 | 12113 |
| | 20 | 2 | 52.1 | Fraser & Neave | Diversified | 590 | 2728 | 839 | 1491 | 6547 | 8365 |
| | 21 | 39 | 5.9 | Singapore Telecommunications | Telecommun. | 577 | 4811 | 50 | 2490 | 411 | 11279 |
| | 36 | 1 | 60.1 | Creative Technology | Electronics | 224 | 445 | 638 | 658 | 883 | 2678 |
| Thailand | 46 | 29 | 12.8 | Charoen Pokphand | Food | 82 | 642 | 109 | 857 | 1077 | 8440 |
| Brazil | 11 | 15 | 28.0 | Souza Cruz SA | Tobacco | 935 | 1246 | 316 | 3784 | 63 | 11387 |
| | 16 | – | 3.7 | Petroleo Brasileiro SA | Petroleum refining | 715 | 30162 | 2316 | 26396 | 24 | 50295 |
| | 31 | 26 | 14.3 | Sadia Concordia SA Industria e Commercio | Food | 313 | 1405 | 567 | 2784 | 57 | 32357 |
| | 39 | 36 | 7.3 | Companhia Cervejaria Brahma | Food | 187 | 1755 | 80 | 1249 | 476 | 9606 |
| | 48 | 28 | 13.2 | Usiminas-Usinas Siderurgicas de Minas GE | Steel | 63 | 3949 | 564 | 2280 | 1375 | 10448 |
| | 50 | 13 | 31.1 | Aracruz Celulose SA | Paper | – | 2593 | 482 | 529 | na | 3378 |
| Chile | 27 | 18 | 24.2 | CMPC Empresas SA | Paper | 352 | 2612 | 380 | 891 | 1718 | 10465 |
| Mexico | 3 | 8 | 36.6 | Cemex SA | Cement | 2847 | 7893 | 744 | 2101 | 8073 | 20997 |
| | 9 | 19 | 22.2 | Grupo Televisa SA | Media | 1371 | 3260 | 286 | 1288 | na | 21600 |
| | 30 | 35 | 8.4 | Empresas Ics Sociedad Controlladora SA | Construction | 321 | 3264 | 95 | 1386 | 2136 | 25267 |
| | 33 | – | na | China Foreign Trade Transportation Corp | Transportation | 300 | – | 300 | na | na | na |
| | 35 | 27 | 13.3 | Grupo Industrial Bimbo SA de CV | Food | na | 1221 | 252 | 1252 | na | 42463 |
| | 44 | 9 | 35.1 | Grupo Sidek | Tourism | 114 | 2831 | 25 | 575 | 10438 | 10774 |
| | 49 | 32 | 10.6 | Vitro Societad Anonima | Non-metallic | 52 | 4338 | 800 | 2872 | 1000 | 36694 |

Source: UNCTAD, World Investment Report 1996, Table I.13

Note: Index of transnationality is calculated as the average of foreign assets/total assets and foreign employment/total employment ratios.

managed by a foreign consultancy group (Swan Hunters). It has since been listed on the Singapore Stock Exchange with diversified share-holdings, although the Singapore government through its various agencies retains a controlling interest. It has also developed into a conglomerate with net assets of S$5.9 billion and turnover of S$2.4 billion in 1995. From its core business, it has expanded into offshore and specialized shipbuilding, engineering, shipping and logistics,telecommunications, property and hotel development, banking and financial services; also, from a Singapore operation, it has become a regional conglomerate. Keppel is a key player in the government's regionalization drive. Its ownership advantages lie in its experience and reputation as a leading Asian shipyard, its experience in infrastructural development in Singapore, and its financial and managerial resources. Keppel's involvement in the Philippines is most visible in shipyards and Kepphil Shipyard is listed on the Manila Stock Exchange; as expansion prospects for Keppel's core shipbuilding and ship repair business in Singapore became constrained by shortage of waterfront space, shortage of labour and rapidly rising labour costs, the Philippines became a choice location. Keppel is also increasingly involved in property and infrastructure-related developments, including the development of industrial parks and tourism parks in Suzhou, Batam, Bintan and Vietnam. In Suzhou, Keppel plays an active role in the consortium developing the 70 sq km industrial park. In Vietnam, Keppel is engaged in the construction of the Saigon Centre in Ho Chi Minh City, a complex of offices, retail space and service apartments. Keppel is also involved in property and hotel developments in the Philippines, Indonesia and Myanmar.

*Asia Pacific Breweries*
Asia Pacific Breweries (APB) is part of the Fraser and Neave group with its core business in beer and soft drinks. Its regionalization efforts are 'a combination of opening several new markets and territories in the Asia Pacific region and successfully defending the leadership position of its brand names in the more mature markets'. Regional growth has been spearheaded by two flagship brands of beer, namely, Tiger and Heineken. Tiger Beer has repeatedly won international recognition, the latest being the Grand Gold Medal in the 34th International Monde Selection Award in Brussels in June 1995. APB operates 15 breweries in nine countries in the Asia Pacific region. Earlier investments have matured and there is strong local competition; APB's operations in Malaysia have been organized under Guinness Anchor Berhad (listed in the Kuala Lumpur Stock Exchange) which managed to retain its leading position in the Malaysian malt liquor market. In Thailand, a new

brewery producing Heineken beer opened in 1995 and is targeted at the middle and upper market segments of the Thai beer market. More exciting growth prospects for APB are new investments in the emerging economies of Indochina, Myanmar and China. Through aggressive brand building and sales promotion, Tiger has established a strong foothold among consumers in Vietnam, Cambodia and Myanmar. Exports from Singapore have been followed by establishment of breweries in these countries. APB found that 'going regional is a costly business and we are fortunate to be working from a strong financial base and so are able to undertake this expansion without impairing Group earnings . . . Finding the right local partners is essential to the success of our regionalisation' (*Annual Report* 1995).

*Creative Technology*
Creative is an electronics multimedia company incorporated in Singapore in 1983. While its principal executive offices are located in Singapore, the headquarters for Creative's principal US subsidiary, Creative Labs Inc, is located in California, and the headquarters for European subsidiaries is located at Creative Labs in the UK. Unlike Keppel and Asia Pacific Breweries, which catered to the domestic market and then regionalized, Creative Technology adopted a global strategy from the start and is Singapore's most internationalized corporation. Also unlike Keppel and Asia Pacific Breweries, whose core businesses represented Singapore's traditional industries, Creative's core business represents the cutting edge of technology. Creative's principal activities are the design, manufacture and distribution of digitized sound and video boards, computers and related multimedia products. More specifically, Creative develops, manufactures and markets a family of sound and video multimedia products for PCs under the Blaster family name. Creative's Sound Blaster sound platform consists of a sound card or chipset, software drivers and bundled software applications that enable PCs to produce high quality audio for entertainment, education, music and productivity applications. The 'Blaster' has become an established brand name among consumers worldwide and the Sound Blaster has become an industry standard. With more than 15 million units sold by 1995, Sound Blaster is the best selling sound platform for PCs, and more than 10,000 Sound Blaster compatible software titles have been developed. Creative has a world-wide distribution network, powerful technologies, product development resources, and low cost manufacturing. It markets its products in North America, Europe and Asia through a worldwide network of distributors; it also markets its products through OEMs. Of its sales in 1995, only 2.2 per cent are in Singapore; the US is its major market with a sales share of

48.3 per cent in the US, followed by Europe with 29.7 per cent and the Asia Pacific (excluding Singapore) with 19.8 per cent. Creative has made a number of acquisitions and investments in pursuit of its strategy of strengthening its product range and technology base. In 1995 Creative achieved sales of over US $1.2 billion and continued to lead the traditional multimedia market with a market share of over 65 per cent. Creative has suffered a series of setbacks in 1996. Internal disagreements have led to the departure of two of the three founding members. Some of its corporate acquisitions and inventory decisions have proven to be serious management errors that severely undermined its bottom line. In a highly competitive business with short product cycles, the company is also under severe pressure to market new innovative products to maintain market share.

# V  Conclusion

The ASEAN region has been a major recipient of FDI to the developing world until recent years. This reflected ASEAN's highly favourable investment climate, which in turn reflected the region's economic buoyancy and rapidly growing market, its cost competitiveness and its FDI-friendly policies. However, its investment share and investment competitiveness are being challenged by new players in the field, particularly China. Within the ASEAN region, the new players, Vietnam and the Philippines, are also attracting considerable investor interest.

ASEAN has undertaken several initiatives which directly or indirectly aim at promoting FDI and intra-ASEAN investment inflows. It is not yet evident whether the formation of the ASEAN Free Trade Area (AFTA) has changed investor perceptions of ASEAN as an integrated market or production base as there has been no sharp acceleration in investment inflows. Investment growth in the ASEAN growth triangles is mixed – the southern growth triangle does not have the scale and synergy of the Hong Kong–Taiwan–South China economic zone and is facing serious labour shortages, while the northern growth triangle and eastern growth area have to overcome serious infrastructural inadequacies. ASEAN is now considering the establishment of an ASEAN Investment Area to complete the ASEAN Free Trade Area and promote FDI and intra-ASEAN investments. Freer trade and freer investments are crucial to provide the market attractions for FDI. However, ASEAN countries individually and collectively also need to improve supply-side conditions, that is, cost competitiveness and productivity, particularly improvements in infrastructure and human resources.

ASEAN would also need to nurture more home-grown multinationals to reduce dependence on foreign multinationals and to enable ASEAN companies to join the mainstream of globalization. At issue is how these home-grown multinationals are to be nurtured. That some multinationals and would-be multinationals are of ethnic Chinese origin and are perceived to form exclusionary business networks can heighten political sensitivity in several ASEAN countries. That ASEAN firms receive preferential treatment over non-ASEAN firms will raise the issue of the 'non-level playing field' and heighten demands for national treatment and MFN treatment among foreign MNCs and foreign governments. Such concerns can be minimized by policies encouraging partnerships, joint ventures, strategic alliances and business networking between the indigenous enterprises and the 'overseas Chinese' enterprises, and between ASEAN enterprises and non-ASEAN enterprises.

**Note**

1    Balance of payments data on FDI flows do not take into account the full extent of foreign participation and control; they understate resources and facilities owned and controlled by foreigners, by excluding foreign participation not accompanied by financial inflows. Also, published data usually do not show sectoral breakdowns or country sources. FDI data compiled by investment boards and agencies based on approvals or commitments overstate actual or realized investments. Also, stock data are often derived from cumulations of annual flow data from a certain time period; for example, Indonesia's FDI stock represents cumulative approved FDI since June 1967, Thailand's since 1970. Definitions of FDI also differ. First, some countries define direct investment to include equity only, while others include reinvested earnings and loans (Indonesia). Second, some countries define firms as foreign when the foreign equity share exceeds 50 per cent (Singapore) and others when it exceeds 25 per cent (Thailand). Third, some countries include the total equity of 'foreign firms' as foreign equity and fail to deduct the local equity component (Indonesia); further, the measurement based on equity capital ignores foreign participation in minority-owned joint ventures, production sharing arrangements, licensing arrangements and strategic alliances. Fourth, some countries measure FDI in terms of equity capital (Malaysia), others in gross fixed assets (Singapore) or net assets (Malaysia). Fifth, the sectoral coverage varies – Indonesia's BKPM data exclude the banking, insurance, oil and gas sectors, Malaysia's are confined to manufacturing in Peninsular Malaysia. Sixth, Indonesia, Malaysia and the Philippines do not compile outward investment statistics and these have to be derived from host country sources; for Singapore, it includes investments by foreign MNCs based in Singapore, and in Thailand the outward FDI stock refers to cumulative outflows since 1978.

## References

Asia Pacific Breweries Limited (1995) *Annual Report*.

Asia Pacific Economic Co-operation, Economic Committee (June 1995) *Foreign Direct Investment and APEC Economic Integration*, Singapore: APEC Secretariat.

Chia Siow Yue (1995) 'Towards Greater Coherence in Foreign Investment Policies', in K. Fukasaku, M. Plummer and J. Tan (eds), *OECD and ASEAN Economies: The Challenge of Policy Coherence*, Paris: OECD Development Centre.

—— (May 1996) 'Intra-ASEAN Direct Investment: Present, Future Direction and Policy Implications.' Paper presented at the Seminar on the Promotion of Foreign Direct Investment in the Context of ASEAN Investment Area organized by the ASEAN Secretariat and the Thailand Board of Investment, Bangkok.

—— (1996) 'The Electronics Industry in Singapore'. Paper prepared for the ASEAN Industries Project commissioned by the ASEAN Secretariat.

Creative Technology Limited (1995) *Annual Report*.

Dobson, Wendy and Chia Siow Yue (eds) (1996, forthcoming). *East Asian Integration and Multinationals*, Singapore: Institute of Southeast Asian Studies.

Dunning, John (1980) 'Towards an Eclectic Theory of International Production: Some Empirical Tests', *Journal of International Business Studies*, vol. 11.

JETRO (March 1995) *JETRO White Paper on Foreign Direct Investment 1995*, Tokyo: Japan External Trade Organisation.

Keppel Corporation Limited (1995) *Annual Report*.

Lee Tsao Yuan (1993) *Overseas Investment: Experience of Singapore Manufacturing Companies*, Singapore: Institute of Policy Studies.

Malaysian Industrial Development Authority (1996) *Statistics on the Manufacturing Sector, 1990–1994*.

Odle, Maurice (1996) 'ASEAN's Place in Global Foreign Investment Trends'. Paper presented at the Training Workshop for ASEAN Investment Policy Making Officials on International Investment Scenario and International Business Practices, Manila, September.

Oman, Charles (1994) *Globalisation and Regionalisation: The Challenge for Developing Countries*, Paris: OECD.

Research Institute for International Investment and Development, Overseas Investment Analysis Division (August 1995) *Japan's Outward Foreign Direct Investment during Fiscal 1994*, Tokyo.

Singapore, Department of Statistics (March 1997) *Foreign Direct Investment Activities of Singapore Companies 1995*, Occasional Paper on Financial Statistics.

Singapore, Department of Statistics (1995) *Foreign Equity Investment in Singapore, 1990–1992*.

Tejima, Shigeki (1995) *Japan's FDI in 1990s and Implications in the Asia Pacific Region*. Paper presented at the Australia-Japan Business Outlook Conference.

UNCTAD Division on Transnational Corporations and Investment (1996) *World Investment Report 1996: Investment, Trade and International Policy Arrangements*, New York: United Nations.

Yeung, Henry Wai-Chung (1995) *Hong Kong Transnational Corporations in ASEAN: A Business Network Approach*. Ph.D. thesis submitted to the School of Geography, University of Manchester.

# 4

# The Chinese Economic Area and Foreign Direct Investment

## Sung Yun-wing

## 1 Introduction

The Chinese Economic Area (CEA) includes Hong Kong, Macau, Taiwan and Mainland China. In terms of the degree of economic integration, there are three concentric layers of the CEA, with the Hong Kong–Guangdong economic nexus or Greater Hong Kong as the core, Greater South China (GSC) covering Hong Kong, Guangdong, Fujian and Taiwan as the inner layer, and Greater China covering Hong Kong, Taiwan and China as the outer layer. Hong Kong is the pivot for the integration of the Chinese Economic Area. Since the inauguration of China's open policy and economic reforms in 1979, extremely intense trade and investment flows have developed in the CEA and the Area has become a very dynamic region with substantial impacts on world trade and investment.

Table 4.1 shows the basic economic indicators of the CEA. The GDP of Taiwan is 1.8 times that of Hong Kong. Comparing the GDP of Hong Kong and Taiwan to that of China or Guangdong or Fujian is not very meaningful because the GDPs of China, Guangdong, and Fujian are biased downwards due to price differences. Comparison of export values may be more meaningful. China's 1995 exports of US $148.8 billion far surpassed Taiwan's exports of US $111.7 billion and also vastly surpassed Hong Kong's domestic exports (i.e., exports made in Hong Kong) of US $30 billion. Hong Kong's total exports (i.e. including re-exports) of US $172 billion still exceeded China's exports by a large margin, but that was only because Hong Kong was re-exporting

**Table 4.1**   Basic indicators of Greater China, 1995

| Indicators | Hong Kong | Taiwan | Macau* | China | Guangdong | Fujian |
|---|---|---|---|---|---|---|
| Area (sq.km) | 1068 | 35961 | 19 | 960000 | 177901 | 121400 |
| Population (mn) | 6.19 | 21.30 | 0.41 | 1211 | 66.68 | 32.3 |
| GDP (US$bn) | 142.0 | 257.2 | 6.5 | 691.4 | 65.1 | 26.3 |
| Per capita GDP (US$) | 23019 | 12490 | 16164 | 571 | 949 | 814 |
| GDP growth rate (%) | +4.6 | +6.3 | +4.0 | +10.2 | +15 | +15 |
| Exports (US$bn) | 172.3[a] 30.0[b] | 111.7 | 1.87 | 148.8 | 56.6 | 7.9 |

\*   Data are for 1994
[a]   Total exports (including re-export)
[b]   Domestic exports

Source: Data for China, Guangdong and Fujian are obtained from the respective Statistical Yearbooks of China Statistical Publishing House. Data for Hong Kong are obtained from the Hong Kong Monthly Digest of Statistics. Data for Taiwan are taken from the Monthly Bulletin of Statistics of the Republic of China. Data for Macao are taken from the Asia Yearbook published by the Far Eastern Economic Review

Chinese products to third countries and also re-exporting third country products to China. In other words, Hong Kong was China's gateway to the world in commodity trade.

Guangdong's 1995 exports of US $56.6 billion already surpassed the domestic exports of Hong Kong of US $30 billion and was on a par with the exports of Thailand. Fujian was a distant second to Guangdong in terms of economic strength. Fujian's 1995 exports and GDP were only 14 per cent and 40 per cent, respectively, of Guangdong's. Macau's GDP was only 5 per cent of that of Hong Kong and can be regarded as an appendage of the Hong Kong economy. This chapter will concentrate on economic interdependence among China, Hong Kong and Taiwan, or the 'trio', and there will be no separate treatment of Macau.

In 1979, Beijing gave Guangdong and Fujian special packages of policies that vastly increased their autonomy, including their autonomy in managing foreign trade and investment and the authority to operate Special Economic Zones (SEZs). Guangdong operates three SEZs: the Shenzhen and Zhuhai SEZs, which are adjacent to Hong Kong and

Macau respectively; and the Shantou SEZ which has close links to over-seas Chinese populations, including a community in Hong Kong that originated in Shantou. Fujian operates the Xiamen SEZ which is oppo-site Taiwan.

The opening of China coincided with the emergence of severe labour shortages in Hong Kong and Taiwan and the need for the latter two economies to restructure. The export-oriented labour intensive industries of Hong Kong have moved to Guangdong on a large scale. The labour-intensive industries in Taiwan have similarly moved to Guangdong and Fujian.

The impetus of the integration of the GSC came primarily from the economic liberalization of China, and secondarily from the economic liberalization of Taiwan. Despite economic liberalization, there are still many barriers to the economic integration of the trio, foremost among which are the remnants of central economic planning in China and Taiwan's ban on direct business links with the Mainland. Moreover, there is no overall institutional framework co-ordinating the economic integration of the trio. However, geographic and cultural proximity and the huge gains from economic complementarity have overcome the many barriers to economic interactions. Private initiative and market forces have led to extremely intense trade and investment flows among the trio despite the lack of an overall institutional framework.

This chapter is organized as follows. After the introductory section, section II will highlight the role of FDI in the CEA. Section III will analyse trade and investment among the trio in detail. Section IV will analyse the problems and prospects of the CEA and its implications for the world trading system.

## II  FDI: Engine of Growth of the Chinese Economic Area

The economic miracles of the 'take-off' of Hong Kong and Taiwan in the 1950s and 1960s were built on the export of labour-intensive light consumer products, especially to the US market. Hypergrowth in Hong Kong and Taiwan had led to severe labour shortages in the 1970s and 1980s, which created an incentive for manufacturers to invest overseas. Though Hong Kong investors (and to a less extent, Taiwanese investors too) have been investing in low-wage countries for some time, the opening of China in 1979 presented significant new opportunities for investors in Hong Kong and Taiwan. In comparison with the ASEAN, China has the advantage of cultural and geographic proximity. This is especially important for Hong Kong and Taiwan because the manufacturing sectors in both economies are dominated by small firms most of which cannot afford to establish operations in an alien environment. Moreover, Hong Kong is connected to China by land. Hong Kong can thus use trucking to carry semi-manufactures to its subsidiaries across the border. Trucking minimizes turnaround time, which is crucial in vertically-integrated manufacturing. It is no accident that Hong Kong and South China are much more tightly integrated than Taiwan and South China as there is no land bridge connecting Taiwan with the Mainland. Moreover, Taiwan's policy of no direct business links with China is a significant barrier to integration.

Table 4.2 shows China's contracted inward foreign investment by source. In this chapter, the term 'foreign investment' includes FDI and 'other foreign investment'[1] as the latter is similar to FDI in that foreign machinery/technology is made available for the use of the Chinese partner and the foreign partner often has de facto (though not de jure) control of the operation).

Hong Kong is by far the largest investor in China and Taiwan is a distant second while the US and Japan are in the third and fourth places. Their shares in cumulative contracted foreign investment in China were respectively 59 per cent, 7.5 per cent, 7.1 per cent, and 5.4 per cent. The large share of Hong Kong in China's investment conceals an important middleman role of Hong Kong. In China's statistics, investment from Hong Kong includes the investment of the subsidiaries of foreign companies incorporated in Hong Kong. Many multinational companies like to test the Chinese investment environment through investments from their Hong Kong subsidiaries because Hong Kong has the required expertise and is the foremost centre for China's trade and investment. Chinese enterprises also invest in China from their Hong Kong subsidiaries to take advantage of the preferences given to foreign investors. This 'round tripping' of Chinese capital in Hong Kong inflates both the amounts of Hong Kong investment in China and also China's investment in Hong Kong. Unfortunately, there is no reliable estimate on the amount of 'round tripping'.

Though the share of Hong Kong investment in China may be somewhat exaggerated by China's official figures, Hong Kong's share of export-oriented FDI in China is undoubtedly very large as Hong Kong's manufacturers have relocated to China in droves. Whereas the nationality of capital is always problematic, figures on trade flows should be more reliable. In 1995, Hong Kong's imports from China related to outward processing in China were US $51.7 billion (table 4.3), which was 75 per cent of China's exports generated by foreign investment, and 35 per cent of China's total exports. It is no exaggeration to say that the investment from Hong Kong is the crux behind China's spectacular

**Table 4.2** Contracted foreign investment in China by source, 1979-95 (US$ million)

| | 1979-90 | 1991 | 1992 | 1993 | 1994 | 1995 | 1979-95 |
|---|---|---|---|---|---|---|---|
| National Total | 45,244 (100) | 12,422 (100) | 58,736 (100) | 111,967 (100) | 83,088 (100) | 91,917 (100) | 403,374 (100) |
| Hong Kong | 26,480 (58.5) | 7,531 (60.6) | 40,502 (69.0) | 74,264 (66.3) | 47,278 (56.9) | 41,303 (44.9) | 237,358 (58.8) |
| Taiwan | 2,000 (4.4) | 1,392 (11.2) | 5,548 (9.4) | 9,970 (8.9) | 5,397 (6.5) | 5,855 (6.4) | 30,190 (7.5) |
| US | 4,476 (9.9) | 555 (4.5) | 3,142 (5.3) | 6,879 (6.1) | 6,027 (7.3) | 7,475 (8.1) | 28,544 (7.1) |
| Japan | 3,662 (8.1) | 886 (7.1) | 2,200 (3.7) | 3,015 (2.7) | 4,457 (5.4) | 7,752 (8.4) | 21,972 (5.4) |

Note: Figures in brackets indicate percentage share of the national total.
Source: Almanac of China's Foreign Relations and Trade, various issues.

export drive. Taiwan's contribution to China's exports would also be significant as Taiwanese investment also utilizes China as a export platform.

Hong Kong and Taiwanese investors have primarily used investment in China to build up their export network, though they have increasingly branched out to foreign-invested enterprises selling primarily to the domestic market. US and Japanese investors used to concentrate on large-scale, domestically-oriented foreign-invested enterprises, though they have recently been alerted to the value of China as an export platform. By 1996, foreign investment accounted for over half of Chinese exports.

Since Deng Xiaoping's southern tour of 1992 in support of economic reforms, utilized FDI in China has increased by leaps and bounds, rising from US $4.4 billion in 1991 to US $11 billion in 1992 and to US $26 billion in 1993. China and Guangdong attracted so much FDI in 1993 that contracted FDI into the ASEAN decreased (though it rebounded in 1994). The 1993 contracted FDI in Guangdong (US $33.1 billion) exceeded that in the entire ASEAN (US $17.3 billion)! Guangdong accounted for 29.4 per cent of the cumulative utilized FDI in China from 1979–95. The impact of the GSC on East Asia and the world is beyond dispute.

Since 1993, as a recipient of FDI, China has been second only to the US and is by far the first among developing countries. China's utilized FDI in 1994, 1995, and 1996 were US $33.8 billion (+23%), US $37.7 billion (+12%) and US $44 billion (preliminary figure) respectively. Despite the continuing rise in utilized FDI, contracted FDI has been beneath the 1993 peak (US $111.4 billion) for the three consecutive years of 1994 (US $82.7 billion), 1995 (US $91.3 billion) and 1996 (73.5 billion). Since contracted FDI signals future trends, China's annual inward utilized FDI has probably reached a plateau at the current high level of around US $40 billion per year. The growth is expected to be slow partly because the base is already very large. Moreover, China has become more picky and favours high-tech projects instead of the traditional labour intensive processing operations, and other developing countries (notably India and the ASEAN) have improved their investment environment.

Despite the rapid increase in FDI in China, investment from outside Greater China is still disproportionately small. By 1995, the US stock of FDI in the Mainland was only roughly the same as its investment in Hong Kong. External investment in China comes predominately from the CEA. By 1995, the shares of the cumulative contracted investments of the USA and Japan in China were respectively only 7.1 per cent and 5.4 per cent of China's total, while the combined share of Hong Kong and Taiwan was 66.6 per cent of China's total (table 4.2).

The 'Chineseness' of FDI in China shows that China's investment environment is still inadequate by international standards. Investors from Taiwan and Hong Kong have been able to mitigate the inadequacy of legal protection through their kinship networks. However, it must be stressed that the Chinese investment environment is maturing and both the shares of Hong Kong and Taiwan have declined since 1992 (table 4.2).

*Benefits of foreign investment*

Evidence is mounting that the contribution of foreign investment to China's growth is very substantial. As previously mentioned, foreign investment, especially that from Hong Kong and Taiwan, is the crux behind China's spectacular export drive. There have been econometric tests done on the contribution of foreign investment to growth in China in comparison with domestic investment, and foreign investment appeared to be much more potent than domestic investment in China's growth (Qiu 1996; Wei 1995). In Qiu's work, which is the best done so far, the marginal product of FDI was 0.466 whereas the marginal product of domestic investment was only 0.165 (Qiu 1996: 65).

According to the above works, exports also have substantial benefits for China's growth. Using Feder's framework, it was found that exports have significant spillover effects for the non-export sector. An increase of exports by 1 per cent raises the output of the non-export sector by 0.037 per cent (Qiu 1996: 58).

Though foreign investment and exports have undoubtedly brought tremendous benefits to China, it appears that the remnants of China's planned system have significantly limited the size of the benefits that would have accrued to China. For instance, in the case of processing operations, it is known that the processing fee obtained by China is only around 15 per cent of the value of exports, whereas the profit margin and re-export markup earned by Hong Kong is as high as one-third of the value of exports. In China's processing operations, the 'take' of Hong Kong investors/traders is thus much higher than the Chinese manufacturers.

The 'take' of Hong Kong is relatively high because Hong Kong performs a lot of value-adding services for processing operations in China, including product design, marketing or order-taking from importers, sourcing, quality control, trade financing, co-ordination of shipping etc. Hong Kong investors in China often use transfer pricing to transfer the profits of their subsidiaries back to Hong Kong to evade

Chinese controls, and such profits also appear as part of the re-export markup.

The fact that China is dependent on Hong Kong for so many of the above services shows the weakness of the Chinese system. China's processing operations are dependent on Hong Kong's trade financing because of the system of credit rationing in China which favours state-owned enterprises. China depends on external investors to perform international marketing and order-taking from importers partly because it is cumbersome for Chinese nationals to get passports to travel overseas.

Foreign-invested enterprises tend to import most of their raw materials because the quality or reliability of local suppliers is less dependable. The rigidity of China's economic system hampers the development of forward and backward linkages from foreign-invested enterprises to local enterprises and thus limit the potential benefits of foreign investment.

The rigidities of China's economic system are in many ways similar to that in other developing countries, though China's socialist system of central planning made things worse. With economic reforms and liberalization, such rigidities will gradually disappear, though the process will likely take a long time. There are already signs that foreign firms are starting to foster backward and forward linkages with local firms.

## III   Investment and Trade in the Chinese Economic Area

Unilateral policy changes are important in the integration of the trio. China has tailored its open-door policy to build closer links with Hong Kong and Taiwan. Taiwanese businesses enjoy special concessions in China over all other overseas businesses. Since 1980, Taiwanese goods face lower taxes in China and the import controls on Taiwanese goods have been less stringent. A 1988 State Council decree also gave Taiwanese investors favourable treatment over other foreign investors (Sung 1992: 8). Local authorities also tend to give Taiwanese investors more favourable treatment in terms of faster approval process or better supporting services.

Though the Mainland is more open to Taiwan than to any other economy, Taiwan is less open to the Mainland than to other economies. However, Taiwan's ban on direct links with China has softened gradually since 1987.

In July 1987, Taiwan eased its foreign exchange controls, and Taiwanese businesses started to invest indirectly on the mainland via subsidiaries established in Hong Kong or elsewhere. In November of that year, Taiwan allowed its citizens to visit their Mainland relatives and Taiwanese visitors to the Mainland soared. In October 1989, Taiwan promulgated regulations sanctioning indirect trade, investment and technical co-operation with China. Taiwan's policy requires that all trade, investment, and visits have to be conducted indirectly, i.e., via Hong Kong or third places. Taiwan still prohibits investment from the Mainland, though it is reported that the Mainland has invested in Taiwan through its overseas subsidiaries. Some Hong Kong companies in which significant portions of shares are owned by Mainland share-holders (e.g., Cathay Pacific) have also invested in Taiwan.

Taiwan's import controls on Mainland products have been gradually liberalized since 1987. The number of items allowed to be indirectly imported increased from 29 items (July 1987) to 90 items (January 1989) to 155 items (early 1990) and then to 1,654 items by the end of 1993 (Yeh 1995: 62). In 1996, Taiwan liberalized by changing from positive licensing to negative licensing, i.e., imports would be freely allowed unless they fall within the controlled list, though positive licensing was retained for agricultural products.

On paper, Hong Kong businesses receive no favourable concessions in China over other overseas businesses. In reality, due to geographical proximity and kinship links, Hong Kong businesses have a significant advantage, especially in Guangdong. It is also easier for Hong Kong Chinese to visit the Mainland than foreigners as visas are not required. China is thus more open to Hong Kong than to other economies. Hong Kong, as a free economy, is open to the whole world including China. However, Hong Kong's controls on visitors from the Mainland are stricter than the controls on visitors from other places as a result of the fear of illegal immigrants from the Mainland. In co-operation with Hong Kong, Beijing also imposes strict controls on visits to Hong Kong.

China is planning to abolish the special favours for Taiwanese and overseas Chinese investors as part of the reform package to gain entry into the WTO (World Trade Organization). However, Hong Kong residents and Taiwanese will continue to enjoy simpler border formalities and probably special informal treatment from local authorities in Guangdong and in Fujian.

Despite these policy changes, there is an obvious lack of institutional integration among members of the CEA. Due to Taiwan's ban on direct business deals with the Mainland, China and Taiwan are institutionally more closely integrated with most economies than with each other. As China is not a member of the WTO and the Chinese currency is not convertible, Hong Kong is institutionally more closely integrated with most of the economies of the free world than with China. Even though

China will resume sovereignty over Hong Kong in 1997, the lack of institutional integration is likely to persist as it is specified in the Sino-British
Agreement on Hong Kong that Hong Kong will remain a separate
customs territory and will continue to have its own currency. Migration
from China to Hong Kong will be strictly controlled.

Though economic theory concentrates on tariffs, controls on migration, and exchange integration, the effect of geographical and cultural
distances may be even more important. Hong Kong is only half-an-
hour's train ride from China, and Taiwan is quite close to China in
terms of geography. The importance of cultural affinity is quite evident.
People in Hong Kong had their ancestral roots in Guangdong, and
Guangdong is the prime site of Hong Kong's investment in China.
Taiwan also accounted for the bulk of investment in Fujian. It should
be noted that geographic and cultural proximity can enable businessmen to evade the formal barriers to trade and investment. Tariffs can be
evaded through smuggling, and there is rampant smuggling from
Hong Kong and Taiwan to China. The movement of people from Hong
Kong and Taiwan to China is relatively free though movement in the
other direction is highly controlled. However, illegal immigrants from
the Mainland are quite common in Hong Kong and Taiwan, as the
labour markets in the two economies are extremely tight. Though
the Chinese *Yuan* is not convertible, the Hong Kong currency has circu-
lated widely (and unofficially) in Guangdong, especially in the
Shenzhen Special Economic Zone (SEZ). The Hong Kong government
estimated that the amount of Hong Kong dollars circulating in China
amounts to 22 to 25 per cent of the total supply of the Hong Kong currency, or roughly HK $17 billion (US $2.2 billion) *(Hong Kong Economic
Journal,* 5 May 1994). A grey market for *Yuan* had also existed in Hong
Kong for some time. The grey market was turned into an open market
in 1993 when China officially permitted visitors to bring 6,000 *Yuan* outside or into China. Many Hong Kong tourists' shops also accept
payment in *Yuan*.

## Hong Kong's investment in China

Hong Kong investment in China is very diversified, ranging from
small-scale labour intensive operations to large-scale infrastructural
projects. The magnitude of Hong Kong's investment in Guangdong is
very large. In 1995, Guangdong's inward FDI was US $10.2 billion, of
which US $8 billion came from Hong Kong, exceeding total inward FDI
of US $7 billion in Mexico, the second largest recipient of FDI among
developing countries. From 1979–95, Guangdong accounted for 29.4 per

cent of the cumulative utilized FDI in China and Hong Kong accounted for 80 per cent of the utilized FDI in Guangdong. Guangdong accounted for around 40 per cent of Hong Kong's FDI in China.

Hong Kong's industrial investment in Guangdong has transformed Hong Kong manufacturing as well as the entire Hong Kong economy. Presently, Hong Kong manufacturing firms employ more than 3 million workers in Guangdong, while the manufacturing labour force in Hong Kong fell from a record of 905,000 in 1984 to 386,000 in 1995. By moving the labour-intensive processes to Guangdong, Hong Kong can concentrate on the more skill-intensive processes such as product design, sourcing, production management, quality control, and marketing. In short, Hong Kong has become the service centre of an industrialized Guangdong.

Before Deng Xiaoping's 1992 southern tour, the largest corporations in Hong Kong had not been active investors in China, though small- and medium-sized Hong Kong enterprises, especially Hong Kong's labour-intensive manufacturing firms, had invested in China in droves. Deng's tour stimulated a wave of investment by major Hong Kong companies, including listed companies such as Cheung Kong, Hutchison-Whampoa, Sun Hung Kai Properties, New World and Kowloon Wharf, in projects ranging from real estate to infrastructure and commerce.

Hong Kong has become the major funding centre for Chinese firms. The price of China play shares among the listed companies has risen rapidly since the beginning of 1992. A number of China investment funds were established which invested in industries and B shares in Chinese stock markets.

In 1992, China approved the public listing of selected state enterprises in the Hong Kong stock market and their shares are popularly called H-shares. By the end of 1994, 15 such stocks were listed in Hong Kong (Ni 1994: 20) with a market capitalization of US $1.8 billion. Together with 40 listed Hong Kong companies controlled by China (with shares worth US $11.5 billion at the end of 1994), the aggregate capitalization was about 4 per cent of the Hong Kong market (Ni 1994: 10). Besides tapping external funds, listing in Hong Kong also speeds up China's enterprise reforms, since listed firms have to follow international accounting standards.

## China's investment in Hong Kong

In the 1990s, China has become an important investor in the world. According to IMF and UNCTAD sources (*Asian Times*, 8 August 1996), from 1990 to 1994, China's average annual outward FDI reached US $2.4

billion, more than that of Latin America and the Caribbean combined. Hong Kong accounted for 60 per cent of China's outward FDI.

In May 1996, the Hong Kong government published the first surveys (1993 and 1994) of external investment in Hong Kong's non-manufacturing sectors (Census and Statistics Department, Hong Kong, 1996), and these give the first precise data on external investment in Hong Kong. At the end of 1994, China was the third external investor in Hong Kong with a share of net assets of 18.4 per cent, after the UK (28.2%) and Japan (20.7%). The US was a distant fourth with a share of 12.0 per cent. Net assets of Chinese investment totalled US $17.2 billion at the end of 1994.

China's investment in Hong Kong is very diversified, covering nearly all sectors of the Hong Kong economy, namely banking, insurance, entrepôt trade, shipping, aviation, real estate, and manufacturing. China's investment strengthens the ties of Hong Kong to China and enhances the position of Hong Kong as the gateway to China.

Hong Kong's investment in China appeared to be substantially larger than the reverse flow. Hong Kong's utilized direct investment in China amounted to US $60 billion at the end of 1994, exceeding considerably China's investment in Hong Kong of US $17 billion. However, the estimate of Chinese investment in Hong Kong is likely to be biased downwards as there is an incentive for China's local authorities and enterprises to establish unofficial subsidiaries in Hong Kong to evade controls on foreign trade and foreign exchange. Hong Kong's investment in China is significantly exaggerated as it includes the investment from the subsidiaries of other multinationals incorporated in Hong Kong. Moreover, officials in planned economies tend to exaggerate economic performance (the 'success indicators' problem). From anecdotal evidence, it is known that Hong Kong investors often overstate the value of their investments in China with the connivance of local officials. For example, Hong Kong manufacturers tend to put a high value on the outdated machinery that they move to China.

As China continues to liberalize its foreign exchange controls, it is expected that more and more Chinese capital will flow to Hong Kong through official as well as unofficial channels. It is natural for Chinese enterprises and investors to move their capital to Hong Kong, as Hong Kong has stricter protection of property rights than China and the funds can also be used much more flexibly in Hong Kong. In the long run, Chinese investment in Hong Kong may rival Hong Kong's investment in China.

## Investment and trade between China and Hong Kong

Hong Kong's investment in processing operations in China, especially in Guangdong, has generated huge trade flows. Table 4.3 shows Hong Kong's trade involving outward processing in China. In 1995, Hong Kong's imports from China involving outward processing amounted to US $51.7 billion, or nearly 74 per cent of Hong Kong's total imports from China. Guangdong clearly accounted for the bulk of the outward processing operations in China as Hong Kong's imports from *Guangdong* related to outward processing accounted for over 90 per cent of the imports from *China* involving outward processing.

The bulk of Hong Kong's imports involving outward processing were further processed or packaged in Hong Kong for export to third countries. Hong Kong's re-exports of Chinese origin involving outward processing have grown very fast and approached the size of Hong Kong's domestic exports in 1991. By 1995, Hong Kong's re-exports of Chinese origin involving outward processing were US $63.7 billion, which was more than double the domestic exports of Hong Kong (US $29.9 billion) and also exceeded the exports of Thailand (US $56.7 billion). The value of manufacturing output of Hong Kong firms in Guangdong/China clearly exceeded that in Hong Kong by a substantial margin.

Besides outward processing, the decentralization of China's foreign trade has also boosted Hong Kong's trade with China, especially Hong Kong's re-exports of Chinese goods (third country goods) to third countries (China). Decentralization vastly increased the number of trading partners and raised the cost of searching for a suitable trade partner. Intermediation emerged to economize on the cost of search, and this demand for intermediation was channelled to Hong Kong due to its efficiency in trading.

Since 1979, Hong Kong's China-related entrepot trade that was not related to outward processing had also grown very rapidly. Both outward processing and the decentralization of China's foreign trade boosted the share of China's trade conducted via Hong Kong. In 1979, the year of the inauguration of China's open policy, China's goods re-exported via Hong Kong were only 7 per cent of China's total exports, but this share rose rapidly to 47 per cent in 1993. Re-exports of third country goods to China via Hong Kong accounted for only 2 per cent of China's imports in 1979, but this share rose to 36 per cent in 1993, and rose further to 40 per cent in 1996.

**Table 4.3** Hong Kong trade involving outward processing in China (US$ million)

| | | Trade involving outward processing in China | | | | | | |
|---|---|---|---|---|---|---|---|---|
| | | Exports to China | | | Imports from | | Re-exports of China Origin | Hong Kong Domestic Exports |
| | | Domestic Exports | Re-exports | Total | China | Guangdong | | |
| 1989 | | 4,098 | 5,757 | 9,855 | 14,562 | 13,601 | – | 28,731 |
| | (i) | (76.0) | (43.6) | (53.0) | (58.1) | – | – | – |
| 1990 | | 4,676 | 7,125 | 11,800 | 18,629 | 17,592 | – | 28,999 |
| | (i) | (79.0) | (50.3) | (58.8) | (61.8) | – | – | – |
| | (ii) | (14.10) | (23.76) | (19.74) | (27.93) | (29.34) | | (0.93) |
| 1991 | | 5,195 | 9,466 | 14,661 | 25,400 | 24,011 | 28,497 | 29,732 |
| | (i) | (76.5) | (48.2) | (55.5) | (67.6) | – | (74.1) | – |
| | (ii) | (11.10) | (32.86) | (24.25) | (36.35) | (36.49) | – | (2.53) |
| 1992 | | 5,719 | 12,578 | 18,297 | 32,566 | 30,335 | 38,733 | 30,245 |
| | (i) | (74.3) | (46.2) | (52.4) | (72.1) | – | (78.3) | – |
| | (ii) | (10.09) | (32.88) | (24.80) | (28.21) | (26.34) | (35.92) | (1.73) |
| 1993 | | 5,835 | 14,870 | 20,706 | 38,160 | 35,617 | 47,122 | 28,815 |
| | (i) | (74.0) | (42.1) | (47.9) | (73.8) | – | (80.8) | – |
| | (ii) | (2.03) | (18.22) | (13.17) | (17.18) | (17.41) | (21.66) | (-4.74) |
| 1994 | | 5,429 | 18,015 | 23,444 | 45,925 | 43,372 | 54,677 | 28,739 |
| | (i) | (71.4) | (43.3) | (47.7) | (75.9) | – | (82.0) | – |
| | (ii) | (-6.96) | (17.03) | (13.22) | (20.35) | (21.77) | (16.03) | (-0.26) |
| 1995 | | 5,673 | 22,456 | 28,130 | 51,650 | 49,068 | 63,658 | 29,945 |
| | (i) | (71.4) | (45.4) | (49.0) | (74.4) | – | (82.2) | – |
| | (ii) | (4.49) | (24.65) | (19.99) | (12.47) | (13.13) | (16.43) | (4.2) |

(i)  Proportion of outward processing trade in total (%)
(ii) Growth rate (%) over previous year

Source: Hong Kong External Trade, various issues.

## Investment and trade between China and Taiwan

Despite the explosive growth of Taiwanese investment on the Mainland since 1987, the total stock of contracted Taiwanese investment at the end of 1995 was only 12.7 per cent of that of Hong Kong (table 4.2). This indicates that there is considerable potential for further expansion of the Taiwanese share. The 1994 'Thousand Islands' incident[2] and China's hostility towards Lee Teng Hui in 1995 and 1996 slowed down Taiwan's investment in China since 1994.

In the early years, Taiwan's investment was largely in small-scale labour intensive operations producing light manufactures for export. The industries involved include textiles, shoes, umbrellas, travel accessories and electronics. The projects were concentrated in Fujian, Guangdong and particularly in the Xiamen region of Fujian. However, Taiwanese investment was increasing in size and sophistication, with an increasing number of more technology-intensive projects such as chemicals, building materials, automobiles, and electronic products and components. The fields of investment have diversified from manufacturing into real estate, finance, tourism and agriculture. The location of investment has spread inland from the coast.

The surge of Taiwanese investment in the Mainland had raised fears that such investment would lead to the 'hollowing out' of Taiwan industry and also posed security threats. In July 1990, the Taiwan government tried to cool down the Mainland investment boom by improving the investment environment in Taiwan and steering investment away from the Mainland to the ASEAN. Both carrots and sticks were used to prevent Formosa Plastics from implementing its gigantic project to build a naphtha cracking plant in Xiamen. To control the Mainland investment boom, Taiwan does not allow investment in higher-value added industries that are still competitive in Taiwan, though these controls are not always observed.

Taiwan's president visited the ASEAN countries in early 1994 in an effort to improve the investment environment for Taiwanese investors in the ASEAN. The Taiwan government is trying to guide the Mainland investment boom rather than to reverse it. There are very real political differences dividing the Mainland and Taiwan and these differences are not going to disappear overnight. However, if Taiwan continues to liberalize its relations with the Mainland, Taiwan investment in China may rival that of Hong Kong in the long run.

As in the case of Hong Kong investment in China, Taiwan's investment in China has also generated huge trade flows. Chung estimated the exports generated by Taiwanese investment in China in 1992 to be US $9.3 billion or 11.6 per cent of China's total exports (Chung 1994: 10).

*Sung Yun-wing*

Taiwan's exports to China have grown extremely rapidly as Taiwanese firms supply their Mainland subsidiaries with semi-manufactures. The bulk of Taiwan's exports to China consists of machinery and semi-manufactures (Kao and Sung 1995: 79).

Taiwan–Mainland trade has grown extremely fast and is now very substantial. Due to Taiwan's restrictions on the trade, both China's and Taiwan's statistics fail to capture part of the trade routed via third ports, especially via Hong Kong. Statistics on Taiwan–Mainland trade shown in table 4.4 are taken from the author's own work which estimates the part of the trade not captured in official statistics (Sung 1997).

**Table 4.4**   Taiwan–Mainland trade (US$mn)

|       | Taiwan's | | China's | |
|-------|---------|---------|---------|---------|
|       | Exports | Imports | Exports | Imports |
| 1986  | 723     | 151     | 866     | 126     |
|       | (1.8)   | (0.6)   | (2.0)   | (0.4)   |
| 1987  | 1,030   | 303     | 1,228   | 257     |
|       | (1.9)   | (0.87)  | (2.8)   | (0.7)   |
| 1988  | 2,153   | 502     | 2,564   | 418     |
|       | (3.5)   | (1.0)   | (4.6)   | (0.9)   |
| 1989  | 3,174   | 718     | 3,746   | 606     |
|       | (4.8)   | (1.4)   | (6.3)   | (1.2)   |
| 1990  | 4,095   | 1.156   | 4.792   | 990     |
|       | (6.1)   | (2.1)   | (9.0)   | (1.6)   |
| 1991  | 6,793   | 1,842   | 7,880   | 1,584   |
|       | (8.9)   | (2.9)   | (12.4)  | (2.2)   |
| 1992  | 9,273   | 1,952   | 10,751  | 1,685   |
|       | (11.4)  | (2.7)   | (13.3)  | (2.0)   |
| 1993  | 12,174  | 2,328   | 14,051  | 2,029   |
|       | (14.3)  | (3.0)   | (13.5)  | (2.2)   |
| 1994  | 14,028  | 2,976   | 16,190  | 2,602   |
|       | (15.1)  | (3.5)   | (14.0)  | (2.2)   |
| 1995  | 17,056  | 3,787   | 19,629  | 3,317   |
|       | (15.3)  | (3.7)   | (14.9)  | (2.2)   |

Note: Figures in brackets represent percentage share of Taiwan's/China's exports or imports.
Source: Data on Taiwan's trade are taken from Sung (1997: table 7). Data on China's trade are estimated from those of Taiwan's by adjusting for cif and fob price differences.

In 1992, the Mainland surpassed Japan to become the second largest market for Taiwan after the US. In 1995, the market shares of the top four markets of Taiwan, namely, US, China, Japan, and Hong Kong (excluding re-exports elsewhere) in Taiwan's exports were 24 per cent, 15.3 per cent, 10.6 per cent, and 5.0 per cent respectively. Taiwan's exports to the USA have declined in absolute terms since 1987, and the Mainland together with Hong Kong may soon become Taiwan's largest market.

By 1991, the Mainland's imports from Taiwan constituted 13 per cent of the Mainland's total imports, and Taiwan has surpassed Hong Kong and the USA to become the mainland's second largest supplier after Japan, which has a share of 20 per cent. In 1995, the shares of Japan and Taiwan in China's imports were 22 and 15 per cent respectively.

Taiwan's imports from the Mainland are much smaller partly because Taiwan only allows the import of selective commodities from the Mainland. However, the rate of growth has been very high. In 1995, Mainland products accounted 3.7 per cent of Taiwan's imports and the Mainland was the fifth largest supplier of Taiwan after Japan (29.2%), the US (20.1%), Germany (5.5%), and South Korea (4.2%). Taiwan has also become a significant market for the Mainland, accounting for 2.2 per cent of China's exports (table 4.4).

## Investment and trade between Hong Kong and Taiwan

Before 1987, the economic ties between Hong Kong and Taiwan were one-sided due to Taiwan's trade protectionism and foreign exchange controls. Hong Kong was open to Taiwan's exports. In the mid-1970s, Hong Kong became Taiwan's third largest market after the US and Japan, accounting for roughly 7 per cent of Taiwan's exports. However, the barriers against Hong Kong goods in Taiwan were quite high.

As for investment in Taiwan, Hong Kong has been the third largest investor in Taiwan, with a 1989 stock of US $1.2 billion (or 11 per cent share) after the US (US $3 billion) and Japan (US $2.9 billion). Taiwanese investment in Hong Kong was insignificant due to Taiwan's then stringent foreign exchange controls. By the end of 1991, Hong Kong cumulative investment in Taiwan totalled US $1.6 billion (Hong Kong Trade Development Council 1992: 4).

Economic ties between Hong Kong and Taiwan developed extremely rapidly in the late 1980s with the liberalization of Taiwan's imports and foreign exchange controls, the sharp appreciation of the Taiwanese currency, and Taiwan's use of Hong Kong as an intermediary in its interactions with the Mainland.

Many Taiwanese toured Hong Kong on their way to the Mainland and Taiwan became the foremost source of tourists for Hong Kong from 1988 to 1993, accounting for 20 per cent of tourist arrivals in 1993. However, Taiwanese tourist arrivals in Hong Kong stagnated since 1994 due to the 1994 Thousand Islands incident and the heightening of tensions across the Taiwan Straits in 1995.

With Taiwan's trade liberalization, the share of the Taiwan market in Hong Kong's domestic exports jumped from 1 per cent in 1985 to 3.4 per cent in 1995, amounting to US $1,031 million. Since 1986, Taiwan has been the seventh largest market for Hong Kong goods (after China, the US, Singapore, Germany, Japan and the UK).

Hong Kong continued to be an important final market (excluding Taiwanese goods re-exported via Hong Kong) for Taiwan in the 1990s. Taiwan's 1995 exports retained for internal use in Hong Kong were US $6,269 million, or 5.6 per cent of Taiwan's exports. Hong Kong was the fourth largest final market for Taiwan after the USA, the Mainland, and Japan.

After adjusting for the cost of insurance and freight, Hong Kong's 1995 retained imports from Taiwan were US $6,582 million or 8.3 per cent of the total retained imports of Hong Kong. Taiwan is the fourth largest supplier of Hong Kong's retained imports after Japan, the USA and China.

Hong Kong is a very important entrepôt for the re-export of Taiwanese goods, not only to the Mainland but also to the ASEAN and other economies. The 1995 exports of Taiwan to Hong Kong were US $26.1 billion or 23.4 per cent of Taiwan's exports. This is just marginally behind Taiwan's exports to the US (US $26.4 billion or 23.6 per cent of Taiwan's exports). Of Taiwan's 1995 exports to Hong Kong, 24 per cent were consumed in Hong Kong; 65.3 per cent were re-exported or transhipped to China, and 10.7 per cent were re-exported or transhipped elsewhere. Taiwan's exports to Hong Kong are forecasted to surpass those to the US in 1997 (*South China Morning Post*, 21 January, 1997).

Taiwan investment in Hong Kong also soared. Cumulative investment from Taiwan reached an estimated US $2 billion by the end of 1989 and half of the amount was invested after 1987 (Zhou 1992: 167). By the end of 1995, cumulative investment from Taiwan was estimated to be US $4 to 5 billion (*Hong Kong Daily News*, 8 August, 1996). Services accounted for over half of the investment, and export/import trade accounted for over 20 per cent. The rest was mainly in finance and insurance. Taiwan became the fifth largest investor in Hong Kong after the UK, Japan, the Mainland and the US.

Hong Kong is the largest offshore base of Taiwan's finance and shipping industries. Taiwanese operate over 3,000 companies in Hong Kong (including paper companies formed to handle business with the Mainland), with around thirty regional headquarters.

## IV   Problems and Prospects of the CEA

While the growth of the CEA has been extremely rapid, and there have been many rosy projections of the future, the CEA also faces a host of problems, both economic and political. Four problems are discussed below:

1. Difficulty of further reforms of the Chinese economic systems;
2. Problems of adjustment to China's export drive in the world market, especially trade frictions with the US and other OECD countries;
3. Maintaining prosperity in Hong Kong after 1997; and
4. Tensions across the Taiwan Strait.

### *Difficulty of further reforms*

After 18 years of economic reforms and opening, the Chinese reforms have reached a crossroad. Most of the easy reforms (agricultural reforms, privatization of small firms) have been completed, and the remaining reforms (reform of large state-owned enterprises, banking reforms, reforms of the fiscal and monetary system) are going to be much more difficult. The lack of thorough reforms will limit foreign investment in China, especially in industries selling to the domestic market, and also in service sectors such as banking, finance, and telecommunications.

The investment of Hong Kong and Taiwan in China had largely been confined to using China as an export base. This can be attributed to the lack of thoroughness of China's reforms. China merely provides cheap land and labour, and all the other ingredients such as raw materials, management, industrial design, marketing, financing etc. are provided externally. Moreover, the foreign investor can recoup the investment as the product is exported, earning foreign exchange in return. Foreign investors who invest in industries selling to the domestic market find it more difficult to recoup their investment as a result of China's foreign exchange controls. Investors in sectors such as banking, finance, and telecommunications will face a hard time as such sectors tend to be highly regulated. The speed of opening of these sectors to foreign investors will be limited by the pace of China's reforms. For instance, foreign investors have been deeply disappointed over the very slow opening of *Renminbi* business to foreign banks.

## Problems of adjustment in the world market

Though the economies of the CEA are tightly linked, it must be stressed that the CEA is not an inward looking trade bloc. The economic reality of the CEA is that the US is their largest market and Japan is their largest supplier of capital goods and technology. An inward looking trade bloc excluding Japan and the US would be detrimental to the CEA.

However, the dependence of the CEA on the US market is unhealthy and can easily lead to severe trade frictions. Since the relocation of the export-oriented industries of Hong Kong and Taiwan to China, the trade deficit of the US with China has increased tremendously while the bilateral deficits of the US with Hong Kong and Taiwan have declined. On the one hand, the total exports of the CEA to the US have gone up, as the relocated firms often expand in scale with the avail-ability of cheap labour and land in China. On the other hand, the total exports of the US to the CEA have also increased markedly due to Taiwan's trade liberalization and rapid growth in China. The US over-all trade deficit with the CEA stayed roughly constant till 1992, but it rose from US $28.3 billion in 1992 to US $39.6 billion in 1995. (However, the size of the deficit relative to US exports only rose marginally from 6.3 per cent to 6.8 per cent during the period.) In 1995, the US–China bilateral deficit was second only to that of US–Japan. The scale of China's exports has generated problems of adjustment for the US as well as other OECD countries.

These trade frictions can be avoided if China liberalizes its imports of commodities and services. As services usually can only be provided on site, the liberalization of services trade often implies the liberalization of foreign investment in service industries. This will give rise to many opportunities of investment and will also imply a much higher degree of integration for the CEA.

Even if China were to liberalize its imports of goods and services, the industrial bases in Hong Kong and Taiwan are too narrow to meet the demands of China. Hong Kong and Taiwan are not likely to become the foremost suppliers of China. Though China may become the largest market for Hong Kong and Taiwan, the reverse is unlikely to be the case. China has to look out of the CEA for its capital goods, technology, and market. The liberalization of China's imports will thus imply rich opportunities for East Asia and the world.

## Stability of Hong Kong after 1997

Though the economic freedoms of Hong Kong are spelt out in great detail in the Sino-British Declaration on the future of Hong Kong, it must be remembered that 'one country, two systems' is an untried formula and the future stability and prosperity of Hong Kong is not assured. As Hong Kong is the pivot of the economic integration of the CEA, the consequences for China and the CEA can be very serious.

The workability of 'one country, two systems' lies more in the political and social realms than the economic realm. The political problem is that China has to resist the tremendous temptation and pressure to intervene in the internal affairs of Hong Kong. As long as China can respect the autonomy of Hong Kong, the economic fundamentals are likely to work in Hong Kong's favour. As the author has elaborated elsewhere, the prospects of Hong Kong as China's middleman are bright (Sung 1991: 28–42). There are significant economies of scale and economies of agglomeration in trading activity and it is very difficult for other cities such as Singapore or Shanghai to compete with Hong Kong because Hong Kong is the established centre for China's trade. The existence of economies of scale in intermediation would enhance the demand for the middleman as small firms will not be able to trade efficiently.

Traders tend to agglomerate in a city, suggesting that there are significant external economies involved. This implies that once a city acquires a comparative advantage in trade, the advantage feeds upon itself, and more trading firms will come to the city, making the city even more efficient in trade.

As business activities agglomerate, the price of land will rise, thereby checking agglomeration. Trading, business services and financial services will be least affected by rising land prices and wages because such activities are neither land-intensive nor labour-intensive. New York and London long ago lost their comparative advantage in manufacturing, but their positions in trading, business, and finance remain formidable.

Despite the rapid development of Shanghai in recent years, Hong Kong's position as the premier hub of China's trade and investment is secure simply because it is *the* established centre. Although Shanghai is set to become the domestic financial centre of China, it cannot compete with Hong Kong as a regional or international centre. Shanghai cannot become a serious contender as a regional or international financial centre unless the *Renminbi* can achieve convertibility on the capital account which will take quite some time.

The development of infrastructure and services skills is a

time-consuming and capital-intensive process. Moreover, the development of services is highly dependent on the regulatory environment. Given the corrupt, inefficient, and immense bureaucracy in China, the development of an efficient international service centre is very difficult.

The continuing high shares of Hong Kong in China's trade and investment show the importance of economies of scale and agglomeration in trading and service activities. It is amazing that, 17 years after China's opening, Hong Kong's shares are still so large. In 1996, Hong Kong handled 41 per cent of China's trade in the form of re-exports, the highest proportion ever. Shanghai's share was only 17 per cent. Moreover, Shanghai does not have a good port because of the silting of the Yangtze river and ships around 50,000 tons can only enter Shanghai at high tide. Hong Kong's share would be two-thirds if transhipment via Hong Kong and direct shipments by Hong Kong trading companies not touching Hong Kong were included.

Hong Kong's shares in China's trade and investment are so high that they are unlikely to rise further. The shares are likely to decline as China is building many ports and many foreign multinationals are investing in China. In the long run, China is likely to overcome its transportation bottlenecks and acquire modern trading skills. While China may even clean up its bureaucracy, it will still rely on Hong Kong for trade, financial, and business services because of economies of scale and agglomeration.

## Tensions across the Taiwan Straits

China's military exercises in the Taiwan Straits in late 1995 and early 1996 reminded the world that the continuous economic integration of the CEA is not a foregone conclusion. However, the episode did demonstrate that China's naval power is not yet strong enough to carry out an invasion. After the successful re-election of Lee Teng Hui to the Presidency in Taiwan, Beijing conducted a high level meeting on the Taiwan issue in May 1996 and resumed its policy of wooing Taiwanese businessmen.

Taiwan has not reciprocated the recent friendly gestures from Beijing. On 15 August 1996, Lee Teng Hui announced that there should be restrictions on Taiwanese companies which invest in the Mainland (*Hong Kong Economic Journal*, 16 August 1996). Though the precise nature of the restrictions has not been announced, Taiwanese businessmen have reacted unfavourably to the announcement. Formosa Plastics called off a US $3 billion power plant project in China and food giant President Enterprises halted its US $100 million project to set up a power plant in the central city of Wuhan. According to Taiwan's statistics on approvals of Mainland-bound investments, there has been a year-on-year decline of 10 per cent in the last four months of 1996 (though the figure for the entire year 1996 still grew by 13.6%) (*South China Morning Post*, 25 January 1997).

On 22 January 1997, Taiwan and China concluded an agreement in Hong Kong agreeing to allow ships owned by Taiwanese or main-landers that carry flags of convenience to sail direct between Kaohsiung and two Mainland ports in Fujian, Xiamen and Fuzhou. This is a far cry from full-scale direct shipping as Taiwan only allows the ships to carry cargo between China and third countries via Kaohsiung. Direct shipping of Taiwanese cargo to the Mainland and vice versa are not allowed. As the transhipment zone is outside Taiwanese customs, it is not considered to be a violation of Taiwan's general prohibition on direct shipping. The impact on Hong Kong is estimated to be less than 1 per cent of Hong Kong's shipping. However, the impact on Hong Kong of a full-scale development of direct shipping could be more serious as cross Straits transhipment via Hong Kong amounted to 1 million containers in 1995 or 8 per cent of Hong Kong's container throughput (*The Hong Kong Standard*, 23 January 1997). Moreover, the shipping traffic from China to the US could stop in Taiwan rather than in Hong Kong, and Hong Kong is currently the transhipment centre for 80 per cent of all US-bound Mainland cargo.

However, the development of full-scale direct shipping links across the Taiwan Strait will probably be slow due to suspicion on both sides. The Taiwanese government's policy is to delay direct links for as long as possible because it believes that the prohibition on direct links is one of its last bargaining chips.

## Prospects of the CEA

Economic forces point to a rapid continuation of economic integration of the CEA. Though there are political uncertainties such as the stability of China in the post-Deng era, doubts on the viability of Hong Kong after 1997, and possible hostilities over the Taiwan Strait, the economic fundamentals of the CEA are strong.

Due to the many differences in the political, legal and economic systems between the Mainland on the one hand, and capitalist China (Hong Kong and Taiwan) on the other, the economic integration of the Mainland with capitalist China will be highly uneven. Integration will proceed rapidly in some areas but slowly in others. Between the Mainland and capitalist China, controls on movements of goods are relatively liberal whereas controls on capital and foreign exchange are more strict and controls on migration are the most strict. Integration of the commodity market between the Mainland and capitalist China will proceed rapidly due to the relatively mild controls on the flow of goods. However, even for the commodity market, one should distinguish between export-processing industries and import-competing industries. The outward processing operations of capitalist China on the Mainland have developed extremely rapidly because their products are exported and they are not hampered by China's foreign exchange controls. The growth of external investment in China's import-competing industries will necessarily be slower due to China's foreign exchange controls.

The integration of services industries between the Mainland and capitalist China will similarly be slow because most services cannot be exported and are sold in the domestic market. Moreover, services are performed for people and require people to people contacts. The controls of capitalist China on migration from the Mainland will hamper the full integration of services.

The integration of the financial markets between the Mainland and capitalist China will also be quite slow as China's foreign exchange controls on the capital account will likely be quite strict even in the medium term. The integration of the labour markets between the Mainland and capitalist China will probably be very slow due to controls on migration.

## The CEA and the world trading system

The CEA is not an inward looking trade bloc. The entry of the Mainland and Taiwan into the WTO would promote the integration of the trio in many ways. To qualify for membership, the Mainland must radically reform its trading system and Taiwan has to further liberalize its trade. This would allow greater scope for market forces to strengthen the integration of the trio. Membership in the WTO would also give the Mainland and Taiwan some protection against trade protectionism in the US. The synergy of China's cheap labour with Hong Kong's and Taiwan's know-how and capital was the main factor behind China's spectacular export drive, and revoking China's MFN status in the US would be very detrimental to the further integration of the trio. Membership in the WTO for both the Mainland and Taiwan would also strengthen the reformers in the Mainland as well as strengthen the international position of Taiwan. Taipei can thus afford to allow its ties with the Mainland to grow further.

For China, APEC can be a partial substitute for the WTO as China's commitments to the APEC would enhance the credibility of

China's policies of reform and trade liberalization. The APEC opens the markets of its members to Chinese exports and also provides a forum for interactions among the trio.

However, the APEC is at best an imperfect substitute for the WTO. The APEC cannot give China recourse against the protectionist actions of non-APEC members. Moreover, the APEC process is fuzzy and less rule-based in comparison to that of the WTO. For enhancement of credibility of trade liberalization, APEC membership counts much less than WTO membership because APEC allows its members to make vague and fuzzy commitments.

The advantage of the APEC process is its flexibility. The APEC provides China a step by step process to shed many of its GATT-incompatible practices. To use the imagery of Deng Xiaoping, the APEC process provides the stepping stones for China to cross the treacherous river of economic reforms into the land of the WTO.

### Notes

1   Including foreign funds involved in leasing, compensation trade, and processing/assembling operations or processing operations for brevity. 'Other foreign investment' constitutes commercial credit rather than FDI because the Chinese partner legally controls the operation and usually pays for foreign machinery and technical assistance with labour services used in making goods for the foreign partner.
2   In 1994, a group of Taiwanese tourists were murdered in a ship at the Thousand Islands resort in Zhejiang. Connivance of local authorities was suspected and there was widespread protest in Taiwan over China's handling of the case.

### References

Census and Statistics Department, Hong Kong (1996) *External Investments in Hong Kong's Non-manufacturing Sectors, 1993 & 1994.*

Chung, Chin (1994) 'The Changing Pattern of Division of Labour across the Straits: Macro Overview and Sectoral Analysis on the Electronics Industry'. Paper presented to the Conference on The China Circle organized by the Institute on Global Conflict and Co-operation, University of California in Hong Kong, September 1–3 (mimeo).

Hong Kong Trade Development Council (1992) 'Hong Kong's Economic Relationship with Taiwan', Hong Kong, February.

Kao, Chang and Sung, Yun-Wing (1995) *An Empirical Study of Indirect Trade between Taiwan and Mainland China,* Mainland Committee of Taiwan Government, Taipei, September.

Ni, Nick (1994) *Asian Perspectives: China's Expanding Economic Interests in Hong Kong,* Nomura Research Institute Hong Kong Limited, December, vol. 11, no. 6.

Qiu, Hong (1996) 'Openness and Economic Growth in China', M.Phil. thesis, Chinese University of Hong Kong (mimeo).

Sung, Yun-Wing (1991) *The China-Hong Kong Connection: The Key to China's Open Door Policy*, Cambridge: Cambridge University Press.

—— (1992) 'Non-institutional Economic Integration via Cultural Affinity: The Case of Mainland China, Taiwan, and Hong Kong', Hong Kong Institute of Asia-Pacific Studies, The Chinese University of Hong Kong, Occasional Paper no. 13, July.

—— (1997) 'Hong Kong and the Economic Integration of the China Circle', in Barry Naughton (ed.), *The China Circle: Economics and Electronics in the PRC, Taiwan, and Hong Kong*, Brookings Institute (forthcoming).

Wei, Shang-Jin (1995) 'The Open Door Policy and China's Rapid Growth: Evidence from City-Level Data', in Takatoshi Ito and Anne Krueger (eds), *Growth Theories in Light of the East Asian Experience*, Chicago: University of Chicago Press, pp. 73–104.

Yeh, Milton (1995) 'Ask a Tiger for Its Hide? Taiwan's Approach to Economic Transaction across the Straits', in Jane Khanna (ed.), *Southern China, Hong Kong, and Taiwan*, The Centre for Strategic & International Studies, Washington, D.C., pp. 61–70.

Zhou, Ba Jun (1992) *Hong Kong: The Economic Transition Accompanying the Political Transition*, Joint Publishing (HK) Co. Ltd., Hong Kong (in Chinese).

# 5

# Japanese Multinationals and Regional Integration in Asia

## Fukunari Kimura

## I  Introduction

The term 'economic integration' is often used without any formal definition in research papers and journalistic articles. It sometimes refers to a sort of trade policy implemented by governments, or is regarded as a synonym of economic interdependence. To avoid any confusion, the author would like to apply a simple but useful definition proposed by Lloyd (1996). He says that a region is regarded as economically integrated if the Law of One Price prevails in all goods and factors markets in the region. This definition follows a standard theoretical setting of 'an integrated world economy' as in Helpman and Krugman (1985). In a pure economic sense, we are interested in economic integration because it loosely implies efficient resource allocation in the region.

In the actual process of economic integration, foreign direct investment (FDI) plays a crucial role. Even if we have free commodity trade, it does not necessarily guarantee the international price equalization of goods and factors. Because there exist nontradable goods/factors and technologies are different across countries, the process of economic integration must be accompanied by the diversification of channels of international transactions beyond simple commodity trade. In particular, international differences in the rate of return on the services of firm-specific factors may not vanish without FDI. FDI includes not only the movement of physical capital but that of firm-specific technology, managerial ability and others. The enlargement of MNEs' activities therefore can be treated as side evidence of deepening economic integration.

Although it is almost impossible directly to quantify firm-specific productive factors, there are some statistical data which separately report firms by the nationality of ownership. It is widely recognized that firms' behaviour is different across the nationality of firms, and there are also a number of studies which support the intuition. Graham and Krugman (1989) and more formally, Doms and Jensen (1995), for example, investigate the behaviour of foreign-owned firms in the United States in comparison with indigenous firms, showing that firms' behaviour differs by the nationality of firms. There must be a sharper contrast between the two in least-developed countries (LDCs). Okamoto (1994) quantifies the difference between the performance of indigenous firms and that of foreign-owned firms in Malaysia; Malaysia is one of the few LDCs reporting the data of foreign-owned firms separated from those of indigenous firms in the census of manufactures.

This study mainly relies on the operational data of foreign affiliates of Japanese firms (FAJF) in 1991 and attempts to evaluate the degree of economic integration in East Asia. We would have liked to include activities of foreign affiliates of Korean, Taiwanese, or Singapore firms, but most of the operational data used below are not available. In addition, activities of affiliates of these nationals only had small weights as of 1991. A formal analysis on these affiliates is left for future research.

To capture the behaviour of Japanese multinationals, it is useful to reorganize statistical data by firms' nationalities. Baldwin and Kimura (1996) and Kimura and Baldwin (1996) propose a new supplementary statistical framework in which cross-border and foreign affiliate activities are aggregated on an ownership basis, in contrast to the residency approach followed in the balance-of-payments accounts. A nationality is attached to each firm, and the data of transactions of goods and services are recalculated as transactions between different nationalities. Economic activities at each location by each national are counted in terms of the value added. In this chapter, we extend the original two-country model to a three-country setting and apply it for a part of the following analysis. By doing so, export activities and FDI activities by Japanese-owned firms become directly comparable in terms of the value added. In addition, we present estimates of the weight of intra-firm trade in Japan's total commodity trade. By conducting these analyses, we can discuss the degree of economic integration in Asia from the viewpoint of Japanese MNEs.

We also try to quantify the significance of foreign affiliates (particularly FAJF) in hosting Asian economies in terms of FDI, value added, employment, exports and imports. This analysis clarifies behavioural differences between indigenous firms and foreign affiliates and at the same time shows how important the activities of foreign affiliates are in their economies. We discuss the degree of economic integration from the viewpoint of Asian countries other than Japan.

Major conclusions of the data analysis are as follows: In the transactions with Asia, Japanese firms still heavily used commodity trade, which is rather a traditional channel, *vis-à-vis* a channel through their foreign affiliates. This observation suggests that the economic integration of the Asian economies did not go very far as of 1991, even though economic interdependence among countries may have been deepened. From the viewpoint of some Asian countries, however, FAJF played a very important role particularly in trade transactions, which indicates that the activities of foreign affiliates had already been an essential part of their economies.

The chapter is structured as follows: section II analyses the behaviour of Japanese firms with special attention to differences between transactions with Asia and those with the rest of the world. Section III quantifies the significance of foreign affiliates' activities in Asian economies. Section IV concludes the chapter.

# II   Activities of Japanese MNEs in Asia

*Basic statistics of FAJF*

Japan has been one of the few countries which have extensively collected the operational data of foreign affiliates. The International Enterprises Section of MITI (Ministry of International Trade and Industry, Government of Japan) annually distributes questionnaires to parent companies which have foreign affiliates with more than 10 per cent share (hereinafter we call these statistics the AJ series). A detailed survey was initiated in 1980 and has been conducted every three years since then. A shortened format of the questionnaire is applied in the other years. The problem of the survey is that it is a so-called *shounin toukei* (approved statistics) and thus it is not legally mandatory for firms to fill in the questionnaire, which results in unstable sample sets over time, incomplete answers, and low reliability of the answers.

The Research and Statistics Department of the Minister's Secretariat of MITI has recently begun to publish another statistical series covering FAJF. This survey is called the Basic Survey of Business Structure and Activity (hereinafter BS91) and collects some data on FAJF. It only covers large majority-owned foreign affiliates whose parents are also large.[1] However, it is a so-called *shitei toukei* (designated statistics), which means that companies have a legal obligation to return the completed questionnaire. The data seem much more reliable than those of the AJ series. The following analysis, hence, mainly relies on these new statistics for the 1991 fiscal year.[2]

Table 5.1 summarizes the information on the geographical distribution of FAJF.[3] First of all, we would like to note that as of 1991, FAJF in Asia earn only 19.3 per cent of the value added by all FAJF. This share looks small, compared with Asia's shares in Japanese total commodity exports and imports which are 33.6 and 31.5 per cent, respectively (calculated from DOT95). In the case of ASEAN-4, the value added share of FAJF is merely 4.1 per cent while the shares in Japanese total commodity exports and imports are 8.1 per cent and 11.3 per cent. These figures indicate that Japanese firms rely heavily on using a channel of commodity trade instead of a channel through FDI for transactions with Asian countries, relative to transactions with the rest of the world.

Second, ratios of sales by destination provide an impression different from a usual claim; it is often said that Japanese firms extensively utilize Asian unskilled labour to produce products and export them to developed countries, which allows Japan to avoid bilateral trade disputes. The ratio of local sales amounts to 46.9 per cent for FAJF in Asia. The ratio of sales to third countries, which is 34.4 per cent, seems quite large though the estimation in the next subsection shows that about two-thirds of it go to other Asian countries instead of going to the US or Europe.

## Exports versus FDI by Japanese

When Japanese firms plan to sell their products to foreigners, they have several choices: to produce in Japan and export; to establish foreign affiliates for production and sell locally or to the third countries; to establish foreign affiliates for distribution and sell locally through them; and so on. Whether to export or to invest abroad is an important decision for MNEs, but past analyses simply compared the amount of exports with the amount of FDI, which is just like a comparison of apples and oranges. The value added approach proposed by Baldwin and Kimura (1996) and Kimura and Baldwin (1996) provides an useful way to compare the two channels directly.

Since we would like to analyse the relationship of Japanese MNEs with Asian countries, we expand the original two-country setting to a three-country setting. Figure 5.1 illustrates the framework. Three rectangles represent Japan, Asia and the rest of the world (ROW) in the geographical sense.[4] In addition, we define three nationals: Japanese, Asians and foreigners (the national of ROW). 'Japanese' consist of

**Table 5.1** Geographical distribution of foreign affiliates of Japanese firms and their characteristics (1991)

| | Share (%) in terms of: | | | | Number of employees per affiliate | Value added ratio (%) | Value added productivity (US dollars) | Ratio of sales by destination (%) | | | Ratio of purchases by origin (%) | |
| --- | --- | --- | --- | --- | --- | --- | --- | --- | --- | --- | --- | --- |
| | number of affiliates [Total: 2,851] | sales [Total: US$ 498 billion] | value added [Total: US$ 98 billion] | number of employees [Total: 919,294] | | | | to local | to Japan | to third countries | from local | from other countries |
| World total | 100.00 | 100.00 | 100.00 | 100.00 | 322 | 19.69 | 106,718 | 65.47 | 14.24 | 20.29 | 27.84 | 72.16 |
| Asia | 33.29 | 16.71 | 19.26 | 42.00 | 409 | 22.71 | 48,946 | 46.91 | 18.72 | 34.37 | 24.45 | 75.55 |
| Asian NIEs | 18.55 | 13.85 | 14.98 | 16.86 | 293 | 21.3 | 94,848 | 46.69 | 18.5 | 34.81 | 21.41 | 78.59 |
| Korea | 2.31 | 1.33 | 4.17 | 2.33 | 324 | 82.05 | 190,983 | 80.92 | 9.70 | 9.37 | 33.98 | 66.02 |
| Taiwan | 6.84 | 1.91 | 3.30 | 6.64 | 313 | 34.03 | 53,081 | 65.84 | 15.21 | 18.95 | 39.78 | 60.22 |
| Hong Kong | 3.09 | 5.09 | 2.14 | 2.35 | 246 | 8.28 | 96,998 | 48.45 | 19.70 | 31.85 | 10.63 | 89.37 |
| Singapore | 6.31 | 5.85 | 5.38 | 5.54 | 283 | 18.09 | 103,578 | 33.06 | 20.03 | 46.91 | 26.62 | 73.38 |
| ASEAN4 | 12.77 | 2.74 | 4.10 | 22.95 | 580 | 29.55 | 19,081 | 47.62 | 19.45 | 32.94 | 41.22 | 58.78 |
| Malaysia | 6.00 | 1.29 | 2.13 | 10.22 | 550 | 32.42 | 22,252 | 32.85 | 19.69 | 47.46 | 42.10 | 57.90 |
| Thailand | 3.96 | 1.04 | 1.31 | 7.05 | 573 | 24.76 | 19,838 | 60.99 | 19.51 | 19.50 | 42.67 | 57.33 |
| Philippines | 1.09 | 0.18 | 0.26 | 2.50 | 743 | 28.06 | 11,110 | 43.85 | 25.55 | 30.60 | 23.67 | 76.33 |
| Indonesia | 1.72 | 0.22 | 0.40 | 3.18 | 597 | 36.67 | 13,486 | 74.81 | 12.53 | 12.66 | 44.20 | 55.80 |
| China | 1.68 | 0.11 | 0.16 | 2.13 | 409 | 28.43 | 8,120 | 55.67 | 29.72 | 14.61 | 33.99 | 66.01 |
| North America | 34.06 | 49.11 | 42.31 | 29.70 | 281 | 16.97 | 152,046 | 77.39 | 12.44 | 10.17 | 34.45 | 65.55 |
| United States | 31.22 | 45.89 | 40.09 | 27.77 | 287 | 17.21 | 154,093 | 77.29 | 12.19 | 10.51 | 34.95 | 65.05 |
| Canada | 2.84 | 3.22 | 2.22 | 1.93 | 219 | 13.55 | 122,581 | 78.80 | 15.87 | 5.32 | 27.58 | 72.42 |

**Table 5.1** (Continued)

| | number of affiliates [Total: 2,851] | Share (%) in terms of: sales [Total: U.S. $ 498 billion] | value added [Total: U.S. $ 98 billion] | number of employees [Total: 919,294] | Number of employees per affiliate | Value added ratio (%) | Value added productivity (U.S. dollars) | Ratio of sales by destination (%) to local | to Japan | to third countries | Ratio of purchases by origin (%) from local | from other countries |
|---|---|---|---|---|---|---|---|---|---|---|---|---|
| Europe | 24.13 | 27.13 | 33.21 | 19.39 | 262 | 24.10 | 182,809 | 59.33 | 9.47 | 31.20 | 17.22 | 82.78 |
| EC12 | 23.04 | 26.75 | 32.72 | 19.10 | 268 | 24.09 | 182,822 | 59.01 | 9.46 | 31.53 | 17.21 | 82.79 |
| United Kingdom | 6038 | 12.24 | 14.65 | 8.00 | 404 | 23.56 | 195,374 | 56.69 | 7.35 | 35.96 | 13.12 | 86.88 |
| France | 3.33 | 2.08 | 3.40 | 2.26 | 219 | 32.17 | 160,758 | 73.51 | 12.96 | 13.52 | 25.99 | 74.01 |
| Germany | 6.07 | 6.18 | 7.05 | 4.48 | 238 | 22.44 | 167,989 | 68.39 | 9.05 | 22.56 | 13.20 | 86.80 |
| Latin America | 3.79 | 1.82 | 2.34 | 5.70 | 509 | 25.38 | 43,763 | 47.83 | 28.66 | 23.51 | 27.18 | 72.82 |
| Mexico | 0.70 | 0.49 | 0.66 | 2.47 | 1135 | 26.48 | 28,683 | 65.10 | 11.60 | 23.30 | 26.85 | 73.15 |
| Brazil | 1.68 | 0.58 | 1.01 | 2.71 | 518 | 33.93 | 39,663 | 29.09 | 41.84 | 29.06 | 42.40 | 57.60 |
| Oceania | 4.52 | 4.65 | 2.67 | 2.63 | 193 | 11.32 | 108,598 | 54.06 | 37.30 | 8.64 | 29.81 | 70.19 |
| Australia | 3.61 | 4.45 | 2.47 | 2.17 | 194 | 10.91 | 121,060 | 53.20 | 37.87 | 8.93 | 29.74 | 70.26 |
| others | 0.21 | n.a. | n.a. | n.a. | n.a. | n.a. | n.a. | n.a. | n.a. | n.a. | n.a. | n.a. |

Note: This covers foreign affiliates of Japanese firms that include affiliates in which Japanese have more than 50% share and have a capital of more than 1 million dollars.
It only covers affiliates which are in mining, manufacturing and commerce sectors.
It only covers those whose parent companies employ more than 50 persons, have a capital of more than 30 million yen and are in mining, manufacturing, wholesale and retail trade, and restaurants.
Value added is calculated as sales minus purchases.
Value added ratio is defined as value added divided by sales.
Value added productivity is defined as value added divided by the number of employees.
The data are slightly biased because no data other than the number of affiliates are available for countries hosting a small number of affiliates.
Data source: BS91.

Japanese-owned firms located in Japan, households and governments located in Japan, and majority-owned foreign affiliates of Japanese firms (FAJF) located in Asia and ROW.[5] Note that 'Japanese' in this definition is different from those on the residency basis or those in the sense of factor holders; we treat FAJF as controlled by Japanese and count all the activities of FAJF as Japanese. Asians and foreigners are defined in a

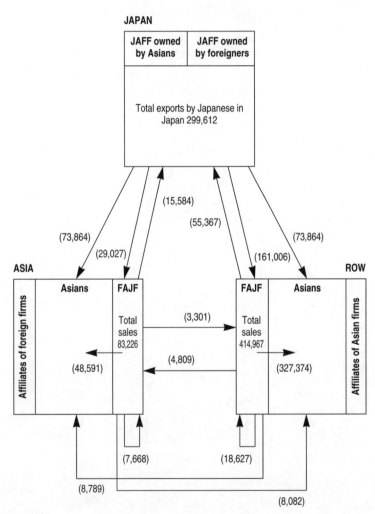

**Figure 5.1**    Sales to foreigners by Japanese: Three-country setting (1991) (in millions of US dollars)

Data sources: Same as table 5.2.

symmetric way. Three nationals reside in three different locations as drawn in figure 5.1. Therefore, if we draw an arrow for each transaction, there would be 81 arrows ($_9P_2$ + 9 or 9 ˘ 9). The numbers shown for 14 arrows in figure 5.1 stand for the estimated amount of sales by Japanese.[6]

Since numbers in figure 5.1 are the amount of gross sales, they do not

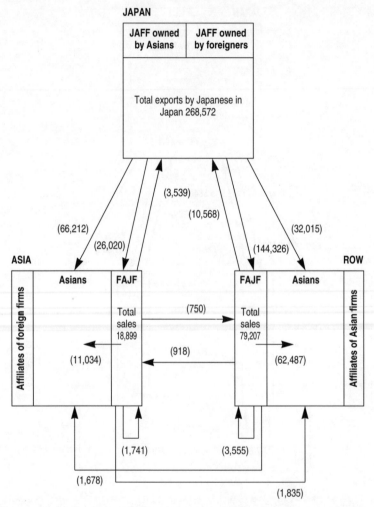

**Figure 5.2**  Japanese value added embodied in sales to foreigners by Japanese: Three-country setting (1991) (in millions of US dollars)

Data sources: Same as table 5.2.

**Table 5.2** Exports versus FDI by Japanese-owned firms in Asian countries, 1991 (in millions of US dollars)

| Partner country | World total | Asia | Korea | Taiwan | Hong Kong | Singapore | Malaysia | Thailand | Philippines | Indonesia | China |
|---|---|---|---|---|---|---|---|---|---|---|---|
| 1. Japanese value added in exports of Japanese-owned firms | 268,572 | 268,572 | 268,572 | 268,572 | 268,572 | 268,572 | 268,572 | 268,572 | 268,572 | 268,572 | 268,572 |
| 1-1. In exports to FAJF | 170,345 | 170,345 | 170,345 | 170,345 | 170,345 | 170,345 | 170,345 | 170,345 | 170,345 | 170,345 | 170,345 |
| 1-1-1. Located in p.c. | 170,345 | 26,020 | 308 | 1,971 | 10,838 | 9,136 | 1,442 | 1,279 | 286 | 217 | 142 |
| 1-1-2. Located in ROW | — | 144,326 | 170,038 | 168,374 | 159,507 | 161,209 | 168,904 | 169,066 | 170,060 | 170,128 | 170,204 |
| 1-2. In exports to p.c. nationals | 98,227 | 66,212 | 17,699 | 14,410 | 3,807 | 1,825 | 5,415 | 7,188 | 2,100 | 4,819 | 7,572 |
| 1-2-1. Located in p.c. | 98,227 | 66,212 | 17,699 | 14,410 | 3,807 | 1,825 | 5,415 | 7,188 | 2,100 | 4,819 | 7,572 |
| 1-2-2. Located in ROW | — | n.a. | n.a. | n.a. | n.a. | n.a. | n.a. | n.a. | n.a. | n.a. | n.a. |
| 1-3. In exports to foreigners | — | 32,015 | 80,528 | 83,817 | 94,420 | 96,402 | 92,812 | 91,038 | 96,126 | 93,408 | 90,655 |
| 1-3-1. Located in p.c. | — | n.a. | n.a. | n.a. | n.a. | n.a. | n.a. | n.a. | n.a. | n.a. | n.a. |
| 1-3-2. Located in ROW | — | 32,015 | 80,528 | 83,817 | 94,420 | 96,402 | 92,812 | 91,038 | 96,126 | 93,408 | 90,655 |
| 2. Value added by FAJF in p.c. | 98,105 | 18,899 | 4,087 | 3,239 | 2,099 | 5,275 | 2,091 | 1,285 | 256 | 394 | 159 |
| 2-1. In goods and services sold to Japanese | 22,873 | 60,030 | 600 | 685 | 569 | 1,545 | 1,063 | 457 | 121 | 100 | 59 |
| 2-1-1. Located in Japan | 13,972 | 3,539 | 397 | 493 | 413 | 1,056 | 412 | 251 | 65 | 49 | 47 |
| 2-1-2. Located in p.c. | 8,901 | 1,741 | 139 | 90 | 43 | 73 | 47 | 53 | 8 | 20 | 4 |
| 2-1-3. Located in ROW | — | 750 | 64 | 103 | 112 | 416 | 604 | 153 | 48 | 30 | 7 |
| 2-2. In goods and services sold to p.c. nationals | 75,233 | 11,034 | 3,169 | 2,043 | 974 | 1,671 | 640 | 730 | 105 | 275 | 84 |
| 2-2-1. Located in Japan | n.a. | n.a. | n.a. | n.a. | n.a. | n.a. | n.a. | n.a. | n.a. | n.a. | n.a. |
| 2-2-2. Located in p.c. | 75,233 | 11,034 | 3,169 | 2,043 | 974 | 1,671 | 640 | 730 | 105 | 275 | 84 |
| 2-2-3. Located in ROW | — | n.a. | n.a. | n.a. | n.a. | n.a. | n.a. | n.a. | n.a. | n.a. | n.a. |
| 2-3. In goods and services sold to foreigners | — | 1,835 | 319 | 511 | 556 | 2,059 | 388 | 98 | 31 | 20 | 17 |
| 2-3-1. Located in Japan | — | n.a. | n.a. | n.a. | n.a. | n.a. | n.a. | n.a. | n.a. | n.a. | n.a. |
| 2-3-2. Located in p.c. | — | n.a. | n.a. | n.a. | n.a. | n.a. | n.a. | n.a. | n.a. | n.a. | n.a. |
| 2-3-3. Located in ROW | — | 1,835 | 319 | 511 | 556 | 2,059 | 388 | 98 | 31 | 20 | 17 |

# Table 5.2 (Continued)

| Partner country | World total | Asia | Korea | Taiwan | Hong Kong | Singapore | Malaysia | Thailand | Philippines | Indonesia | China |
|---|---|---|---|---|---|---|---|---|---|---|---|
| 3. Value added by FAJF in ROW | — | 79,207 | 94,018 | 94,866 | 96,006 | 92,830 | 96,014 | 96,820 | 97,850 | 97,711 | 97,946 |
| 3-1. In goods and services sold to Japanese | — | 15,042 | 22,130 | 22,201 | 22,138 | 21,299 | 21,855 | 22,430 | 22,761 | 22,770 | 22,822 |
| 3-1-1. Located in Japan | — | 10,568 | 13,453 | 13,493 | 13,392 | 12,887 | 13,605 | 13,735 | 13,915 | 13,919 | 13,932 |
| 3-1-2. Located in p.c. | — | 918 | n.a | n.a. | n.a. | n.a. | n.a. | n.a. | n.a. | n.a. | n.a. |
| 3-1-3. Located in ROW | — | 3,555 | 8,698 | 8,708 | 8,746 | 8,412 | 8,250 | 8,695 | 8,846 | 8,850 | 8,890 |
| 3-2. In goods and services sold to p.c. nationals | — | 1,678 | n.a. | n.a | n.a | n.a | n.a | n.a | n.a | n.a | n.a |
| 3-2-1. Located in Japan | — | n.a | n.a | n.a | n.a | n.a | n.a | n.a | n.a | n.a | n.a |
| 3-2-2. Located in p.c. | — | 1,678 | n.a | n.a | n.a | n.a | n.a | n.a | n.a | n.a | n.a |
| 3-2-3. Located in ROW | — | n.a | n.a | n.a | n.a | n.a | n.a | n.a | n.a | n.a | n.a |
| 3-3. In goods and services sold to foreigners | — | 62,487 | 71,887 | 72,665 | 73,868 | 71,531 | 74,159 | 74,390 | 75,089 | 74,941 | 75,124 |
| 3-3-1. Located in Japan | — | n.a | n.a | n.a | n.a | n.a | n.a | n.a | n.a | n.a | n.a |
| 3-3-2. Located in p.c. | — | n.a | n.a | n.a | n.a | n.a | n.a | n.a | n.a | n.a | n.a |
| 3-3-3. Located in ROW | — | 62,487 | 71,887 | 72,665 | 73,868 | 71,531 | 74,159 | 74,390 | 75,089 | 74,941 | 75,124 |

Definitions

FAJF: Foreign affiliates of Japanese firms that include affiliates in which Japanese have more than 50% share and that have a capital of more than 1 million dollars.
FAJF only covers affiliates which are in mining, manufacturing and commerce sectors.
FAJF only covers those whose parent companies employ more than 30 million yen and are in mining, manufacturing, wholesale and retail trade, and restaurants.

JAFF: Japanese affiliates of foreign firms with more than one-third shares, that report their direct investment to MITI and have foreign participation in management.
Coverage of affiliates' data is 51.9% in terms of number of affiliates.

p.c.: The partner country of region concerned.
ROW: All countries other than Japan and a partner country (region).
Japanese: Households and governments in Japan + all firms located in Japan − JAFF + FAJF.
Asians: Households and governments in p.c. + Asian-owned firms located in p.c. + affiliates of firms owned by p.c. nationals in Japan and ROW.
Foreigners: Households and governments in ROW + foreign-owned firms located in ROW + affiliates of foreign firms in Japan and p.c.
0.1036 is the import inducement coefficient of export in Japan obtained from IO90 (pp. 321, 388). See the text for detail.

Notes:
1) Data from BS91, AJ91 and AF91 are for the 1991 fiscal year (April 1991 to March 1992) while the other data are for the 1991 calendar year. Data from AJ92 are for the 1992 fiscal year.
2) Data reported in yen are converted to US dollars by using the exchange rate (rf for 1991 in IFS94).
3) The data purchases from Japan and from ROW by FAJF are obtained from AJ91.
4) Since the ratios of intra-group sales are not available for 1991, those in the year 1992 (from AJ92) are used.

Method of estimation

1.	([Japanese total exports] – [Exports by JAFF]) x (1-0.1036) = [1-1.] + [1-2.] + [1-3.]
1-1	[1-1-1.] + [1-1-2.]
1-1-1.	([Imports from Japan by FAJF in p.c. (using the ratio of import from Japan by FAJF in ASEAN, NIEs, or Asia)] – [Imports from JAFF by FAJF in p.c. (n.a.)]) x (1-0.1036)
1-1-2.	([Imports from Japan by FAJF in ROW] – [Imports from JAFF by FAJF in ROW (n.a.)]) x (1-0.1036)
1-2.	[1-2-1.] + [1-2-2.]
1-2-1.	([Japanese exports to p.c.] – [Exports to p.c. by JAFF (available only for exports to Asia)]) x (1-0.1036) – [1-1-1.] – [1-3-1.]
1-2-2.	[Japanese exports to p.c. nationals located in ROW (n.a.)] x (1-0.1036)
1-3.	[1-3-1.] + [1-3-2.]
1-3-1.	[Japanese exports to foreigners located in p.c. (n.a.)] x (1-0.1036)
1-3-2.	([Japanese exports to ROW] – [Exports to RWO by JAFF]) x (1-0.1036) – [1-1-2.] – [1-2-2.]
2.	[Sales by FAJF in p.c.] – [Purchases by FAJF in p.c.] = [2-1.] + [2-2.] + [2-3.]
2-1.	[2-1-1.] + [2-1-2.] + [2-1-3.]
2-1-1.	[2.] x [Ratio of sales to Japan by FAJF in p.c.] – [2-2-1.] – [2-3-1.]
2-1-2.	[2.] x [Ratio of local sales by FAJF in p.c.] x [Ratio of sales to FAJF in local sales by FAJF in p.c. (proxy: ratio of intra-group sales in local sales by FAJF in p.c. (proxy: ratio of intra-group sales in local sales by FAJF in NIEs, ASEAN, or Asia)]
2-1-3.	[2.] x ([Ratio of sales to ROW by FAJF in p.c.] x [Ratio of sales to FAJF in ROW in sales to ROW by FAJF in p.c. (proxy: ratio of intra-group sales in sales to ROW by FAJF in NIEs, ASEAN, or Asia)]
2-2.	[2-2-1.] + [2-2-2.] + [2-2-3.]
2-2-1.	[Value added in goods and services sold to JAFF (owned by p.c. nationals) by FAJF in p.c. (n.a.)]
2-2-2.	[2.] x [Ratio of local sales by FAJF in p.c.] – [2-1-2.] – [2-3-2.]
2-2-3.	[Value added in goods and services sold to p.c. nationals located in ROW by FAJF in p.c. (n.a.)]
2-3.	[2-3-1.] + [2-3-2.] + [2-3-3.]
2-3-1.	[Value added in goods and services sold to JAFF (owned by foreigners) by FAJF in p.c. (n.a.)]
2-3-2.	[Value added in goods and services sold to foreigners located in p.c. by FAJF in p.c. (n.a.)]
2-3-3.	[2.] x Ratio of sales to ROW by FAJF in p.c.] – [2-1-3.] – [2-2-3.]
3.	[Sales by FAJF in ROW] – [Purchases by FAJF in ROW] = [3-1.] + [3-2.] + [3-3.]
3-1.	[3-1-1.] + [3-1-2.] + [3-1-3.]
3-1-1.	[3.] x [Ratio of sales to Japan by FAJF in ROW] – [3-2-1.] – [3-3-1.]
3-1-2.	[3.] x ([Ratio of sales to p.c. by FAJF in ROW (available only for sale to Asia)] x [Ratio of sales to FAJF in local sales by FAJF in ROW (proxy: ratio of intra-group sales in sales to p.c. by FAJF in ROW (proxy: ratio of intra-group sales in local sales by FAJF in RWO)]
		Asia by FAJF in ROW)]
3-1-3.	[3.] x [Ratio of local sales by FAJF in ROW] x [Ratio of sales to FAJF in local sales by FAJF in ROW (proxy: ratio of intra-group sales in local sales by FAJF in ROW (n.a.)]
3-2.	[3-2-1.] + [3-2-2.] + [3-2-3.]
3-2-1.	[Value added in goods and services sold to JAFF (owned by p.c. nationals) by FAJF in ROW (n.a.)]
3-2-2.	[3.] x [Ratio of sales to p.c. by FAJF in ROW (available only for sale to Asia)] – [3-1-2.] – [3-3-2.]
3-2-3.	[Value added in goods and services sold to p.c. nationals located in ROW by FAJF in ROW (n.a.)]
3-3.	[3-3-1.] + [3-3-2.] + [3-3-3.]
3-3-1.	[Value added in goods and services sold to JAFF (owned by foreigners) by FAJF in ROW (n.a.)]
3-3-2.	[Value added in goods and services sold to foreigners located in p.c. by FAJF in ROW (n.a.)]
3-3-3.	[3.] x ([Ratio of local sales by FAJF in ROW] + [Ratio of sales to ROW by FAJF in ROW]) – [3-1-3.] – [3-2-3.]

Data sources
	Data for FAJF: BS91.
	Data for JAFF: AF91.
	Cross-border trade data: DOT95.
	Exchange rate: IFS94.
	By-origin purchases and sales to Asia by FAJF: AJ91.
	Ratios of intra-firm trade by FAJF: AJ92.

necessarily reflect the importance of each transaction. For example, when a Japanese firm located in Japan exports a product through its wholesale affiliates located abroad, the sales are counted twice in this figure; once for an arrow from Japanese parents to FAJF and another for one from FAJF to foreigners abroad. One of the ways to weigh each transaction is to introduce a value added concept. Figure 5.2 presents the Japanese value added contents of each transaction at the origin of each arrow (see also Asia's column in table 5.2). Japanese value added in exports of Japanese-owned firms is calculated by subtracting the import component in the remaining exports. The proportion of the import component in exports (10.36%) is obtained from the 1990 non-competitive-import-type input-output table (IO90). Assuming that the ratio of value added to sales is the same no matter where the sales destination is, we obtain the Japanese value added in exports of Japanese-owned firms to FAJF in Asia (US $26,020 million), to FAJF in ROW (US $144,326 million), to Asians in Asia (US $66,212 million), and to foreigners in ROW (US $32,015 million). There is no information on exports to foreigners in Asia or exports to Asians in ROW.

Value added earned by FAJF in Asia (US $18,899 million) is calculated as sales minus purchases. Assuming again that the ratio of value added to sales (22.7%) is the same no matter where the sales destination is, we obtain the value added by FAJF in goods and services sold to Japanese located in Japan (US $3,539 million), to Japanese located in Asia (US $1,741 million), to Japanese located in ROW (US $750 million), to Asians located in Asia (US $11,034 million), and to foreigners located in ROW (US $1,835 million). Data are not available for sales by FAJF to Asians in Japan and ROW, or those to foreigners in Japan and ROW. Value added by FAJF in ROW in goods and services sold to various places is estimated in the same way, using the ratio of value added to sales, 19.1 per cent.

Although these figures are only approximate estimates with a number of reservations on the data set, the value added account provides useful insights on the activities of Japanese MNEs. We know that some foreign affiliates carry out extensive production activities while others simply work as marketing branches without adding much value. To discuss the weights on various channels of activities assigned by MNEs, it is convenient to look at the value added contents embodied in goods and services sales.

By using the figures in table 5.2, table 5.3 presents estimates of the value added contents embodied in sales by Japanese to Asians in Asia and to foreigners in ROW. The Japanese value added contents of indirect channels are estimated as follows: In the case of US $15,192 million (to produce in Japan and to distribute through FAJF in Asia), we multiply Japanese value added in exports of Japanese-owned firms to

**Table 5.3** Major channels for Japanese firms to sell products abroad (1991)

| | Value added contents (Millions of US dollars) | Share (%) |
|---|---|---|
| For Japanese firms to sell products to Asians in Asia (total of below): | 97,174 | 100.00 |
| To produce in Japan and export directly | 66,212 | 68.14 |
| To produce in Japan and distribute through FAJF in Asia | 15,192 | 15.63 |
| To produce in Japan and distribute through FAJF in ROW | 3,058 | 3.15 |
| To produce in Asia and sell locally | 11,034 | 11.35 |
| To produce in ROW and export to Asia | 1,678 | 1.73 |
| | | |
| For Japanese firms to sell products to foreigners in ROW (total of below): | 212,723 | 100.00 |
| To produce in Japan and export directly | 32,015 | 15.05 |
| To produce in Japan and distribute through FAJF in ROW | 113,860 | 53.53 |
| To produce in Japan and distribute through FAJF in Asia | 2,526 | 1.19 |
| To produce in ROW and sell locally | 62,487 | 29.37 |
| To produce in Asia and export to ROW | 1,835 | 0.86 |

Notes:
Minor indirect channels such as 'to produce in Japan and to distribute through FAJF in ROW and then through FAJF in Asia' are omitted.
The above figures are estimated based on table 5.2.

FAJF in Asia (US $26,020 million) by the proportion of sales to Asians in Asia by FAJF in Asia (11,034 / 18,899). Similar calculation applies for other indirect channels. The table shows a sharp contrast in the choices of transaction channels: Japanese firms put much weight on direct exports when selling products to Asians, while they rely more on a channel through FAJF in ROW. It is often said that Japanese firms export a large portion of their products through their wholesale foreign affiliates, but our estimates indicate that it is not the case when selling products to Asians. At the same time, the value added portion generated by FAJF in ROW is also large when selling to foreigners. Both manufacturing FAJF and wholesale FAJF play important roles in ROW. However, this is not the case in selling to Asians. Moreover, it is necessary to stress that in selling products to foreigners in ROW, selling through FAJF in Asia has a very small portion.

Table 5.2 also presents estimated results for three-country models, each of which includes Japan, one East Asian country, and the ROW. Table 5.4 presents some figures calculated from table 5.2. The first three rows show the value added contents in sales by Japanese to Japan through FAJF in each partner country. The figures are negligible except for those of Hong Kong and Singapore. Considerable amounts of value added contents are first exported from Japan to Hong Kong (US $2,135 million) and Singapore (US $1,830 million) and then are exported back to Japan. These figures suggest the existence of a division of labour in the production process or some sort of strategic manoeuvre by Japanese MNEs for exchange rate hedging, tax evasion or something. The 4th row to the 7th row present weights of major channels for Japanese to sell to each partner country in terms of value added contents. To produce in Japan and directly export is a dominant channel for all partner countries except Hong Kong and Singapore. Large amounts of value added contents earned by Japanese in Japan are sold through FAJF in Hong Kong (US $5,030 million) and Singapore (US $2,894 million), which indicates that FAJF in these countries work as wholesale branches. The last three lines present the value added contents in sales by Japanese to ROW through FAJF in each partner country. Again, figures are small for all countries except Hong Kong and Singapore. FAJF in Hong Kong and Singapore also work as wholesale branches and assembly plants to sell products to ROW (US $2,872 million and US $3,566 million). The characteristics of FAJF in Hong Kong and Singapore thus are widely different from those in other Asian countries. A difference between FAJF in Hong Kong and those in Singapore is that the latter earn more value added, which indicates that the FAJF activities in Singapore contain a more extensive production process.

In summary, Japanese-owned firms still use a traditional direct

**Table 5.4** Major channels for Japanese firms to sell products through partner countries (1991)

| Partner country | Korea Value added contents (in millions of dollars) | Korea Share (%) | Taiwan Value added contents (in millions of dollars) | Taiwan Share (%) | Hong Kong Value added contents (in millions of dollars) | Hong Kong Share (%) | Singapore Value added contents (in millions of dollars) | Singapore Share (%) |
|---|---|---|---|---|---|---|---|---|
| For Japanese firms to sell products to Japanese in Japan (total of below): | 46 | 100.00 | 793 | 100.00 | 2,548 | 100.00 | 2,886 | 100.00 |
| To produce in Japan and distribute through FAJF in p.c. | 30 | 7.00 | 300 | 37.84 | 2,135 | 83.77 | 1,830 | 63.40 |
| To produce in p.c. and export to Japan | 397 | 93.00 | 493 | 62.16 | 413 | 16.23 | 1,056 | 36.60 |
| For Japanese firms to sell products to p.c. nationals in p.c. (total of below): | 21,107 | 100.00 | 17,697 | 100.00 | 9,811 | 100.00 | 6,390 | 100.00 |
| To produce in Japan and export directly to p.c. | 17,699 | 83.86 | 14,410 | 81.43 | 3,807 | 38.80 | 1,825 | 28.56 |
| To produce in Japan and distribute through FAJF in p.c. | 239 | 1.13 | 1,243 | 7.03 | 5,030 | 51.27 | 2,894 | 45.29 |
| To produce in p.c. and sell locally | 3,169 | 15.01 | 2,043 | 11.54 | 974 | 9.93 | 1,671 | 26.15 |
| For Japanese firms to sell products to foreigners in ROW (total of below): | 343 | 100.00 | 821 | 100.00 | 3,429 | 100.00 | 5,626 | 100.00 |
| To produce in Japan and distribute through FAJF in p.c. | 24 | 7.00 | 311 | 37.84 | 2,872 | 83.77 | 3,566 | 63.40 |
| To produce in p.c. and export to ROW | 319 | 93.00 | 511 | 62.16 | 556 | 16.23 | 2,059 | 36.60 |

| Partner country | Malaysia Value added contents (in millions of dollars) | Malaysia Share (%) | Thailand Value added contents (in millions of dollars) | Thailand Share (%) | Philippines Value added contents (in millions of dollars) | Philippines Share (%) | Indonesia Value added contents (in millions of dollars) | Indonesia Share (%) | China Value added contents (in millions of dollars) | China Share (%) |
|---|---|---|---|---|---|---|---|---|---|---|
| For Japanese firms to sell products to Japanese in Japan (total of below): | 695 | 100.00 | 500 | 100.00 | 138 | 100.00 | 77 | 100.00 | 89 | 100.00 |
| To produce in Japan and distribute through FAJF in p.c. | 284 | 40.81 | 250 | 49.88 | 73 | 52.78 | 27 | 35.51 | 42 | 47.09 |
| To produce in p.c. and export to Japan | 412 | 59.19 | 251 | 50.12 | 65 | 47.22 | 49 | 64.49 | 47 | 52.91 |
| For Japanese firms to sell products to p.c. nationals in p.c. (total of below): | 6,496 | 100.00 | 8,646 | 100.00 | 2,322 | 100.00 | 5,245 | 100.00 | 7,731 | 100.00 |
| To produce in Japan and export directly to p.c. | 5,415 | 83.35 | 7,188 | 83.14 | 2,100 | 90.47 | 4,819 | 91.87 | 7,572 | 97.94 |
| To produce in Japan and distribute through FAJF in p.c. | 441 | 6.80 | 727 | 8.41 | 117 | 5.03 | 151 | 2.89 | 75 | 0.97 |
| To produce in p.c. and sell locally | 640 | 9.86 | 730 | 8.45 | 105 | 4.50 | 275 | 5.24 | 84 | 1.09 |
| For Japanese firms to sell products to foreigners in ROW (total of below): | 656 | 100.00 | 196 | 100.00 | 65 | 100.00 | 30 | 100.00 | 31 | 100.00 |
| To produce in Japan and distribute through FAJF in p.c. | 268 | 40.81 | 98 | 49.88 | 34 | 52.78 | 11 | 35.51 | 15 | 47.09 |
| To produce in p.c. and export to ROW | 388 | 59.19 | 98 | 50.12 | 31 | 47.22 | 20 | 64.49 | 17 | 52.91 |

Notes:   'p.c.' denotes a partner country.   'ROW' denotes all countries other than Japan and a partner country.

'Foreigners' means nationals of ROW.   Minor indirect channels are omitted.

All figures are estimated based on table 5.2.

export channel, rather than utilizing their foreign affiliates, when selling products to Asia, which indicates that economic integration has not yet advanced very far. Among East Asian countries, Hong Kong and Singapore play special roles in distributing Japanese products to the world.

## Intra-group transactions

The next question is what proportion of transactions with FAJF are between firms and affiliates under the same parent companies. We here use the ratios of intra-group transactions reported in AJ86, 89 and 92.[7] Intra-group trade is defined as trade transactions among related companies which include parent companies, affiliates in which the parent companies have more than 10 per cent share, and foreign firms in which affiliates have more than 50 per cent share. We compare Japan's total exports and imports, exports and imports by FAJF, and intra-group exports and imports. These estimates are imprecise to some extent due to the data quality problem. Aside from the instability of the sample in the AJ series, exports and imports by FAJF may count transactions through Japanese trading companies, which potentially makes these figures overstated.

Table 5.5 presents the estimated figures. It separately lists figures for partner regions of Asian NIEs, ASEAN-4, Asia as a whole, and the world total. The figures are unstable over time, and compared with the 1991 figures by BS91, the proportions of exports and imports through FAJF in total exports to the world seem too small. In 1989, imports from FAJF in Asian NIEs are larger than Japan's total imports from Asian NIEs, which is obviously an anomaly. Despite such shakiness of the estimation, we can still pick up the overall tendencies. First, on the export side, exports to FAJF and intra-group trade have much smaller shares in total exports in the case of Asian countries than in that of the world total. This is consistent with our observation in the last subsection. Second, on the import side, transactions through FAJF as well as intra-group transactions have extremely large shares in the case of imports from Asian NIEs while those are much less significant in the case of imports from ASEAN-4. The former may reflect extensive market control by general trading companies or some sort of hedging behaviour of Japanese producers which have wholesale headquarters in Hong Kong and other places. The latter indicates that there is weaker control by Japanese company groups in ASEAN countries. In addition, Japan's imports of oil and natural gas from Indonesia may push down these figures to some extent.

**Table 5.5** Japanese trade transactions with FAJF and intra-group trade (in millions of US dollars and percentages)

| | 1986 | | 1989 | | 1992 | |
|---|---|---|---|---|---|---|
| Japan's exports to Asian NIEs | 34,754 | (100.00) | 45,851 | (100.00) | 73,808 | (100.00) |
| Exports to FAJF in Asian NIEs | n.a. | – | 9,782 | (21.34) | 15,134 | (20.50) |
| Intra-group exports to Asian NIEs | n.a. | – | 6,955 | (15.17) | 12,727 | (17.24) |
| Japan's imports from Asian NIEs | 14,470 | (100.00) | 23,565 | (100.00) | 26,580 | (100.00) |
| Imports from FAJF in Asian NIEs | n.a. | – | 24,078 | (102.18) | 22,286 | (83.84) |
| Intra-group imports from Asian NIEs | n.a. | – | 7,873 | (33.41) | 13,416 | (50.47) |
| Japan's exports to ASEAN4 | 8,662 | (100.00) | 14,474 | (100.00) | 28,030 | (100.00) |
| Exports to FAJF in ASEAN4 | 2,121 | (24.48) | 5,637 | (38.95) | 5,946 | (21.21) |
| Intra-group exports to ASEAN4 | 1,169 | (13.49) | 2,678 | (18.50) | 4,870 | (17.37) |
| Japan's imports from ASEAN4 | 16,075 | (100.00) | 18,924 | (100.00) | 27,456 | (100.00) |
| Imports from FAJF in ASEAN4 | 2,633 | (16.38) | 2,063 | (10.90) | 5,068 | (18.46) |
| Intra-group imports from ASEAN4 | 1,475 | (9.17) | 1,102 | (5.82) | 3,887 | (14.16) |
| Japan's exports to Asia | 60,722 | (100.00) | 72,146 | (100.00) | 119,392 | (100.00) |
| Exports to FAJF in Asia | 6,694 | (11.02) | 15,158 | (21.01) | 21,724 | (18.20) |
| Intra-group exports to Asia | 3,648 | (6.01) | 9,580 | (13.28) | 17,988 | (15.07) |
| Japan's imports from Asia | 41,405 | (100.00) | 56,740 | (100.00) | 77,259 | (100.00) |
| Imports from FAJF in Asia | 9,632 | (23.26) | 26,441 | (46.60) | 27,196 | (35.20) |
| Intra-group imports from Asia | 5,433 | (13.12) | 9,069 | (15.98) | 17,433 | (22.56) |
| Japan's total exports to the world | 241,813 | (100.00) | 239,762 | (100.00) | 344,985 | (100.00) |
| Total exports to FAJF | 77,924 | (32.22) | 155,273 | (64.76) | 118,286 | (34.29) |
| Total intra-group exports | 56,963 | (23.56) | 110,244 | (45.98) | 94,274 | (27.33) |
| Japan's total imports | 146,498 | (100.00) | 183,013 | (100.00) | 236,317 | (100.00) |
| Total imports from FAJF | 41,640 | (28.42) | 111,096 | (60.70) | 91,675 | (38.79) |
| Total intra-group imports | 16,240 | (11.09) | 43,661 | (23.86) | 38,779 | (16.41) |

Note: Data in yen are converted into US dollars by using exchange rates shown in AJ86, 89, and 92.
Sources: AJ86, 89, 92, DOT93, 95, IFS96.

Market control by firm groups in East Asian countries has been one of the major concerns for firms in other regions which try to penetrate into the growing Asian market. As for Japan's exports, the grip of Japanese firms seems weaker when selling to Asia than when selling to ROW. Japanese firms use a direct export channel extensively, and we do not observe any evidence on *keiretsu* in the international context. However, Japan's imports from Asian NIEs (probably from Hong Kong and Singapore) are dominated by transactions through FAJF and intra-group transactions. This may suggest the existence of an entry barrier for firms in ROW to penetrate into the Japanese market.

## III   The Weight of Japanese MNEs in the Asian Economies

In this section, we try to quantify the importance of Japanese MNEs in the Asian economies. FDI is not a simple international capital movement, but it carries firm-specific elements including technology and managerial ability. Since it is ultimately interpreted as the movement of firm-specific productive factors, it is not easy to measure its effect on host countries' economies in statistical data. The author believes that the best strategy for research in the long run is to reorganize enterprise/ establishment censuses in host countries so as to separate firms into indigenous ones and foreign-owned ones and to measure the differences in operational performances between them. Malaysia and Singapore have already started collecting information on indigenous and foreign-owned firms separately. More serious microeconomic studies on the influence of FDI activities are expected in the future. In this chapter we look at some macro-level data and attempted to quantify the weights of FDI (particularly those of FAJF) in host countries.

Table 5.6 presents ratios of inward and outward FDI to gross fixed capital formation (GFCF) for each East Asian country, which are compiled by UNCTAD (United Nations Conference on Trade and Development). Ratios of GFCF to GDP are also listed. In 1993, ratios of inward FDI to GFCF are particularly high in Singapore (43.3%) and Malaysia (23.7%). By combining these with GFCF/GDP ratios, we obtain that ratios of inward FDI to GDP are as high as 12.4 and 8.1 per cent, respectively, which indicates that the impact of inward FDI on macroeconomic growth must also be enormous. China follows with the ratio of inward FDI to GFCF being 20 per cent, though a sudden drop of GFCF from 1992 to 1993 looks anomalous. In other East Asian countries, ratios of inward FDI to GFCF are somewhere between 0 per cent and 7 per cent, or ratios of inward FDI to GDP are less than 2 per cent.

In these countries, the impact of inward FDI is not very large in terms of the flow of funds.

As for the outward FDI, Japan has undoubtedly been the country with the largest figures both in flows and stocks, but some East Asian countries are activating outward FDI recently. In 1993, ratios of outward FDI to GFCF in Taiwan, Singapore, and Malaysia are 6.4, 4.9, and 6.2 per cent, respectively. The absolute sizes of outward FDI stocks of these countries are probably not very large yet. However in the future, we would need to pay attention to these figures. Korea's outward FDI has recently drawn attention, but as of 1993, the ratio of outward FDI to GFCF was only 0.9 per cent.

The operational data of foreign affiliates provide a pretty different impression. Table 5.7 presents the shares of FAJF in each East Asian country in terms of value added, employment, exports, and imports. The denominator of each weight is a macroeconomic figure for each country. As for the value added weights, Singapore and Malaysia are again high; FAJF generate 13.5 and 4.4 per cent of their GDP, respectively. These figures are fairly large if we take into account that the sample set of BS91 excludes small-scale affiliates and the indirect effect of affiliates on the rest of the economy. The ratio is 2.7 per cent in Hong Kong, and they are less than 2 per cent in other countries. The weights in terms of employment are in general smaller than those in terms of value added because FAJF are usually more capital-intensive and have higher productivity than the indigenous firms. It is 3.9 per cent in Singapore, 1.3 per cent in Malaysia and less than 1 per cent in the other countries. In terms of export and import operations, weights of FAJF are much larger: 33.1 per cent of exports and 26.5 per cent of imports are handled by FAJF in Singapore. Hong Kong and Malaysia also heavily rely on FAJF (13.3 per cent and 20.7 per cent for Hong Kong and 12.6 per cent and 6.9 per cent for Malaysia). Taiwan, Thailand, and the Philippines also export and import through FAJF to a large extent. Overall, the figures in table 5.7 indicate that the behaviour of FAJF widely differs from that of indigenous firms in each country.

In summary, FAJF play a very important role, particularly in trade operations of these countries. Affiliates of other countries' MNEs are also supposed to have considerable significance in these Asian economies. In addition, although it is not easy to quantify, MNEs probably contribute to technology advancement of indigenous companies.

## IV   Conclusion

This chapter mainly relies on the 1991 data of FAJF and tries to quantify the weights of the sales channels as well as measuring the significance

**Table 5.6** Inward and outward foreign direct investment in East Asian countries (in percentages)

|  |  | 1981–85 av. | 1986–90 av. | 1991 | 1992 | 1993 |
|---|---|---|---|---|---|---|
| Japan | Inward FDI/GFCF | 0.1 | 0.1 | 0.1 | 0.2 | 0.0 |
|  | Outward FDI/GFCF | 1.5 | 4.1 | 2.9 | 1.5 | 1.1 |
|  | GFCF/GDP | 29.0 | 30.0 | 31.8 | 30.8 | 30.1 |
| Korea | Inward FDI/GFCF | 0.5 | 1.2 | 1.0 | 0.5 | 0.4 |
|  | Outward FDI/GFCF | 0.3 | 0.6 | 1.2 | 0.9 | 0.9 |
|  | GFCF/GDP | 29.2 | 32.6 | 37.6 | 36.6 | 35.5 |
| Taiwan | Inward FDI/GFCF | 1.5 | 3.7 | 3.0 | 2.4 | 2.4 |
|  | Outward FDI/GFCF | 0.4 | 12.7 | 4.4 | 4.6 | 6.4 |
|  | GFCF/GDP | 23.0 | 22.4 | 23.9 | 17.9 | 17.5 |
| Hong Kong | Inward FDI/GFCF | 6.9 | 12.9 | 2.3 | 7.7 | 7.1 |
|  | Outward FDI/GFCF | 1.1 | 1.6 | 1.7 | −0.5 | 0.6 |
|  | GFCF/GDP | 27.3 | 27.2 | 28.3 | 27.8 | 24.5 |
| Singapore | Inward FDI/GFCF | 17.4 | 35.0 | 32.7 | 36.2 | 43.3 |
|  | Outward FDI/GFCF | 1.7 | 6.2 | 3.0 | 4.0 | 4.9 |
|  | GFCF/GDP | 46.6 | 37.6 | 35.4 | 38.3 | 28.6 |
| Malaysia | Inward FDI/GFCF | 10.8 | 11.7 | 24.0 | 26.0 | 23.7 |
|  | Outward FDI/GFCF | 2.5 | 3.1 | 2.5 | 2.3 | 6.2 |
|  | GFCF/GDP | 34.0 | 27.7 | 35.3 | 34.3 | 34.1 |
| Thailand | Inward FDI/GFCF | 3.0 | 6.5 | 5.6 | 4.9 | 3.6 |
|  | Outward FDI/GFCF | 0.0 | 0.4 | 0.5 | 0.3 | 0.5 |
|  | GFCF/GDP | 24.9 | 29.3 | 36.9 | 39.1 | 38.7 |
| Philippines | Inward FDI/GFCF | 0.8 | 6.7 | 6.0 | 2.0 | 5.9 |
|  | Outward FDI/GFCF | 0.1 | 0.0 | 0.3 | 0.1 | 0.0 |
|  | GFCF/GDP | 24.7 | 19.7 | 20.0 | 21.7 | 24.0 |
| Indonesia | Inward FDI/GFCF | 0.9 | 2.1 | 3.6 | 5.1 | 4.8 |
|  | Outward FDI/GFCF | 0.0 | 0.0 | 0.0 | 0.1 | 0.0 |
|  | GFCF/GDP | 28.0 | 33.0 | 35.1 | 27.3 | 29.1 |
| China | Inward FDI/GFCF | 0.9 | 2.1 | 3.3 | 7.8 | 20.0 |
|  | Outward FDI/GFCF | 0.2 | 0.5 | 0.7 | 2.8 | 3.2 |
|  | GFCF/GDP | 32.4 | 38.8 | 34.9 | 33.0 | 25.2 |

GFCF: Gross fixed capital formation.
GDP: Gross domestic product.
Data source: WIR95.

of FAJF in Asian economies. We found that Japanese firms still heavily use commodity trade channels rather than utilizing channels through foreign affiliates when they sell their products to Asia, which shows a sharp contrast with their behaviour when they sell to the rest of the world. When selling products to North America and Europe, Japanese firms look at their large and mature markets which deserve considerable marketing efforts through foreign branches. Production operation by FAJF is also extensive in North America and Europe, which is motivated partly by potential protectionism in these countries and more importantly by the favourable environment for production, including the quality of labour, the procurement of intermediate products, infra-

**Table 5.7** Weights of foreign affiliates of Japanese firms in East Asian countries, 1991 (in percentages)

|  | Value added | Employment | Exports | Imports |
|---|---|---|---|---|
| Korea | 1.56 | 0.11 | 1.32 | 0.72 |
| Taiwan | 1.77 | 0.72 | 4.10 | 5.76 |
| Hong Kong | 2.69 | 0.69 | 13.26 | 20.74 |
| Singapore | 13.50 | 3.90 | 33.10 | 26.52 |
| Malaysia | 4.44 | 1.29 | 12.61 | 6.89 |
| Thailand | 1.49 | 0.22 | 7.13 | 5.96 |
| Philippines | 0.62 | 0.10 | 5.82 | 3.89 |
| Indonesia | 0.34 | 0.04 | 0.93 | 1.47 |
| China | 0.04 | 0.00 | 0.35 | 0.41 |

Note: The denominators of value added weights are GDP on the factor price basis except Malaysia, Indonesia, and China for which they are GDP on the market price basis.
Data sources: BS91, WT95, TAIWAN92.

structure, and others. Compared with North America and Europe, the Asian market still seems so immature and small in size that the full scale of operations in production and distribution by MNEs is not realized. In addition, the governments of Asian countries often impose legal restrictions on foreign majority ownership, which may impede the activities of MNEs. It seems that a full utilization of firm-specific factors is yet to come in Asia.

On the other hand, from the viewpoint of Asian economies, the involvement of FAJF in their economies has already become large. In particular, the international trade operations conducted by FAJF have considerable shares in their economies. Through their operations, FAJF contribute to the advancement of economic integration.

Japanese firms have so far conducted most of the intra-regional FDI operations in Asia, and thus this chapter concentrated on analysing their behaviour. In the future, however, outward FDI by other Asian economies will surely have heavier weights. Although it is difficult to capture their foreign operations in statistics, it is important and necessary to expand the scope of research.

### Notes

The original version of this chapter was presented at the symposium, Beyond Regionalism: European and Asian Multinationals in a Globalising Economy, held at OECD Development Centre, Paris, on 7–8October 1996. The author is grateful to Prof. Saucier and other participants in the symposium. He also would like to thank Profs. Sazanami, Urata, Itoh, and participants in a seminar at Fukushima University and in the Keio Economic Association Conference at Hakone for useful comments.

1    See the precise description of the coverage at the bottom of table 5.1.
2    MITI plans to conduct this survey annually beginning in the 1994 fiscal
     year.
3    In the same year, the data of the AJ series cover 8,505 affiliates instead of
     2,851 reported in table 5.1. However, the sales figures in the AJ series are
     $659 billion, which is not that much larger than $498 billion in BS91. See
     table 1 in Kimura and Baldwin (1996) for details.
4    Asia stands for Asian countries east of Pakistan throughout this chapter.
5    We here use the criterion of majority ownership to classify the nationality
     of firms. What we really want to capture is who is controlling the firm, even
     though it is not directly observable in statistics.
6    Most of the data in figure 5.1 were obtained from BS91. To supplement the
     information on sales proportions by destination, AJ91 was used. Since the
     data of transactions among FAJF are not available, the information on the
     proportion of intra-group transactions is used as a proxy. Exports by
     Japanese affiliates of foreign firms (JAFF), which must be subtracted from
     exports to calculate 'Japanese' exports, are obtained from AF91. To be
     precise, we should consider the JAFF component and the FAJF component
     in these exports, but the data are not available. Cross-border trade data and
     exchange rates are from DOT95 and IFS94, respectively.
7    Volume 2 of BS91 also provides exports to and imports from 'related'
     companies (defined as foreign affiliates where Japanese parent companies
     have more than 20 per cent stock share) by the parent companies. However,
     these obviously include exports and imports through trading companies
     and thus have a double-counting problem for our purposes. In addition,
     exports by destination and imports by origin are not reported. Therefore,
     we present figures drawn from AJ86, 89 and 92.

### References

Baldwin, Robert E. and Kimura, Fukunari (1996) 'Measuring US International
    Goods and Services Transactions'. NBER Working Paper 5516 (March).
Council of Economic Planning and Development, Republic of China (1992)
    *Taiwan Statistical Data Book 1992.* Taipei: Council of Economic Planning and
    Development, Republic of China [TAIWAN92].
Doms, Mark and Jensen, J. Bradford (1995) 'A Comparison between the
    Operating Characteristics of Domestic and Foreign Owned Manufacturing
    Establishments in the United States'. Presented in the NBER-CRIW
    Conference on Geography and Ownership as Bases for Economic Accounting,
    Washington, D.C., 19–20 May.
Graham, Edward M. and Krugman, Paul R. (1989) *Foreign Direct Investment in
    the United States.* Washington, D.C.: Institute for International Economics.
Helpman, Elhanan and Krugman, Paul R. (1985) *Market Structure and Foreign
    Trade: Increasing Returns, Imperfect Competition, and the International Economy.*
    Cambridge, Mass.: The MIT Press.
International Monetary Fund (1993) *Direction of Trade Statistics Yearbook 1993.*
    Washington, D.C.: International Monetary Fund [DOT93].
International Monetary Fund (1994) *International Financial Statistics Yearbook
    1994.* Washington, D.C.: International Monetary Fund [IFS94].
International Monetary Fund (1995) *Direction of Trade Statistics Yearbook 1995.*
    Washington, D.C.: International Monetary Fund [DOT95].

International Monetary Fund (1996) *International Financial Statistics*, 49, no. 6 (June) [IFS96].

Kimura, Fukunari and Baldwin, Robert E. (1996) 'Application of Nationality-Adjusted Net Sales and Value Added Framework: The Case of Japan'. NBER Working Paper No. 5670 (July).

Lloyd, P. J. (1996) 'International Trade and Economic Regionalisation'. Paper presented at the Conference on India's New Economic Policy, New Delhi, 11–14 March.

Management and Coordination Agency, Government of Japan (1994) *1990 Input-Output Tables: Explanatory Report*. Tokyo: Management and Co-ordination Agency, Government of Japan [IO90].

Ministry of International Trade and Industry, Government of Japan (1989) *Dai 3 kai kaigai toushi toukei souran* (*The 3rd Statistics on Japanese Direct Investment Abroad*). Tokyo: Printing Office, Ministry of Finance, Government of Japan [AJ86].

Ministry of International Trade and Industry, Government of Japan (1991) *Dai 4 kai kaigai toushi toukei souran* (*The 4th Statistics on Japanese Direct Investment Abroad*). Tokyo: Printing Office, Ministry of Finance, Government of Japan [AJ89].

Ministry of International Trade and Industry, Government of Japan (1993a) *Dai 22 kai wagakuni kigyou no kaigai jigyou katsudou* (*The 22nd Survey of Foreign Affiliates of Japanese Firms*). Tokyo: Printing Office, Ministry of Finance, Government of Japan [AJ91].

Ministry of International Trade and Industry, Government of Japan (1993b) *Dai 26 kai gaishi-kei kigyou no doukou* (*The 26th Survey of Japanese Affiliates of Foreign Firms*). Tokyo: Printing Office, Ministry of Finance, Government of Japan [AF91].

Ministry of International Trade and Industry, Government of Japan (1994a) *Dai 5 kai kaigai toushi toukei souran* (*The 5th Statistics on Japanese Direct Investment Abroad*). Tokyo: Printing Office, Ministry of Finance, Government of Japan [AJ92].

Ministry of International Trade and Industry, Government of Japan (1994b) *Results of the Basic Survey of Business Structure and Activity, 1992. Volume 2: Report by Diversification of Business Activities*. Tokyo: Shadan Houjin Tsuusan Toukei Kyoukai [BS91 (Volume 2)].

Ministry of International Trade and Industry, Government of Japan (1994c) *Results of the Basic Survey of Business Structure and Activity, 1992. Volume 3: Report by Subsidiary Companies*. Tokyo: Shadan Houjin Tsuusan Toukei Kyoukai [BS91 (Volume 3)].

Okamoto, Yumiko (1994) 'Impact of Trade and FDI Liberalisation Policies on the Malaysian Economy'. *The Developing Economies* 32, no. 4 (December), pp. 460–78.

United Nations Conference on Trade and Development, Division on Transnational Corporations and Investment (1995) *World Investment Report 1995: Transnational Corporations and Competitiveness*. New York: United Nations [WIR95].

The World Bank (1995) *World Tables 1995*. Baltimore: The Johns Hopkins University Press [WT95].

# 6

# Monetary Co-operation and Integration in East Asia

## Kiichiro Fukasaku and David Martineau

## I  Introduction

Europe and East Asia provide two divergent examples of regional economic integration.[1] In Europe, economic integration has been deepening and widening among the member states of the European Union (EU) as a result of the 'EC 1992' process (1985–92), and this process has been accompanied by a parallel move on the monetary front following the creation of the European Monetary System in 1979. More recently, the ratification of the Maastricht treaty has paved a way for EU member states to create a monetary union by the turn of this century. Accordingly, the move towards irrevocably fixed exchange rates, the introduction of a single currency and the creation of a European Central Bank for conducting common monetary and exchange-rate policies have come to the top of political and economic agenda.

By contrast, economic integration in East Asia has been primarily market-driven, unleashed by unilateral liberalization of trade and investment in an increasing number of developing economies of the region.[2] Given the growing importance of intra-regional trade and investment flows in recent years, these economies are also beginning to embrace the so-called 'open regionalism' and taking new policy initiatives.[3] The recent move by the ASEAN member states to establish a free trade area in most products by 2000 (except for Vietnam) can be seen as an important step towards deeper integration in the region. This trend is likely to be strengthened by the APEC initiatives which aim at establishing 'free and open trade and investment' by 2010 (for developed members) or 2020 (for the others), as declared by APEC leaders at Bogor in November 1994.[4] At the same time, APEC Finance Ministers have been involved in annual consultations on macroeconomic, financial, exchange-rate and other policies including capital flows and capital market development.

While the question of monetary or currency union is not – and will not be – an issue for APEC members nor for the economies of East Asia in the near future, there has been growing concern over the impact of financial liberalization and increased capital flows on macroeconomic stability in the region.[5] The Mexican financial crisis in late 1994 provides a stark reminder that large and volatile capital flows in the wake of financial liberalization can create substantial problems for macro-economic management in emerging market economies. Although the currency and stock markets in most East Asian economies proved rather resilient to adverse repercussions from Mexico, once the initial shocks were absorbed, this incident reminds them that a successful programme of economic liberalization requires greater discipline in macroeconomic policies.[6]

In this context, the Third Report of the APEC Eminent Persons Group has drawn particular attention to the financial dimension in pursuing the long-term goal of the Bogor Declaration, urging APEC Finance Ministers to provide strong support for the new initiatives at the IMF to respond to 'any such crisis that carries systemic implications' (APEC 1995: 33–5). More recently, suggestion has been made that there is a need for establishing a regional institution to facilitate closer co-operation among the central banks in East Asia with the aim of preventing future financial crises and helping them to develop more efficient domestic financial systems.[7]

Does East Asia need a regional institution or mechanism for monetary policy co-operation as it heads for deeper economic inte-gration? What are the economic conditions for an effective monetary policy co-operation? Does East Asia meet such conditions? It is the purpose of this chapter to address these questions by examining the nature and extent of financial interdependence in the region and by discussing their implications for regional monetary co-operation.

The rest of the chapter is organized as follows. In section II, we review main characteristics of macroeconomic and financial developments in East Asia in recent years. We apply a 'Granger causality' test to nominal interest-rate links across the Pacific to examine the nature and extent of financial interdependence in the region. In section III we examine the long-run relationships between money, income and interest rates in East Asian economies by using cointegration techniques developed by Engle and Granger (1987), Johansen (1988) and others. The stability and predictability of money demand are a precondition for the effectiveness of monetary policy and regional monetary co-operation. Finally, some concluding remarks will be presented in section IV.

## II   Reasons for Monetary Co-operation in East Asia

Recently there has been growing debate over whether there is a case for creating a common currency area in East Asia, and in particular, a yen bloc (see, for example, Frankel 1993a; Frankel and Wei 1993 and 1994; Goto and Hamada 1994; Ito 1994; Melvin, Ormiston and Peiers 1994; and Bénassy-Quéré 1996). While the broad consensus is that there is little evidence or justification for creating a yen bloc, Goto and Hamada (1994) argue that economic preconditions for creating a currency union in East Asia are at least as favourable as those in Europe.[8] The results of their principal component analysis also indicate that linking a common East Asian currency to the US dollar or to the yen may not be necessary.[9] We want to carry forward this debate by examining whether there is any economic reason for conducting monetary co-operation in East Asia. Generally speaking, regional monetary co-operation may be useful only if the economies of the region share a common policy objective and are exposed to common external shocks. There is, however, a paucity of empirical research on this issue in the context of East Asia. We attempt to fill this gap, although a full analysis of it is beyond the scope of the chapter, since it requires a detailed study of both organizational and technical dimensions involving monetary policy co-operation.

Exchange-rate movements are of great concern for policy-makers in export-oriented East Asian economies, as their financial and currency markets are becoming more open and influenced by large fluctuations of the dollar–yen rates. They are particularly concerned about any real appreciation of their national currencies against the currencies of their main export markets which will have a negative impact on international competitiveness. However, this is not the only concern for policy-makers of this region, especially those of the ASEAN region, because their current account positions are also constrained by servicing external debt (table 6.1).

For example, when its domestic currency depreciates in real terms, the country's export competitiveness will improve, but at the same time, the burden of servicing its external debt will also increase. Countries such as Indonesia and the Philippines whose external debt represents around 60 per cent of their respective GNP are very sensitive to any large depreciation of their national currencies *vis-à-vis* the currency of

**Table 6.1** Macroeconomic indicators for selected ASEAN economies

| | Current account % of GDP, (average 1993–5) | Net external debt % of GNP, 1994 | Currency composition of long-term debt 1994 (%) | | |
| | | | US Dollar | Yen | Multiple currency |
|---|---|---|---|---|---|
| Indonesia | −1.8 | 57.4 | 20.3 | 37.7 | 26.8 |
| Malaysia | −6.1 | 36.9 | 21.6 | 39.4 | 23.2 |
| Philippines | −5.2 | 59.3 | 30.3 | 38.1 | 25.7 |
| Thailand | −5.2 | 43.1 | 24.4 | 53.1 | 16.2 |

Sources: ADB Asian Development Outlook 1995–96 and World Bank World Debt Tables, 1996

denomination of their debt, and such sensitivity increases, as the debt-GNP ratio rises.[10]

More generally, a stable exchange rate is of common interest to those economies that have a large tradable sector. These economies tend to set their exchange rates in line with their main trading partners as an intermediate target for monetary policy. In the case of European countries with strong trade and investment links with Germany, exchange-rate targeting with the mark has been used as a nominal anchor for monetary policy. Likewise, many East Asian economies for which the United States has been the dominant economic partner have adopted, *de facto* or *de jure*, an exchange-rate targeting regime with the US dollar as an anchor for domestic stabilization policy.

However, the trade and investment linkages have been intensifying within East Asia over the past decade. This raises the question of which currency they should be targeting. Although pegging to a basket of key currencies, which normally includes the US dollar, the mark and the Japanese yen, has been increasingly adopted by East Asian economies, the currency weights actually used do not necessarily reflect the relative importance of economic relationships.[11] Focusing on ASEAN economies, figure 6.1 indicates this preference of maintaining an exchange-rate targeting regime with the US dollar.[12] But, since the late 1980s, such exchange-rate policies have led to an impressive nominal depreciation of their currencies against the Japanese yen, which in turn has increased the weight of the debt service in their current account deficits. Bénassy-Quéré (1996) argues that while East Asian economies as a whole would be better off with a peg to the Japanese yen, they individually have a strong incentive for pegging their currencies to the US dollar in order to maintain export competitiveness relative to other economies of the region.

## Inflation Convergence and Monetary Co-operation

The starting point of our discussion is to presume that the primary goal of monetary policy for East Asian economies is to provide a stable monetary environment over the medium term. Because this is a *sine qua non* for keeping low to moderate inflation over the medium term, which is a cornerstone of East Asia's 'miracle' stories (World Bank 1993). High and volatile inflation is inconsistent with outward-oriented growth policy. High inflation leads to real exchange-rate appreciation and a corresponding loss of international competitiveness. Excessive volatility in inflation and thus in exchange rates is also harmful to domestic investment by raising uncertainties and risks. Furthermore, maintaining a stable monetary environment is a prerequisite for the continuation of financial reforms that East Asian economies have been undertaking over the past decade and a half.[13]

Table 6.2 compares both growth and inflation performance of selected Asia-Pacific economies over the period 1970–94. Despite major disturbances on the world economic scene during this period, most East Asian economies (except the Philippines) have achieved remarkable growth performance and at the same time, managed to bring the high inflation of the 1970s down to below 10 per cent in the 1980s and 1990s. In particular, Chinese Taipei, Malaysia, Singapore and Thailand have

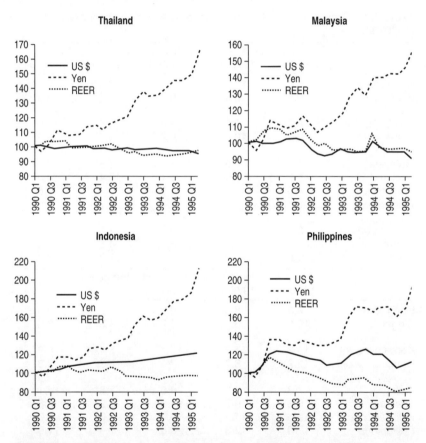

**Figure 6.1**  Exchange rates and real effective exchange rates for selected ASEAN economies
(Period 1990 Q1 – 1995 Q1; Index 100 = 1990 Q1)

Sources: IMF, International Financial Statistics and authors' own calculations.

been most successful in keeping annual rates of inflation below 5 per cent. Singapore has proved to be most 'inflation-averse' over the period. Even in the case of China, Indonesia and the Philippines, recent inflation episodes are considered to be moderate by developing-country standards.

Table 6.3 shows the degree of price and exchange-rate volatility for selected Asia-Pacific economies over the past ten years. The degree of volatility each year is defined as the standard deviation from mean of annual percentage changes in consumer prices (and exchange rates)

**Table 6.2** Growth and inflation in selected Asia-Pacific economies (1970–94)

| | Average annual percentage change in real GDP | | | | |
|---|---|---|---|---|---|
| | 1970–75 | 1975–80 | 1980–85 | 1985–90 | 1990–94 |
| Hong Kong | 6.4 | 11.6 | 5.5 | 7.5 | 5.6 |
| Singapore | 9.5 | 8.6 | 6.2 | 7.9 | 8.4 |
| Korea, Rep. of | 8.9 | 7.5 | 8.4 | 10.0 | 7.0 |
| Chinese Taipei | 8.9 | 10.6 | 6.7 | 9.1 | 6.8 |
| Malaysia | 7.4 | 8.5 | 5.1 | 6.8 | 8.3 |
| Thailand | 5.6 | 7.9 | 5.4 | 10.4 | 8.3 |
| Indonesia | 8.0 | 7.9 | 4.7 | 6.3 | 6.8 |
| Philippines | 6.1 | 6.2 | −1.4 | 4.7 | 1.5 |
| United States | 2.3 | 3.2 | 2.5 | 2.6 | 2.3 |
| Japan | 4.4 | 4.6 | 3.7 | 4.5 | 1.4 |
| China | n.a. | n.a. | 10.1 | 7.8 | 11.7 |

| | Average annual percentage change in CPI[1] | | | | |
|---|---|---|---|---|---|
| | 1970–75 | 1975–80 | 1980–85 | 1985–90 | 1990–94 |
| Hong Kong | 8.8 | 8.3 | 9.2 | 7.0 | 9.5 |
| Singapore | 10.5 | 3.7 | 3.2 | 1.3 | 2.8 |
| Korea, Rep. of | 15.3 | 17.2 | 7.1 | 5.4 | 6.6 |
| Chinese Taipei | 12.2 | 8.7 | 3.9 | 2.2 | 3.8 |
| Malaysia | 7.3 | 4.5 | 4.6 | 1.8 | 4.1 |
| Thailand | 9.8 | 9.7 | 4.9 | 3.9 | 4.6 |
| Indonesia | 19.5 | 14.6 | 9.7 | 7.5 | 8.8 |
| Philippines | 17.0 | 12.3 | 20.5 | 7.8 | 11.0 |
| United States | 6.8 | 8.9 | 5.5 | 4.0 | 3.2 |
| Japan | 11.4 | 6.6 | 2.8 | 1.3 | 1.7 |
| China | n.a. | n.a. | 3.5 | 10.1 | 10.5 |

[1] Consumer price index, except for China in which retail price index was used.
Sources: IMF, national statistics.

**Table 6.3**   Volatility of consumer prices and exchange rates in selected Asia-Pacific economies (1985–94)

|                | CPI  | US $ | NEER | REER |
|----------------|------|------|------|------|
| Hong Kong      | 0.73 | 0.92 | 3.15 | 2.92 |
| Singapore      | 0.44 | 2.17 | 1.25 | 1.23 |
|                |      |      |      |      |
| Korea          | 0.77 | 1.94 | 2.81 | 2.62 |
| Chinese Taipei | 0.94 | 3.28 | 3.93 | 4.40 |
|                |      |      |      |      |
| Indonesia      | 1.14 | 6.03 | 7.19 | 6.46 |
| Malaysia       | 0.90 | 2.31 | 3.78 | 2.79 |
| Thailand       | 0.76 | 2.08 | 2.05 | 2.20 |
| Philippines    | 3.76 | 6.22 | 6.42 | 5.09 |
|                |      |      |      |      |
| United States  | 0.44 | n.a. | 2.57 | 3.36 |
| Japan          | 0.50 | 5.57 | 4.70 | 4.73 |

Sources: IMF, national statistics, author's own calculations.

calculated for each quarter over the corresponding quarter of the previous year. Exchange-rate volatility is expressed in terms of three indicators, dollar exchange rates, nominal effective exchange rates (NEER) and real effective exchange rates (REER).[14] It should be noted at the outset that the interpretation of table 6.3 is not straightforward, because the stability of nominal and real exchange rates can not be maintained simultaneously when national rates of inflation tend to diverge significantly from international ones.

Hong Kong provides a special case of a fixed exchange-rate regime in an open economy. Since 17 October 1983, the Hong Kong dollar has been pegged to the US dollar at the rate of HK $7.80 per US $1. With virtually no restriction on international capital mobility, Hong Kong can not have an independent monetary policy but imports the effects of US monetary policy.

In the case of Indonesia and the Philippines, which are considered to be 'inflation-prone' among East Asian economies, the degree of volatility for both consumer prices and exchange rates is considerably greater than that in Singapore. In these countries, there have been successive rounds of currency devaluation over the past ten years to avoid real exchange-rate appreciation but without major success.

As seen above, the relative success of many developing economies in East Asia in achieving low inflation and high growth, compared with those in Latin America and elsewhere, owes much to a high degree of economic openness and thus low incentives to inflate (Fukasaku and Hellvin 1996). Glick, Hutchison and Moreno (1995) argue that a pegging exchange rate can not be seen as an effective means to control inflation in East Asian economies. Rather, openness serves as an effective constraint for the government not to take an inflationary policy (Romer 1993; Moreno 1994). But in the longer run, a gradual convergence of inflation rates within the region would be necessary, should these economies seek greater financial interdependence in the coming years.

This point may be explained more articulately in the context of the 'new view' of monetary co-operation that addresses credibility issues (de Grauwe 1996). The central insight of this view can be formulated as follows. When two countries with different reputations concerning inflation (say, Singapore and the Philippines) decide to co-operate, the high-inflation country is likely to benefit from the reputation of the low-inflation country. On the other hand, the low-inflation country will be 'hurt' by the bad reputation of the high-inflation country, leading to a welfare loss. Thus a country, like Singapore, may have no incentive to co-operate with the high-inflation economy, unless it can impose some conditionality. This conditionality is likely to define the 'common' monetary policy which is likely to be as tight as Singapore's. The high-inflation country that lacks credibility in anti-inflationary policies may find it difficult to converge, without monetary co-operation. Since economic agents are sceptical about the credibility of disinflationary policies, it would be difficult for the monetary authorities to reduce inflationary expectations so that the nominal interest rates remain high. Following de Grauwe (1996), the decline in the observed inflation is not matched by a decline in the expected inflation. As a result, it would be difficult for the country with a bad reputation to converge to the equilibrium level of low inflation in the country with good reputation.

From this viewpoint, it would be beneficial for the East Asian economies to seek closer monetary co-operation in the region, including both 'inflation-averse' and 'inflation-prone' economies. On the one hand, it would help the latter economies to address more readily both inflation and external debt problems, because they could improve their credibility in conducting monetary policy. On the other hand, the former economies would also benefit from the reduced political risk of countries of bad reputation being left out completely. The issue of policy credibility is likely to increase in importance as the degree of financial interdependence deepens in the region.

## The Degree of Financial Interdependence

As discussed above, maintaining a stable monetary environment is extremely important both for macroeconomic stability and growth and for a successful financial reform. But, this condition may have become more difficult to meet as a result of financial reform itself. Financial reform in East Asia has been taking place on many fronts simultaneously, including privatizing state-owned banks; easing entry restrictions for both domestic and foreign firms; expanding the range of financial services and instruments; relaxing interest rate controls; removing restrictions on international capital flows; and strengthening prudential regulations and legal systems (ADB 1995).

While the scope and speed of financial reform differ considerably across countries, its direction has been towards less resort to direct controls on interest rates and credit allocation and more use of market-based instruments in conducting monetary policy. For example, unlike the 1970s, most East Asian economies have maintained positive interest rates throughout the 1980s and 90s (see the next section). As a result of financial liberalization and deregulation since the early 1980s, the degree of integration of domestic financial markets has increased substantially in East Asia, as domestic institutional rates in both deposit and loan markets have been progressively adjusted to changes in money market rates (de Brouwer 1995).

Meanwhile, East Asia has experienced a surge in private capital flows. Although direct investment is the largest flow of private capital to East Asia, net portfolio flows to East Asia have been growing rapidly, rising from $2.4 billion in 1990 to $25.3 billion in 1994 (Riedel 1995). As restrictions on foreign ownership of domestic stocks are being reduced and capital-account liberalization is proceeding, East Asian economies continue to be major recipients of portfolio investment. For example, strong economic growth and ongoing financial liberalization have made Malaysia and Thailand most attractive locations for portfolio flows, together with China and Korea (Chee 1993; Khan and Reinhart 1995; and Kohsaka 1996). In addition, international bond issues have become an important source of external financing in several East Asian economies, including China. Although the size of the East Asian bond market is still very small, representing only 2 per cent of the world bond market, the growth of this market has been impressive during the first half of the 1990s. The outstanding value of the East Asian bond market (excluding Chinese Taipei) increased from $167 billion in 1989 to $338 billion in 1994 (World Bank 1995). Similarly, the development of equity markets in East Asia has been remarkable as well.[15] Given the region's high savings rate, the further development of domestic capital markets, especially bond markets, is likely to stimulate intra-regional capital flows among East Asian economies.

*Money Market Rate Determination: Integration with a Reference Rate*
A common approach to measuring the degree of financial market integration is to test the extent to which domestic interest rates tend to move

in parallel with foreign interest rates. One group of empirical studies focused on an investigation of the relative influence of US and Japanese interest rates on East Asian interest rates (Chinn and Frankel 1993 and 1995; Glick and Hutchison 1990; and Glick and Moreno 1994). Another group of studies examined the extent to which domestic interest rates are driven by offshore reference rates. For example, the studies compiled by Cole, Scott and Wellons (1995) show that in Hong Kong after 1982, SIBOR (Singapore Interbank Offered Rate for the US dollar) drove HIBOR (Hong Kong Interbank Offered Rate for US dollar) but not vice versa and that HIBOR drove domestic market rates. This is another indication of the influence of foreign interest rates on local ones. They also found that LIBOR has become a reference rate for Indonesia and SIBOR for Malaysia. Not surprisingly, for countries with foreign exchange controls, like Korea and Chinese Taipei, they did not identify any significant foreign reference rates.

To test the degree of integration of financial markets (both regionally and internationally) in East Asian economies, we applied 'Granger causality' tests on domestic money market rates.[16] We focus on the impact of money market rates from the United States, Japan, Hong Kong and Singapore on other East Asian economies. Since financial integration is going on in this region, we divide the sample period (1980–95) into two sub-periods, 1980–87 and 1988–95, before and after liberaliza-

**Table 6.4**   Granger causality tests for nominal interest rates (monthly data, period 1980 M1–1995 M2)

| Country | Before liberalisation | After liberalisation |
|---|---|---|
| Hong Kong | **Singapore*** | USA**, Korea**, Chinese Taipei*, Malaysia** |
| Singapore | **USA***, Hong Kong* | **USA*** |
| Korea | USA* | **Singapore*** |
| Chinese Taipei | – | – |
| Malaysia | **Japan*** | USA*, Japan*, Hong Kong*, Thailand*, Philippines** |
| Thailand | Philippines* | **Japan*, Singapore**** |
| Indonesia | **Singapore*** | **Singapore***, Philippines* |
| Philippines | Indonesia* | **Japan*, Singapore**** |

Notes: Before liberalisation (1980: 1–1987: 12), After liberalisation (1988: 1–1995: 12)
** Significant at 1% level, * at 5%.
For each causality test, we use a 12-lag structure, the maximum number of observations is 94, the minimum one is 62.
Sources: The author's own calculations.

tion.[17] The summary results of 'Granger causality' tests are reported in table 6.4. It shows both expected and unexpected results.

*Before Liberalization*
Interest rate co-movements are limited in the first sub-period because of the low degree of openness of financial markets. There are three main points to make. First, US interest rates had a significant influence on interest rates in two countries, Singapore and Korea, but not in Hong Kong. Second, domestic interest rates in Chinese Taipei were neither 'Granger-causing' nor 'caused' by foreign interest rates. Third, the direct influence of Japanese interest rates was limited only to the case of Malaysia; while the co-movement of interest rates was found significant among four other ASEAN countries (Indonesia, Philippines, Singapore and Thailand).

*After Liberalization*
Domestic interest rates in East Asian economies tend to show strong co-movements with each other as well as with the interest rates of the United States and Japan. The United States and Japan are now 'Granger-causing' three domestic interest rates, respectively: Hong Kong, Singapore and Malaysia (United States), and Malaysia, Thailand and the Philippines (Japan). This indicates the further internationalization of financial markets in East Asia.

Compared with the previous period, the number of co-movement cases among East Asian economies doubled from 11 to 22. Because of its influence on four domestic interest rates at the 5 per cent level (Korea, Thailand, Indonesia and Philippines), and one in Malaysia at the 10 per cent level (but not included in table 6.4), Singapore can be considered to be a key reference rate in this region. What is surprising is that Hong Kong does not exert any significant influence on domestic interest rates in the region except those in Malaysia. Despite the financial opening, albeit gradual, in Chinese Taipei since the 1980s, its interest rates were found not to linked to other interest rates except those in Hong Kong.

The above results are largely consistent with the results of Glick and Moreno (1994) who argue that the impact of foreign interest rates is likely to be large in economies where 'access to domestic financial markets has been relatively open and the monetary authorities have tended to limit changes in the exchange rate' (p. 46). Our results also show that ASEAN markets have become well integrated on the monetary front. Hong Kong's relative insignificance as a reference rate may be explained by its growing links with China where domestic inflationary pressures have been high, thereby pushing up interest rates in Hong Kong, as shown by figure 6.2. In addition, there might be a growing risk premium in Hong Kong, as 1997 approaches. Otherwise it seems difficult to explain such a widening gap in interest rates, given Hong Kong's fixed exchange-rate regime *vis-à-vis* the US dollar.

In short, the combination of ongoing financial liberalization, increased capital flows and greater influence of foreign interest rates has altered significantly the environment in which monetary policy is conducted in East Asia. No country can conduct a satisfactory monetary policy, ignoring its impact on exchange rates and paying no attention to macroeconomic developments in other countries of the region. This is particularly the case for ASEAN countries whose financial markets are more open than those in Chinese Taipei and Korea. How have these financial developments affected the effectiveness of monetary policy in East Asia? What are their implications for monetary policy co-operation? These are the questions to which we turn in the next section.

## III    Effectiveness of Monetary Policy in the Wake of Financial Liberalization

Before discussing the effectiveness of domestic monetary policy in a world of growing financial interdependence, it may be useful to distin-

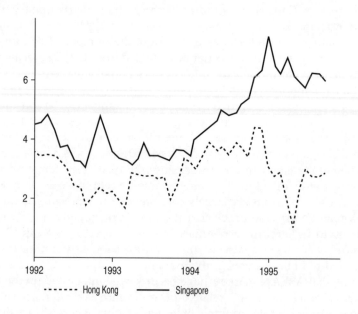

**Figure 6.2**   Comparison of nominal interest rate levels (Singapore and Hong Kong, 1992–95)

guish three major types of financial regimes in East Asia (Basu 1995). The first type consists of two city-states, Hong Kong and Singapore, whose financial regimes have been relatively liberal since the mid-1970s, characterized by open capital accounts, the absence of interest-rate controls, and extensive foreign participation in the financial sector, though entry into commercial banking is regulated by the issuing of licences by the monetary authorities. A second type includes Indonesia, Malaysia, the Philippines and Thailand whose financial markets have been liberalized considerably in recent years, and as a result, there are relatively few controls on international capital flows; restrictions on foreign ownership of local stocks have been eased; and interest subsidies are generally low or have been reduced (except for Indonesia) though directed credit programmes have continued. A third type comprises Chinese Taipei and Korea whose financial markets were characterized in the 1970s and early 1980s by a system of 'financial repression' with extensive use of subsidised and directed credit, interest-rate ceilings and closed capital accounts. While considerable progress has been made since then to liberalize financial markets and deregulate capital flows, they are the least integrated into international financial markets (ibid., p. 5).

**Table 6.5**   Real money market rates in selected Asia-Pacific economies (1970–94)

|  |  | \multicolumn{5}{c}{Average Annual Rates} |
|---|---|---|---|---|---|---|
|  |  | 1970–75 | 1975–80 | 1980–85 | 1985–90 | 1990–94 |
| Hong Kong | (c) | n.a. | n.a. | 2.32 | −0.55 | **−4.25** |
| Singapore | (a) | n.a. | −2.83 | 9.84 | 6.30 | **7.39** |
| Korea, Rep. of | (a) | n.a. | 2.16 | 9.71 | 9.36 | **11.21** |
| Chinese Taipei | (a) | −2.00 | 0.52 | 8.18 | 7.93 | **7.63** |
| Malaysia | (a) | n.a. | n.a. | n.a. | 3.16 | **4.00** |
| Thailand | (a) | n.a. | 1.68 | 12.56 | 5.44 | **6.63** |
| Indonesia | (a) | n.a. | −10.77 | 4.36 | 4.45 | **9.02** |
| Philippines | (b) | n.a. | −1.27 | 5.81 | 10.33 | **12.27** |
| United States | (b) | −2.75 | −0.83 | 8.76 | 5.33 | **4.02** |
| Japan | (b) | −1.12 | 1.72 | 7.47 | 7.03 | **6.70** |

(a) Annual percentage change in wholesale price index.
(b) Annual percentage change in producer price index.
(c) Annual percentage change in consumer price index.
Note: Money market rates are taken from IMF, IFS line 60b (short-term money market rates) or 60c (treasury bill rates) except for Hong Kong (three-month Hong Kong dollar inter-bank offered rates) and Taiwan (91–180 day commercial paper rates in the secondary market).
Sources: IMF, IFS CD-ROM; national statistics.

Despite these differences in domestic financial systems, the East Asian economies have in common that unlike in the 1970s, they have kept positive real interest rates almost throughout the 1980s and 1990s (table 6.5).[18]

This has contributed significantly to the 'deepening' of financial markets, as measured by M2/GDP (figure 6.3). In contrast to the movement of the M1/GDP ratio, which reflects the degree of an economy's monetization, the M2/GDP ratios in East Asian economies tend to rise rapidly with the growth of per capita income, partly because of increased propensities to hold time, savings, and foreign-currency deposits. The exceptionally high ratios in Hong Kong and Chinese Taipei are due to the fact that M2 includes both domestic and foreign (US dollar) currency deposits.

Thus, an important question to be asked about the effectiveness of monetary policy is whether these financial developments have changed significantly the long-run relationships between monetary aggregates, income and interest rates. One interesting finding by earlier studies (Aghevili et al. 1979; Tseng and Corker 1991) is that as expected, interest rates have become increasingly important as a determinant of money demand for both narrow and broad money (M1 and M2) since the 1980s. At the same time, at least one monetary aggregate appears to have maintained stable long-run relationships with income and interest rates. In what follows, we extend this analysis by using time-series data covering the whole period of financial liberalization (1980–94) and by testing how foreign interest rates may have affected domestic money demand.

## Cointegration Test

Standard classical estimation methods, usually used in applied econometrics, are based on the assumption that the means and variances of the variables are constant and independent of time. However, applications of the unit root tests show that these assumptions are not satisfied by a large number of macroeconomic and financial time-series. These tests have also shown that using classical estimation methods – such as the ordinary least squares (OLS) – to estimate the relationship between non-stationary variables gives misleading inferences. This is known as the 'spurious regression problem'. If the means and variances of the non-stationary variables change over time, all the computed statistics in the regression model fail to converge to their true values. Furthermore, conventional tests of null hypotheses will be biased towards rejecting the null hypotheses between dependent and independent variables.

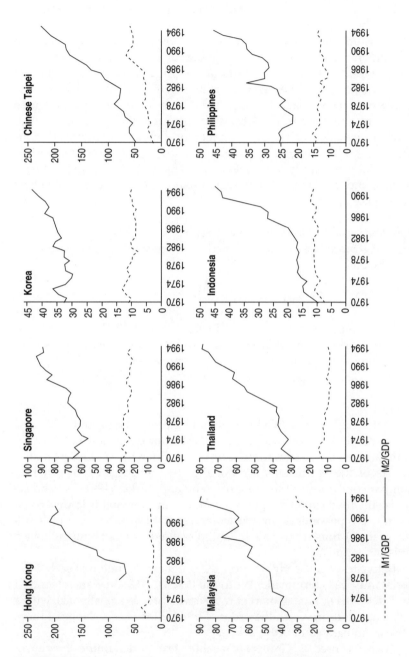

**Figure 6.3** Narrow and broad money as percentage of GDP (1970–94)

In this context, the cointegration methods have important implications. They can be viewed as a technique to estimate the long-run
relationship between non-stationary variables. In our study, there are
broadly two major steps in applying unit root and cointegration
techniques. First, unit root tests are applied to determine whether
the variables in the regression equation are stationary. Second, cointegration regressions are estimated. These cointegration regressions
represent the long-run relationship between these variables. The
problem is that these cointegration relationships are not causal relationships. Therefore, theoretical insights are used to determine 'what causes
what'. Here we apply the Engle and Granger (1987) method[19] of esti-
mating the existence of long-run relationships between monetary
aggregates, income and interest rates.

*Specification of the Money Demand Function*
The long-run money demand function to be estimated in our study is
specified as:

(A)      $M = c + \alpha Y + \beta r$

where $M$ represents real money demand, $Y$ real GDP and $r$ nominal
money market rates (that is, interest rates on alternative assets).
Variables other than interest rates are expressed in logarithms. A priori,
$\alpha$ is expected to be positive and $\beta$ is expected to be negative.[20]

*Estimation*
As noted above, we followed both Engle and Granger (1987) and
Johansen (1988) procedures. These two approaches are not directly
comparable (the assumptions are quite different, so the estimated
values of the coefficients are not directly comparable). In order to
compare our results with those of Tseng and Corker (1991), we choose
to use the Engle and Granger method. But this method is known to be
a little bit pessimistic in particular cases (it rejects too much cointegration), thus we use the Johansen method as a tool (known to be a
little bit optimistic).[21]

Before testing on cointegration, the order of integration of each time-
series must be determined.[22] We found that $M1$, $M2$ and $Y$ are integrated
of order 1 (I(1)). Money market rate series r are also mostly I(1), with a
few exceptions in which the order of integration is zero. None of these
series is integrated of order 2.

Then we used a 'Granger causality' test to determine the causal
relationships among these three variables. In most cases (except in the
Philippines), there is strong evidence that income and money market

rate series cause both *M1* and *M2*. At the first stage of the Engle and Granger procedure, the regression equation (A) is estimated by ordinary least squares (OLS). The residuals of this regression are then tested for stationarity[23] to determine whether this equation might represent a cointegrating relationship between money demand, income and interest rates. If this is the case – that is, the residuals follow white noise processes (mean equal to zero and standard deviation constant and finite over time) – the OLS estimates of the coefficients are consistent and converge rapidly to the true values of the parameters. If the stationarity is rejected, the data do not support the existence of a stable relationship in the long run.[24]

*Empirical Results*

Table 6.6 presents the OLS estimates of coefficients of the money demand functions for individual East Asian economies and the results of the ADF test for cointegration developed by Engle and Granger (1987). For the reasons discussed above, we also present the results of the cointegration test based on the Johansen method. To test relative influence of foreign interest rates in the region, we also estimated equation (A) including foreign interest rates (respectively from the United States, from Japan, from Hong Kong and from Singapore) as a substitute for the domestic one. We present only the best estimations we obtained using Singapore's interest rate (the others are less significant and are available on request).

The cointegration test normally requires a fairly large number of observations to obtain convincing results. But, with a small sample size, as in the case of this study (50 to 60 observations in most cases), this test poses some problem in deciding whether or not there is a cointegrating relationship between the variables, when the test statistic values are close to the 10 per cent critical values. This suggests that there may be cases in which a certain degree of 'judgement' is required. In coping with this problem, we set the following rules.

First, if both the ADF test and the Johansen likelihood ratio indicate the existence of a cointegrating relationship, then the cointegration status is clearly 'yes'. On the contrary, if both indicate the non-existence of such relationship, the cointegration status is clearly 'no'. There are, in fact, five cases in which the ADF test indicates 'no' while the Johansen likelihood ratio shows 'yes'. In these cases, we put 'Doubt' in the column of 'cointegration status'.

Second, we also put 'Doubt' in the column of 'cointegration status' in the case of 'low statistical power' (see Engle and Granger 1987): when the residuals in equation (A) are stationary but with a strong autoregressive component, the tests would be biased towards incorrectly

Table 6.6 Long-run relationships between money, income and interest rates[1] (selected East Asian economies, maximum period: 1980:Q1–1995:Q1)

| | | | Domestic interest rates | | | | | | Singapore's interest rates | | | |
|---|---|---|---|---|---|---|---|---|---|---|---|---|
| | | Obs. | Income elasticity | Interest rates semi-elasticity | ADF[2] | Johansen[3] | Cointegration[4] status | Obs. | Income elasticity | Interest rates semi-elasticity | ADF[2] | Johansen[3] | Cointegration[4] status |
| Hong Kong | M1 | 53 | 1.06 | -0.02 | 2.65 | 39.37** | Yes | 61 | 1.03 | -0.02 | <Crit. Val. | 32.34* | Doubt |
| | M2 | 53 | 1.26 | -0.01 | 1.93* | 57.34** | Yes | 61 | 1.27 | -0.06 | 1.96* | 31.82* | Yes |
| Singapore | M1 | 59 | 1.19 | -0.02 | 2.05* | 36.96** | Yes | – | – | – | – | – | – |
| | M2 | 59 | 1.41 | -0.02 | 2.24* | 34.85* | Yes | – | – | – | – | – | – |
| Korea | M1 | 61 | 1.34 | -0.03 | 2.74* | 43.62** | Yes | 61 | 1.04 | -0.05 | 2.52* | 33.51** | Yes |
| | M2 | 61 | 0.89 | -0.08 | 3.43* | 34.03* | Yes | 61 | 1.72 | -0.06 | 3.21* | 38.72** | Yes |
| Chinese Taipei | M1 | 53 | 1.32 | n.s. | <Crit. Val. | <Crit. Val. | No | 53 | 1.42 | -0.19 | <Crit. Val. | 33.51** | No |
| | M2 | 53 | 1.41 | n.s. | <Crit. Val. | 35.24 | Doubt | 53 | 1.54 | -0.21 | 1.96 | 29.38* | Doubt |
| Malaysia | M1 | 53 | 1.21 | n.s. | <Crit. Val. | 39.03** | Doubt | 56 | 1.18 | n.s. | <Crit. Val. | 28.72* | Doubt |
| | M2 | 53 | 1.17 | n.s. | 2.2 | 26.63 | Doubt | 56 | 1.04 | -0.04 | 2.05* | 36.83** | Yes |
| Thailand | M1 | 56 | 1.57 | -0.04 | 1.91 | 47.6** | Yes | 53 | 1.42 | -0.03 | 1.62 | 29.62* | Yes |
| | M2 | 56 | 1.64 | -0.01 | 1.77 | 53.59** | Yes | 53 | 1.51 | -0.03 | 1.65 | 31.91* | Yes |
| Indonesia | M1 | 56 | 0.89 | n.s. | <Crit. Val. | 26.74* | Doubt | 53 | 0.92 | -0.18 | 1.65 | 33.09** | Yes |
| | M2 | 56 | 0.93 | n.s. | 2.11 | 25.51* | Yes | 53 | 0.98 | -0.28 | 1.778 | 31.98* | Doubt |
| Philippines | M1 | 56 | 1.04 | n.s. | 2.53 | 32.78* | Yes | 58 | 0.93 | -0.02 | 2.77 | 30.99* | Doubt |
| | M2 | 56 | 1.29 | n.s. | 2.72 | 31.43* | Yes | 58 | 0.92 | -0.06 | 2.52 | 32.81* | Doubt |

[1] See Annex 1 for detailed definitions and sources.
[2] ADF <Crit. Val. = less than 10% significance level; ADF = 10%; ADF* = 5%; ADF** = 1%
[3] LR <Crit. Val. = less than 10% significance level; LR = 10%; LR* = 5%; LR** = 1%
[4] If both Johansen test and ADF test reject the null hypothesis (no cointegration relationship), we indicate 'Yes', 'No' in the reverse case. 'Doubt' if the LR accepts cointegration and the ADF test rejects it, in the case of 'Low Statistical Power', and in the case of 'Spurious Regression'.
Note: All the estimated coefficients are significant at the 5% level, n.s. = Not significant.
Source: Author's own calculations.

rejecting cointegration. We found three such cases.

Finally, when there is no 'Granger causality' evidence between the variables, 'spurious regression' problems arise. In this case we also put 'Doubt' in the column of 'cointegration status'. This applies only to the Philippines case (*M1* and *M2*) using Singapore's interest rates as a substitute for the domestic one.

Table 6.6 shows several interesting results about cointegration tests. First of all, our results are largely in line with what the theory predicts with expected signs of both income and interest-rate coefficients. While the range of the estimated income elasticities (0.89 to 1.64) is similar to those in Tseng and Corker (1991, table 1), the estimated semi-elasticities of interest rates tend to be smaller in our results. However, their study did not find a cointegrating relationship in the case of Korea, but in our results such relationship (with respect to both domestic and Singapore's interest rates) clearly exists. An interesting point in this respect is that as indicated by the results of 'Granger causality' tests reported in table 6.4, Korea's interest rates tended to co-move with Singapore's interest rates during the period 1988–95, and this corresponds with the fact that from 1986 the Bank of Korea activated the monetary stabilization bond market as an instrument for open market operations (Kang 1995). Second, in the case of Chinese Taipei, we failed to find a cointegrating relationship in a clear manner. The lack of a stable long-run relationship between monetary aggregates, income and interest rates may reflect that the domestic money market rates we used are not appropriate as a proxy for the rate of return on alternative assets (Chiu and Hou 1993). Third, as expected the Johansen procedure tends to find cointegrating relationships much more frequently than the Engle–Granger method. Fourth, domestic interest rates were found to be statistically insignificant in four economies, that is, Chinese Taipei, Indonesia, Malaysia and the Philippines. However, when we used Singapore's interest rates instead of domestic interest rates, we found better results in the case of three ASEAN countries. This seems consistent with the relative openness of ASEAN financial markets and the growing importance of Singapore as the region's financial centre.

## IV   Concluding Remarks

Until quite recently there was strong doubt as to whether the geographical definition of 'East Asia' can be considered to be *one* region in an economically meaningful sense. With sustained high growth and unilateral liberalization of trade and investment in the 1970s and 1980s, the region appears to have emerged in the 1990s as an entity comprising economies with common economic goals and policy instruments, despite large differences in political and social conditions.

As we reviewed in section II, maintaining price stability has come to the top of economic priorities in most East Asian economies. At the same time, the move towards freer financial markets and increased capital mobility have led to greater financial interdependence both within the region and across the Pacific, as observed by co-movements in nominal interest rates (table 6.3). Under more flexible exchange-rate regimes, monetary policies in East Asian economies (except Hong Kong) have been effective in reducing high inflation or maintaining low to modest inflation. In this sense, these economies have come to share a common policy ground for regional monetary co-operation. Conversely, it can be argued that the move towards closer monetary co-operation among the central banks of the region is expected to increase the policy credibility of a few 'inflation-prone' economies without undermining that of other 'inflation-averse' economies. In order to make AFTA and APEC work, it would be necessary for the member countries to take a closer look at each other's macroeconomic policy developments.

In this context, closer co-operation among central banks in the region would be desirable. Our analysis of Granger causality and cointegration tests indicates that this is an issue of particular importance for ASEAN countries, since they are now seeking both deeper integration among the existing members and further enlargement of ASEAN membership in the near future. Macroeconomic stability and monetary co-operation will become even more important, since three prospective members of ASEAN (Cambodia, Laos PDR and Myanmar) have much higher rates of inflation.

## Appendix: Data Sources and Definitions

Prior to analysis, money and income data were seasonally adjusted using the X11 filter. This seasonal adjustment was carried out because of a lack of data for some series and because, for many countries, quarterly income data were interpolated from annual observations implying pre-filtering of some of the variables.

### M1–M2

Both narrow money – currency plus demand deposits – and broad money – narrow money plus quasi money – were analysed separately, as in Tseng and Corker (1991). The definitions of narrow money and broad money correspond closely, in most cases to the aggregates M1 and M2. The data for narrow and quasi money were taken from the International Monetary Fund's *International Financial Statistics* (*IFS*), lines 34 and 35 respectively, except for Chinese Taipei from *Quarterly National Economic Trends* and Hong Kong from *Hong Kong Monthly Digest of Statistics*. The M1 and M2 series are divided by GDP deflators to obtain real monetary balance.

## GDP–GDP Deflator

Income and prices were proxied by GDP and GDP deflators, respectively. Data for real and nominal GDP were taken from *IFS* lines 99 b.p and 99b, except for Chinese Taipei from *Quarterly National Economic Trends* and Hong Kong from *Hong Kong Monthly Digest of Statistics*.

## Interest Rates

Nominal market interest rates on alternative assets were generally proxied by money market rates taken from (where available) *IFS* line 60b except for Chinese Taipei from *Quarterly National Economic Trends* and Hong Kong from *Hong Kong Monthly Digest of Statistics*. Real interest rates were proxied by nominal market interest rates divided by the Wholesale Price Index taken from *IFS* line 63 (except Malaysia-GDP deflator). For Chinese Taipei, we used nominal market interest rates divided by GDP deflator and for Hong Kong we used nominal market interest rates divided by the Consumer Price Index from *Hong Kong Monthly Digest of Statistics*.

### Acknowledgements

The authors are grateful to the Economic Services Branch of the Central Government Office of Hong Kong for providing us with statistical materials. The authors would like to thank the staff members of the OECD Development Centre and Menzie Chinn and Richard Pomfret for helpful comments and suggestions on an earlier draft. The views expressed here, however, are those of the authors alone and do not represent those of the Organisation to which they belong.

### Notes

1   See Pelkmans and Fukasaku (1995) for a detailed account of the economic integration process both in Europe and in Asia.
2   Unless otherwise noted, 'East Asia' refers to a group of nine economies, namely, China, Chinese Taipei, Hong Kong, Indonesia, Republic of Korea (hereafter, Korea), Malaysia, the Philippines, Singapore and Thailand. In much of the chapter, however, China will be excluded from our study because of the lack of sufficient time-series data on a monthly/quarterly basis.
3   See Pelkmans and Fukasaku (1995) for a critical view of 'open regionalism'.
4   To be sure, the Bogor Declaration has set out three goals. Two others are

to pursue (1) expansion and acceleration of trade and investment facilitation programmes and (2) intensified development co-operation to attain sustainable growth, equitable development and national stability.

5   See, for example, Corbo and Hernandez (1994), Goldstein (1995), Khan and Reinhart (1995), Reisen (1995) and Wang and Shilling (1995). See also Fukasaku and Hellvin (1996) for a review of private capital flows in the 1990s and policy responses undertaken by several emerging economies in Asia and Latin America.

6   See Genberg and Nadal de Simone (1993) on the importance of macroeconomic discipline in implementing regional integration arrangements.

7   In his speech delivered in September 1995, the Governor of the Reserve Bank of Australia argued in favour of creating a new BIS-type institution for the Asian region as a forum for discussions and deliberations in such policy areas as financial liberalization and its macroeconomic and regulatory implications. He stated that such a regional institution would allow central banks to have more structured and sustained discussion, experience sharing, monitoring, research and co-operation than is possible under the current, informal arrangements (*Reserve Bank of Australia Bulletin*, October 1995, as reprinted in *BIS Review*, November 1995). See also *Nihon Keizai Shimbun*, 30 September 1995, and *Financial Times*, 21 November 1995. It should be noted in this conjunction that the central banks of five Asian economies (Australia, Hong Kong, Indonesia, Malaysia and Thailand) agreed in November 1995 to set up bilateral repo agreements which allowed them to borrow from each other to bolster foreign reserves in times of currency crisis and defend their own currencies (*Financial Times*, 21 November 1995). More recently, Japan, Hong Kong and Singapore have reached an agreement allowing the Bank of Japan to ask them to intervene in the foreign exchange markets on its behalf (*Financial Times*, 21 February 1996).

8   Their argument is based on an examination of three criteria for an optimal currency area, that is, the degree of synchronization of macroeconomic disturbances, the degree of openness and the degree of factor mobility. See also Ito (1994).

9   See also Williamson (1995).

10  Bénassy-Quéré (1996) shows that with a 60 per cent debt-GNP ratio, a 10 per cent depreciation against the currency of denomination induces a rise in the debt by 6 per cent of GNP. Conversely, the real depreciation raises external competitiveness. With a debt ratio of around 20 per cent, the net effect of the depreciation on the current account will be positive only if the sum of the price elasticities of exports and imports exceeds 1.3 (instead of 1 without external debt).

11  Two recent studies, Frankel and Wei (1993) and Bénassy-Quéré (1996) suggest that the weight of the US dollar is predominant in estimated currency baskets for Asian economies.

12  In figure 6.1, a decline in exchange rates implies an appreciation of the domestic currency concerned, and vice versa.

13  See, for example, Fry (1995) on this point.

14  REERs were calculated by using consumer price index and covering 11 OECD Member countries and 8 East Asian economies.

15  The total size of East Asian stock markets as measured by market capitalization increased from 4.9 per cent of the world stock market in 1989 to 8.7

per cent in 1994 (IFC, *Emerging Stock Markets Fact Book 1995*, pp. 14–15). There are, however, substantial differences in real (and nominal) return on equity investment across countries (Engel and Rogers 1994.) See also Feldman and Kumar (1994) on low correlation of stock prices.

16    We applied a test of 'Granger causality' to nominal interest rates, defined as 'money market rates' in IMF, *International Financial Statistics*, except for Hong Kong and Taiwan where data was taken from national sources (see Appendix 1 for details).

17    Strictly speaking, most of the money markets in our study were liberalized during the 1983–6 period. But, to have enough data in each sub-period, we cut our sample in late 1987. This choice can easily be justified by the delay between a measure and the effectiveness of this measure. One can consider that 'free' money market rates took effect in 1988.

18    Hong Kong is an exception, partly due to rising costs in non-tradable sectors, and partly because of strong inflationary pressures from China.

19    This method is used to compare our results with a previous IMF study on financial liberalization in Asian countries (Tseng and Corker 1991).

20    Equation (A) assumes that money holdings adjust instantaneously to desired levels following a change in incomes or interest rates. In practice, as is well explained in Tseng and Corker (1991, p. 13), this would not be the case. In the short run, most theoretical models assume that money demand depends on expected incomes and interest rates rather than on actual values. Tseng and Corker (1991) used an error correction dynamic specification defined as 'a more general, intertemporal version of the partial adjustment assumption'. The Johansen procedure deals with this problem assuming a lag structure (of fourth order) in the estimated equation.

21    See Banerjee et al. (1995) and Hatanaka (1996) for a complete discussion.

22    A test for unit roots was performed using the Dickey-Fuller test (DF), the augmented Dickey-Fuller (ADF) test and the Phillips and Perron test (PP) with four lagged differences.

23    The stationarity is tested using the DF test, the ADF test and the PP test (4 lags). In order to simplify the presentation we just indicate the ADF test.

24    This could be the case if ongoing financial liberalization strongly altered the institutional environment and thus affected the long-run stability of money demand.

## References

ADB (1995) *Asian Development Outlook 1995 and 1996* (Part III), Manila.

Aghevili, B. et al. (1979), 'Monetary Policy in Selected Asian Countries', *IMF Staff Papers*, vol. 26, no. 4, pp. 775–824.

Ariff, M. (1996) 'Effects of Financial Liberalization on Four Southeast Asian Financial Markets, 1973–94', *ASEAN Economic Bulletin*, vol. 12, no. 3, March.

APEC (1995) *Implementing the APEC Vision*, Third Report of the EPG, Singapore, August.

Basu, P.K. (1995) 'Financial Flows and Financial Market Integration in the Asia-Pacific', Paper presented at 2nd APEC Round Table on *Facilitating Interdependence in the Asia-Pacific*, 23–24 June, Singapore.

Banerjee, A. et al. (1993) *Co-integration, Error-Correction and the Econometric Analysis of Non-stationary Data*, Oxford: Oxford University Press.

Bénassy-Quéré, A. (1996) 'Exchange Rate Regimes and Policies in Asia', CEPII, Paris, January (mimeographed).

Chee, P.L. (1993) 'Flows of Private International Capital in the Asia and Pacific Region', *Asian Development Review*, vol. 11, no. 2, pp. 104–39.

Cheng, H.-S. (ed.) (1988) *Monetary Policy in Pacific Basin Countries*, Boston: Kluwer Academic Publishers.

Chinn, M.D. and J.A. Frankel (1993) 'Financial Links Around the Pacific Rim: 1982–1992', CIDER Working Paper No. C93-023, University of California at Berkeley, October.

—— (1995) 'Who Drives Real Interest Rates Around the Pacific Rim: the U.S. or Japan?', Pacific Basin Working Paper No. PB95–02, Federal Reserve Bank of San Francisco, March.

Chiu, P.C.H. and T.-C. Hou (1993) 'Prices, Money and Monetary Policy Implementation Under Financial Liberalisation: the Case of Taiwan', in H. Reisen and B. Fischer (eds), *Financial Opening: Policy Issues and Experiences in Developing Countries*, OECD Development Centre Documents, Paris, pp. 173–200.

Cole, C.D., H.S. Scott, and P.A. Wellons (eds) (1995) *Asian Money Markets*, New York: Oxford University Press.

Corbo, V. and L. Hernandez (1994) 'Macroeconomic Adjustment to Capital Inflows: Latin American Style versus East Asian Style', World Bank Policy Research Working Paper No. 1377, Washington, D.C., November.

de Brouwer, G. (1995) 'The Liberalisation and Integration of Domestic Financial Markets in Western Pacific Economies', AJRC, Australian National University, Canberra, August (mimeo).

de Grauwe, P. (1996) 'Monetary Union and Convergence Economics', *EuropeanEconomic Review*, 40, 1091–1101.

Engel, C. and J.H. Rogers (1994) 'Relative Returns on Equities in Pacific Basin Countries', in Glick and Hutchison (eds), pp. 48–67.

Engle, R. and C. Granger (1987) 'Cointegration and Error Correction: Representation, Estimation and Testing', *Econometrica*, vol. 55, no. 2, pp. 251–76.

Feldman, R.A. and M.S. Kumai (1994) 'Emerging Equity Markets: Growth, Benefits and Policy Concerns', IMF PPAA/94/7, Washington, D.C., March.

Frankel, J.A. (1993a) 'Is Japan Creating a Yen Bloc in East Asia and the Pacific?', CIDER Working Paper no. C93–007, University of California at Berkeley.

—— (1993b) 'Recent Changes in the Financial Systems of Asia and Pacific Countries', CIDER Working Paper No. C93–031, University of California at Berkeley.

Frankel, J.A. and S.-J. Wei (1993) 'Emerging Currency Blocs', CIDER Working Paper No. C93–026, University of California at Berkeley, October.

—— (1994) 'Yen Bloc or Dollar Bloc?: Exchange Rate Policies of the East Asian Economies', in T. Ito and A.O. Krueger (eds), *Macroeconomic Linkage: Savings, Exchange Rates and Capital Flows*, Chicago: University of Chicago Press, pp. 295–333.

Fry, M.J. (1995) *Money, Interest Rate and Banking in Economic Development* (chapter 19) 2nd edn, Baltimore: Johns Hopkins University Press.

Fukasaku, K. and L. Hellvin (1996) 'Stabilisation with Growth: Implications for Emerging Economies', Paper presented to a joint OECD-KDI-ICEG Conference on *Growth and Competition in the New Global Economy*, Seoul, June.

Genberg, H. and F. Nadal De Simone (1993) 'Regional Integration Agreements and Macroeconomic Discipline', in K. Anderson and R. Blackhurst (eds), *Regional Integration and the Global Trading System*, London: Harvester Wheatsheaf, pp. 167–95.

Ghosh, A.R. and P.R. Masson (1994) *Economic Co-operation in an Uncertain World*, Oxford: Blackwell Publishers.

Glick, R. and M.M. Hutchison (1990) 'Financial Liberalisation in the Pacific Basin: Implications for Real Interest Rate Linkages', *Journal of Japanese and International Economics*, vol. 4, no. 1, pp. 36–48.

Glick, R. and R. Moreno (1994) 'Capital Flows and Monetary Policy in East Asia', Proceedings of the 11th Pacific Basin Central Bank Conference on *Monetary and Exchange Rate Management with International Capital Mobility*, 31 October–2 November, Hong Kong.

Glick, R., M. Hutchison, and R. Moreno. 'Is Pegging the Exchange Rate a Cure for Inflation? – East Asian Experiences'. Working Paper 95-08. Centre for Pacific Basin Monetary and Economic Studies. Federal Reserve Bank of San Francisco. August 1995.

Goldstein, M. (1995) 'Coping with Too Much of a Good Thing: Policy Responses for Large Capital Inflows in Developing Countries', Policy Research Working Paper No. 1507, World Bank, September.

Goto, J. and K. Hamada (1994) 'Economic Preconditions for Asian Regional Integration', in T. Ito and A.O. Krueger (eds), *Macroeconomic Linkage: Savings, Exchange Rates and Capital Flows*, Chicago: University of Chicago Press, pp. 359–85.

Hatanaka, M. (1996) *Time-Series-Based Econometrics: Unit Roots and Cointegration*, New York: Oxford University Press.

Ito, T. (1994) 'On the Possibility of a Yen Bloc', in R. Glick and M.M. Hutchison (eds), *Exchange Rate Policy and Interdependence: Perspectives from the Pacific Basin*, Cambridge: Cambridge University Press, pp. 317–43.

Johansen, S. (1988) 'Statistical Analysis of Cointegration Vectors', *Journal of Economic Dynamics and Control*, vol. 12, pp. 231–54.

Johansen, S. and K. Juselius (1990) 'Maximum Likelihood Estimation and Inference on Cointegration: with Applications to the Demand for Money', *Oxford Bulletin of Economics and Statistics*, vol. 52, pp. 169–210.

Kang, M-S. (1995) 'Money Markets in Korea', in C.D. Cole, H.S. Scott and P.A. Wellons (eds), pp. 159–208.

Kohsaka, A. (1996) 'Interdependence through Capital Flows in Pacific Asia and the Role of Japan', in T. Ito and A.O. Krueger (eds) *Financial Deregulation and Integration in East Asia*, Chicago: University of Chicago Press, pp. 107–42.

Khan, M.S. and C.M. Reinhart (eds) (1995) *Capital Flows in the APEC Region*, IMF.

Melvin, M., M. Ormiston and B. Peiers (1994) 'Economic Fundamentals and a Yen Currency Area for Asian Pacific Rim Countries', in R. Glick and M.M. Hutchison (eds), *Exchange Rate Policy and Interdependence: Perspectives from the Pacific Basin*, Cambridge: Cambridge University Press, pp. 344–61.

Moreno, R. (1994) 'Explaining Asia's Low Inflation', *FRBSF Weekly Letter*, No. 94-38.

Pelkmans, J. and K. Fukasaku (1995) 'Evolving Trade Links between Europe and Asia: Towards 'Open Continentalism'?', in K. Fukasaku (ed.) (1995) *Economic Co-operation and Integration in Asia, Proceedings of the International Forum on Asian Perspectives*, jointly organized by Asian Development Bank and OECD Development Centre, 1–2 July, Paris.

Reisen, H. (1995) 'Managing Temporary Capital Inflows: Lessons from Asia and

160 *Kiichiro Fukasaku and David Martineau*

Latin America', OECD Development Centre (mimeo), March.

Riedel, J. (1995) 'Factor Market Integration in Developing Asia', Paper presented at the ADB Conference on *Emerging Global Trading Environment and Developing Asia*, 29–30 May, Manila.

Romer, D. (1993) 'Openness and Inflation: Theory and Evidence', *Quarterly Journal of Economics*, vol. 108, pp. 869–903.

Tseng, W. and T. Corker (1991) *Financial Liberalisation, Money Demand and Monetary Policy in Asian Countries*, IMF Occasional Paper No. 84, Washington, D.C., July.

Wang, Y. and J.D. Shilling (1995) *Managing Capital Flows in East Asia*, World Bank Discussion Paper, Washington, D.C., May.

Williamson, J. (1995) 'Exchange-Rate Policies for East Asian Countries in a World of Fluctuating Rates'. Paper presented at a symposium on *Prospects of Yen–Dollar Exchange Rate and Korea's Exchange Rate Policy*, KDI, Seoul, 12 December.

World Bank (1993) *The East Asian Miracle: Economic Growth and Public Policy*, Oxford: Oxford University Press.

World Bank (1995) *The Emerging Asian Bond Market*, Washington, D.C., June.

# 7

# US and Japanese Multinationals in European Manufacturing: Location Patterns and Host Region/Country Characteristics

Hideki Yamawaki, Luca Barbarito

and Jean-Marc Thiran

## I  Introduction

The formation of the European Union (EU) in 1992 was expected to transform the market structures of European manufacturing industries in several aspects through its creation of a single internal market. One of its potential impacts was to trigger changes in the geographic configuration of economic activities within the EU through increasing foreign direct investment. The elimination of trade restrictions among the member states and thus the creation of the enlarged market must have provided incentives for potential multinational enterprises (MNEs) based both within and outside the EU to organize their pan-European manufacturing activities within the EU and locate their manufacturing facilities at the most efficient sites within the EU. The questions of where potential MNEs locate their production bases within the EU and what factors determine their choices have become, then, particularly relevant inasmuch as they influence the performance of the MNEs' foreign operations in that region, the host country's prospects for regional development, and the extent of geographic specialization and clustering in the EU.

By focusing on the location decisions of non-EU multinational firms in the EU, this chapter addresses the following questions: (1) where do non-EU multinational firms such as US and Japanese firms locate their manufacturing subsidiaries within the EU?; (3) do they locate their subsidiaries in the same location?; and (3) what factors determine their location decisions? In particular, this chapter attempts to answer these questions by using a new data base that covers 450 Japanese affiliates and 3528 US affiliates across 45 regions and 12 member states in the European Union in the early 1990s.

In section II descriptive statistics for Japanese data are presented to show how Japanese direct investment is distributed across countries and regions in the EU. The data show clearly that the distribution pattern varies across member states and regions. In section III the US data are compared with the Japanese data to find the difference and similarity in the subsidiary locations of US and Japanese MNEs. In section IV the characteristics of potential host countries and regions are examined and used to infer their links to the locations of US and Japanese firms in the EU. Finally, a summary and conclusions are presented in section V.

## II    The Location Pattern of Japanese Manufacturing Affiliates[1]

The Japanese statistical source used in this study is a Toyo Keizai directory which lists the manufacturing subsidiaries more than 10 per cent controlled by Japanese firms that were distributed among 15 European countries in 1993. From this list, we selected 432 subsidiaries (95 per cent of all the European manufacturing subsidiaries in Toyo Keizai) which were in the European Union and for which we were able to determine the NUTS-1[2] European region in which they were located, and for which the number of employees was given.[3]

Previous studies on the location decisions of multinational enterprises (MNEs) have shown a pattern which varies across different host countries. This pattern is also present for Japanese MNEs that invest in the EU. Table 7.1 shows the distribution of Japanese manufacturing subsidiaries in the EU represented in our sample. Among the host countries that are most preferred by Japanese MNEs are the United Kingdom, Germany, and France. The United Kingdom is by far the most favoured destination (32.6%), followed by Germany (19.5%), France (12%) and Spain (12.0%). In fact, the United Kingdom and Germany together account for more than half (52.1%) of total

**Table 7.1**  Employment in Japanese subsidiaries in EU-12, 1993

| Country | Employment | % |
|---|---|---|
| United Kingdom | 43626 | 32.6 |
| Germany | 26113 | 19.5 |
| France | 16089 | 12.0 |
| Netherlands | 8695 | 12.0 |
| Portugal | 7221 | 6.5 |
| Belgium | 6886 | 5.1 |
| Italy | 5658 | 4.2 |
| Ireland | 2564 | 1.9 |
| Luxembourg | 575 | 0.4 |
| Greece | 166 | 0.0 |
| Denmark | 131 | 0.0 |
| | | |
| Sub-total UK + Germany | 69739 | 52.1 |
| | | |
| TOTAL | 133752 | 100.0 |

employment of Japanese subsidiaries in EU manufacturing.

While this pattern suggests that country characteristics underlie the choice of host countries, it overlooks the fact that the presence of Japanese MNEs varies widely across regions within each host country. When the European Union is divided into regions according to the NUTS-1 level of regional classification, four regions, West Midlands and South East in the United Kingdom, Bayern in Germany and Ile de France in France, stand out as the most popular destinations of Japanese investors. In fact, these regions account for more than a third of total employment in Japanese subsidiaries in the European Union.

Another important pattern that was observed in our earlier study (Thiran and Yamawaki 1996) is that Japanese subsidiaries are not evenly distributed across regions within a host country. For example, Japanese MNEs are attracted to West Midlands and South East but not at all to East Anglia in the United Kingdom. They invest in Bayern and Hessen but not in Schleswig-Holstein, Rheinland-Pfalz and Saarland in Germany. This variance in the presence of Japanese MNEs among regions within a country persists when the regions are neighbouring geographically as in the cases of West Midlands (16145 employees) and East Midlands (786) in the United Kingdom, and Hessen (5178) and Rheinland-Pfalz (0) in Germany.

Table 7.2 examines the cross-industry difference in the choice of regions by listing the most preferred regions by Japanese MNEs for each industrial sector. The list of regions in table 7.2 confirms our earlier conjecture that the choice of regions varies across industries. For example, the lists of the most favoured regions are different between electric and electronic products, and automobiles. While Japanese electric firms are likely to invest in West Midlands, Bayern and South East, the auto manufacturers tend to choose the southern regions, Este in Spain and Portugal. This pattern of the cross-industry difference in the choice of locations is also present in other manufacturing industries.

Another interesting finding that emerges from table 7.2 is that the geographic concentration of Japanese investment varies across industries. The last column of table 7.2 shows the share of the three largest regions in total employment of Japanese subsidiaries. While food, rubber and plastics, ferrous and non-ferrous metals, stone, clay, and glass, and other transport equipment are industries where more than 70 per cent of Japanese employment is concentrated in three regions, the regional concentration of Japanese investment in the machinery industry is relatively low with approximately 30 per cent of Japanese employment concentrated among three regions.

## III    The Location Pattern of US Manufacturing Affiliates

Is the pattern observed above peculiar to Japanese investment? Do multinational firms based in other non-EU countries choose the same locations as Japanese firms do? To shed some light on these questions a preliminary analysis was conducted by comparing the location pattern of Japanese MNEs with the location pattern of US MNEs. Because of the unavailability of a data source for US MNEs operating in the EU which is similar and comparable to the Japanese data source presented above, we were obliged to identify the locations of US MNEs in European manufacturing industries by reading the corporate directories compiled and provided by the American Chamber of Commerce in each member state. We first classified the geographic locations of US subsidiaries according to the NUTS-1 level of regional classification and then aggregated the recorded number counts of subsidiaries for each EU region. Since this data source did not provide any numbers on sales and employment, we were unable to construct an employment-based variable that was comparable to the variable constructed and presented above for the Japanese MNEs. In what follows, therefore, our analysis is solely based on the comparison between the US subsidiary number count and the Japanese subsidiary number count.[4]

Table 7.3 compares the locations of US and Japanese subsidiaries in seven member states in the EU in the early 1990s. Only seven EU states are used in this comparison because of the lack of US data for the rest of the EU countries including Spain and Portugal. Given the potential bias

**Table 7.2** Most preferred regions by Japanese investors in 1993

| Industry | regions | CRG 3 * |
|---|---|---|
| Ferrous and non-ferrous | Madrid (ESP), Nordrhein-Westfalen (D), Ile de France (F) | 76 |
| Stone,clay,glass | Bruxelles (B), Ile de France (F),West Midlands (GB) | 74 |
| Chemical | Bayern (D), Zuid-Nederland (NL), Bruxelles (B) | 54 |
| Machinery | Niedersachsen (D), Bayern (D), Nord-ovest (I) | 31 |
| Instrument | South East (GB), Nord-ovest (I), Baden-Wuerttemberg (D) | 36 |
| Electrical products | West Midlands (GB), Bayern (D), South East (GB) | 49 |
| Automobile | Este (ESP), Portugal, West-Nederland (NL) | 54 |
| Other transports | Noroeste (ESP), Este (ESP), Lombardia (I) | 73 |
| Food | Ile de France (F), North West (GB), Baden-Wuerttemberg (D) | 92 |
| Textile | South East (GB), Lombardia (I), Portugal | 59 |
| Rubber and plastics | Ile de France (F), Hessen (D), West Midlands (GB) | 91 |
| Miscellaneous | Bayern (D), Lombardia (I), Hessen (D) | 46 |

* CRG3 = Geographical concentration ratio of the three most important regions in terms of employment in Japanese subsidiaries.

due to this data deficiency, one of the most striking results from this analysis is that the most preferred host country within the European Union by the US and Japanese MNEs is identical, namely the United Kingdom. The frequency with which US and Japanese MNEs choose the UK as their prime location is very similar. Thirty-seven per cent of US MNEs and 39 per cent of Japanese MNEs in our sample chose the UK as their prime location. However, the differences between US and Japanese MNEs in their location choices emerge after the UK. While US MNEs tend to invest in the Netherlands (15%), Belgium (12%), and Ireland (11%), Japanese MNEs are more likely to go to Germany (18%) and France (15%).[5] Ireland is generally more favoured by the US investors than by the Japanese investors.

Why do Japanese MNEs prefer Germany and France, while US MNEs prefer the Netherlands, Belgium and Ireland after they choose UK as their prime location? Several possible explanations are considered. First, the composition of industries is different between the US and Japanese samples. In the US sample, the subsidiaries classified in the non-electrical machinery sector constitutes the largest group accounting for 22.4 per cent of the total number of US subsidiaries in the sample. After non-electrical machinery follows chemicals (18.6%) and electrical machinery (12.6%). On the contrary, the largest industrial sector in the Japanese sample is the electrical machinery sector which accounts for 29.6 per cent of the total number of Japanese subsidiaries in the sample. The

**Table 7.3**  US and Japanese subsidiaries in seven EU countries, 1993, in percentages

| US subsidiary | | Japanese subsidiary | |
| --- | --- | --- | --- |
| UK | 37 | UK | 39 |
| Netherlands | 15 | Germany | 18 |
| Belgium | 12 | France | 15 |
| Ireland | 11 | Belgium | 8 |
| Italy | 10 | Netherlands | 8 |
| Germany | 9 | Italy | 8 |
| France | 7 | Ireland | 4 |

Notes: Due to the unavailability of data only seven EU countries are considered in this comparison. The percentage figures are based on the subsidiary number counts in each member state compared.

second and third largest sectors in the Japanese sample are the non-electrical machinery sector (19.4%) and the office and data processing equipment sector (9.0%), respectively. The importance of the chemicals sector is much lower in the Japanese sample (9.0%) than in the US sample (18.6%). To the extent that different industries locate their production bases in different regions and countries, the geographic configurations of US and Japanese MNEs differ in the EU.

A corollary to this explanation is derived from the observation that the MNE in each industry chooses its production location by evaluating the comparative advantages of potential host countries. If the MNE intends to establish a pan-European production and thus export base, the location choice is of particular importance and should be influenced by industry-specific and country-specific factors. An earlier study on the location decision of Japanese MNEs during the late 1980s by Yamawaki (1993) finds evidence that the Japanese manufacturers of electronic and electric equipment are more likely to locate production bases in the European countries where R&D capability is high while car manufacturers tend to choose countries where labour costs are relatively low.

Yet another explanation for the difference and similarity of locations between Japanese and US MNEs may be derived from the observation that they prefer different entry modes. To the extent that Japanese MNEs prefer 'greenfield' investment over acquisitions of local firms more than US MNEs do (Yamawaki 1994), the existence of target firms for acquisitions in a particular country may simply dictate subsidiary locations. In addition, the institutional environment concerning corporate governance in certain Continental countries (e.g., Germany and France) may make acquisitions of local firms harder than in the UK.[6]

To examine further the difference in the choice of locations between Japanese and US MNEs in Europe, we calculated a simple correlation of the regional count of subsidiaries as a percentage of total industry count between the US and Japanese samples. The result of this analysis is presented in table 7.4, for each of the ten industries classified at the two-digit NACE level for which data were available. For the sample of 58 European NUTS-1 regions the simple correlation coefficient varies from the lowest correlation of –0.079 (primary metal) to the highest value of 0.697 (office and data-processing equipment). The correlation coefficients are statistically significant with the exception of three industries (primary metal, motor vehicles, and food) where they are insignificant.

This result confirms our earlier conjecture that the difference and similarity of the geographic configuration of activities between US and Japanese MNEs reflect the underlying difference and similarity of the composition of industries. When the industry difference between the US and Japanese samples is controlled as shown in the results of table 7.4, the frequency of choosing a particular region for production base by the US MNE is significantly correlated with the frequency of the Japanese MNE's choosing the same region. This tendency is strong and highly significant for R&D-intensive industries such as office and data-processing equipment, electrical machinery, and non-electrical machinery. On the contrary, the correlation of locations between the US and Japanese firms becomes weaker for less R&D-intensive industries such as metal products, textiles, and stone, clay, and glass products.

To examine further the location pattern in the R&D-intensive industries table 7.5 presents the distribution of US and Japanese subsidiaries among seven EU states for non-electrical machinery, electrical machinery, and office and data-processing equipment. Two observations appear to emerge from table 7.5. First, as already evidenced in table 7.4, the UK stands out as the major location for US and Japanese investors. The shares that the UK accounts for exceed 40 per cent for both US and Japanese samples in the three industries, excepting only the Japanese sample of non-electrical machinery. The percentage figures for the UK in table 7.5 are much higher than the overall figures (37% for the US sample and 39% for the Japanese sample) presented in table 7.3. In particular, 50 per cent of US subsidiaries in electrical machinery are located in the UK, and 49 per cent of Japanese subsidiaries in office and data-processing equipment are located in the UK.

Furthermore, the US and Japanese subsidiaries that manufacture office and data-processing equipment are more likely to locate in the same region in the UK. Among those Japanese subsidiaries established in the UK, 58 per cent are located in the South East region. Similarly, 49 per cent of the US subsidiaries in office and data-processing equipment located in the UK are found in the same South East region. This observation is consistent with the evidence presented in table 7.4 of the particularly high correlation of locations between the US and Japanese MNEs in this industry. On the contrary, in electrical machinery, Japanese subsidiaries are more geographically dispersed than US subsidiaries. More than 60 per cent of the US subsidiaries in the UK are concentrated in the South East, while the Japanese subsidiaries in the UK are distributed in the South East (26%), Wales (21%), West Midlands (17%), and Scotland (15%).

Second, while they are most concentrated in the UK, the Japanese subsidiaries are also concentrated in Germany. Their shares for Germany exceed 20 per cent in non-electrical machinery (24.1%) and electrical machinery (22.7%) and 15 per cent in office and data-processing (15.4%). On the contrary, the US subsidiaries in these three industries are more evenly distributed among the EU states after the

**Table 7.4**    Simple correlations of US and Japanese subsidiary locations

| Industry | Simple Correlataion (N = 58 regions) |
| --- | --- |
| Primary metal | −0.079 |
| Motor vehicles | 0.051 |
| Food | 0.25 |
| Stone, clay, glass | 0.27 |
| Textile | 0.479 |
| Metal products | 0.488 |
| Chemicals | 0.553 |
| Electrical machinery | 0.642 |
| Non-electrical machinery | 0.67 |
| Office and data processing equip. | 0.697 |

Note: Simple correlations are calculated from the regional count of subsidiaries as percentage of total industry count for the US and Japanese samples.

**Table 7.5**    Distribution of US and Japanese subsidiaries among seven EU countries, 1993 (in percentages)

| Country | NACE 32 Non-electrical machinery | | NACE 33 Office and data-processing equipment | | NACE 34 Electrical machinery | |
| --- | --- | --- | --- | --- | --- | --- |
| | Japan | US | Japan | US | Japan | US |
| Belgium | 3.90 | 11.00 | 7.60 | 6.60 | 5.00 | 5.40 |
| Germany | 24.10 | 11.10 | 15.40 | 11.30 | 22.70 | 9.40 |
| France | 16.00 | 7.70 | 12.80 | 4.40 | 5.10 | 4.70 |
| Ireland | 3.90 | 8.50 | 2.50 | 15.60 | 6.70 | 13.90 |
| Italy | 5.00 | 7.00 | 7.60 | 6.90 | 3.40 | 5.90 |
| Netherlands | 8.10 | 12.90 | 5.10 | 15.00 | 2.50 | 10.50 |
| UK | 38.60 | 41.80 | 48.70 | 40.10 | 44.50 | 50.20 |
| Total of the seven | 100.00 | 100.00 | 100.00 | 100.00 | 100.00 | 100.00 |

Note: Due to the unavailability of data, Denmark, Greece, Spain, Luxembourg and Portugal are not included in this table. The percentage figures are based on the number counts of subsidiaries.

UK. In non-electrical machinery three countries receive more than 10 per cent of total investment each, 11.0 per cent for Belgium, 11.1 per cent for Germany, and 12.9 per cent for the Netherlands. And the other three countries receive similar numbers of US subsidiaries, 7.7 per cent for France, 8.5 per cent for Ireland and 7.0 per cent for Italy. A similar pattern holds for the US subsidiaries in office and data-processing equipment and electrical machinery where the shares for Germany, Ireland and the Netherlands are very comparable.

## IV    Country and Regional Attributes as Determinants of MNEs' Location Decisions

The descriptive analysis in the previous section shows that the extent of US and Japanese direct investments in the European Union differs across countries, regions and industries. In particular, we found that the manufacturing subsidiaries of Japanese MNEs in highly R&D-intensive industries are more concentrated in the UK and Germany than the subsidiaries of US MNEs. Why do the Japanese MNEs in R&D-intensive industries choose the UK and Germany as their prime production location? In this section we attempt to provide an answer to this question by examining the underlying economic attributes of the EU states.

The research design we use in this section is as follows: we first apply a factor analysis to a set of variables which represent country/regional characteristics of the EU member states, to expose the underlying attributes of these countries and regions. We then examine if the UK and German regions, in particular, constitute groups which are distinct from the rest of the EU regions. While this research design does not allow us to establish a direct link of the location choice to the country/regional characteristics, we are able to circumvent the potential problems associated with the multicollinearity among the variables that are constructed at the regional level for a particular country in a multiple regression model as found in our earlier research (Yamawaki, Thiran and Barbarito 1996). Our approach here is therefore to use a factor analysis to complement the regression analysis.[7]

### Previous Studies[8]

The existing literature on the choice of *host countries* by the MNE has identified a number of economic factors as important determinants of the MNE's location decision. These include, among others: (1) labour and other factor costs (e.g., Swedenborg 1979; Dunning 1980; Kravis and Lipsey 1982; and Yamawaki 1993); (2) market size (e.g., Swedenborg 1979; Dunning 1980; Kravis and Lipsey 1982; Veugelers 1991); (3)

technological capability of the host country (e.g., Cantwell 1989; and Yamawaki 1993); (4) the host country's policy towards foreign direct investment; (5) the geographical and cultural distance/proximity between the source and host countries as factors that influence the MNE's choice of host country (e.g., Davidson 1980); and (6) the extent of unionization and the scope of union-bargaining (Bughin and Vannini 1995).[9]

Another strand of empirical literature has addressed the question of whether the characteristics of *host regions* determine the MNE's choice of regions in the host country by examining specifically the entry of MNEs into the US and UK markets. These studies include Coughlin, Terza and Arromdee (1991), Glickman and Woodward (1988), Friedman, Gerlowski and Silberman (1992), and Head, Ries, and Swenson (1995), among others. In general, these empirical studies have examined the effects of the following sets of factors on the MNE's regional choice: (1) labour market characteristics including labour costs, the extent of unionization, and the number of strikes; (2) the existence of transport and other infrastructures; (3) market demand characteristics and the density of manufacturing activity in the region; (4) agglomeration effects; and (5) governmental incentives towards foreign direct investment such as taxation and subsidy.[10]

## Country and Regional Variables

Following the previous literature and given the constraint on data availability, we use the following variables to represent the characteristics of the EU countries/regions:[11]

TAXES = nominal corporate tax rate
PATENTS = cumulated number of patents
GDP/CAP = GDP per capita
LABOUR COSTS = wages per employee
PRODUCTIVITY = value added per employee
SEA = quantity of goods loaded by waterways per capita
AIR = quantity of goods loaded by air per capita
ROAD = length of highways per km square of the area
TRANSPORT = a composite index of SEA, AIR, and ROAD

where PATENTS and TAXES are constructed at the country level, while the rest of the variables are constructed at the NUTS-1 regional level.

PATENTS is a proxy measure for technological capacity of the host country, and TAXES measures the government's incentive towards foreign direct investment. The influence of the labour market environment at the regional level on the location choice is examined through LABOUR COSTS and PRODUCTIVITY. Since the previous literature has suggested that the existence of highly developed transportation infrastructure is a significant incentive to attract foreign direct investment into the region, we use SEA, AIR, and ROAD to identify the existence of such infrastructure in the region. Market conditions at the regional level are measured by GDP/CAP. The previous literature suggests that the extent of the MNE's activity in the region becomes large when the MNE sells its product primarily in the region which grows faster and has higher per capita income and thus sophisticated demand.

*Results of the Factor Analysis of Country/Regional Attributes*

Using GDP/CAP, AIR, ROAD, SEA, TAXES, PATENTS, LABOUR COSTS, and PRODUCTIVITY constructed for 44 regions from six EU states (Belgium, France, Germany, Italy, Spain, and the UK),[12] we extracted principal components[13] and created two factors to expose the underlying attributes of regions. Factor 1 is weighted positively on PRODUCTIVITY (0.94), GDP/CAP (0.76), TAXES (0.74), and TRANS-PORT[14] (0.50). It thus represents the degree of regional economic development. Factor 1 accounts for 41.7 per cent of total variance. Factor 2 has heavy positive weightings on PATENTS (0.92) and LABOUR COSTS (0.70). It therefore represents the region's R&D capability and the existence of skilled workers and engineers.[15] Factor 2 accounts for 30.8 per cent of total variance.

When each of the 44 regions is mapped against these two factors, three distinct groups of regions are statistically identified (figure 7.1). All the regions in Germany and Ile de France in France form one distinctive group of regions where value added per worker is high, GDP per capita is high, better transport infrastructure is available, and technological capability is high, but wages and corporate tax are high. They form a cluster in the north-east cell of figure 7.1. The second distinctive group includes all the regions in the United Kingdom where technological capability is high, and corporate tax is relatively low, but value added per worker is low, GDP per capita is low, and transport infrastructure is relatively inferior. These regions are mapped in the south-east cell of figure 7.1. The last group includes all the rest of the regions in the European Union which are distinguished from the first two groups by lower technological capability and lower labour costs.

Comparison of the cluster of all the German regions plus Ile de France with the cluster of the UK regions indicates clearly that Germany has higher GDP/CAP, PRODUCTIVITY, TRANSPORT, PATENTS, and

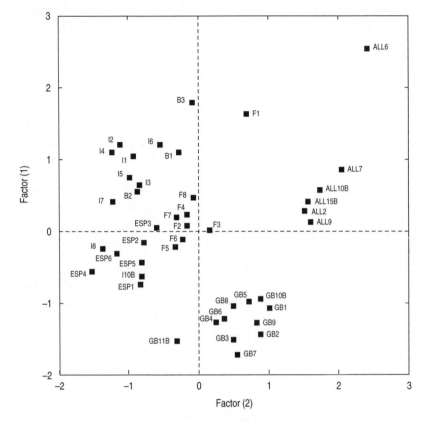

**Figure 7.1** Mapping of 44 European regions

LABOUR COSTS than the UK. Germany has the advantage over the UK in terms of higher labour productivity, higher technological capability, the existence of affluent consumers, and the existence of better transport networks. In other words, the UK has the advantage over Germany in terms of lower labour costs and lower taxes. The UK in turn has higher LABOUR COSTS and PATENTS than the regions of Belgium, France (except Ile de France), Italy, and Spain. The UK thus has the advantage over these EU states in terms of higher technological capability, but is at a disadvantage in terms of higher labour costs.

This finding provides evidence that is consistent with the earlier findings of this chapter that the US and Japanese MNEs that search a host country in the EU are most likely to go to the UK. Their preference for the UK is strong when they originate in R&D-intensive industries. This pattern appears to be well explained by the finding above that the UK has the advantage in lower labour costs and corporate tax rate given that it has a relatively high level of technological capability. While Germany shows similar or even better technological capability in the analysis, it simply is a more expensive place to locate a production base. The strong preference by the Japanese MNEs in R&D-intensive industries for Germany as production location will be presumably explained by its advantage in high technological capability and the existence of skilled workers with high productivity. When the MNE gives these factors more weight than levels of labour costs and tax rate, it must choose Germany over the UK. In particular, if the MNE's motivation is aimed at sourcing local technological capability to augment its resources and capability, then the advantage based on technology and skill will outweigh the advantage based on costs.[16] On the contrary if low labour costs are one of the more important factors to be competitive in the European market, the MNEs are more likely to set up their manufacturing bases in a country such as Spain.[17]

Finally, the mapping of the European regions presented in figure 7.1 shows that a country's regions tend to form a cluster of its own. This finding suggests that in this analysis the country's attributes wield stronger influence in determining the economic performance of its constituent regions than the regions' attributes.[18]

## V    Conclusions

This chapter has identified and compared the location patterns of US and Japanese MNEs in European manufacturing industries. It then inferred the causes of the observed patterns by using a new data set which characterizes country and regional economic conditions in selected EU member states. The most important findings on location patterns are: (1) both US and Japanese MNEs choose the UK as the prime location for their direct investments; (2) generally speaking, the choice of host countries after the UK, however, differs between the US and Japanese firms; (3) the choice of locations varies with the industry; (4) in highly R&D-intensive industries, the US choice of locations and the Japanese choice of locations are more likely to converge than in less R&D-intensive industries; and (5) specifically, in the office and data-processing equipment industry both the US and Japanese subsidiaries are highly concentrated in one region, namely, the South East region in the UK. The result from a factor analysis of the region/country attributes suggests that the strong preference of US and Japanese MNEs for locating their subsidiaries in the UK is motivated by the advantage held by the UK over other EU member states in favourable labour costs and tax rate and relatively high technological capability.

The finding that the location of US and Japanese subsidiaries in the office and data-processing equipment industry tends to converge in a specific region of one country needs special attention inasmuch as such concentration of foreign direct investment changes the geographic configuration of European industry activities. One of the potential impacts of such geographic concentration of business in one region is on the ways in which firms and governments consider their industries. In the office and data-processing equipment industry the US and Japanese MNEs may have considered their industries on a regional level. To the extent this is the case, the recent development of a theory of international trade which emphasizes the importance of regions as units of analysis (Krugman 1991) is of important empirical relevance for the EU industry. In the European common market where national boundaries have become less important in recent years, regional factors should have gained in importance as significant determinants of locations of MNEs' production bases.

Finally, the finding of the convergence of production locations for US and Japanese MNEs in R&D-intensive industry appears to suggest the importance of examining further the questions of (1) whether the potential of agglomeration economies attracts foreign investors to a region where manufacturing activity is dense (e.g. Head, Ries and Swenson 1995); and (2) whether the geographic concentration of industrial activity is linked to the geographic concentration of innovative activity (e.g. Audretsch and Feldman 1996). While this chapter does not seek to ascertain such links that connect the MNEs' location pattern to the existence of agglomeration and knowledge spillover effects, it presents, at least, a factual pattern that evokes the need of future research that examines these questions addressed for European industries.

## Appendix: Sources and Definitions of the Regional and Country Variables

TAXES is the nominal corporate tax rate in 1990 for the EC member states. This variable taken from Commission des Communautés européennes, 1992, *Inventaire des impôts perçus dans les Etats membres des Communautés européennes*, Luxembourg.

PATENTS is the cumulated number of patents granted in the United States to the firms domiciled in an EC country in a specific industry over the 1963–86 period, divided by the total cumulated number of patents for all EC countries in that industry. This variable is constructed from

The US Patent and Trademark Office, 1987, *Patenting Trends in the US: 1963–1986*, Washington, D.C.: US Patent and Trademark Office.

GDP/CAP, AIR, ROAD, and SEA are all obtained from the same statistical source, EUROSTAT, 1990 and 1993, *Regions Statistical Yearbook*, Theme 1, Series A, Luxembourg.

GDP/CAP is an index of regional Gross Domestic Product per capita in 1990 (EC total=100).

AIR is the quantity of goods (in 1000 tons) regionally unloaded in 1990 divided by the population of this region in 1990.

SEA is the quantity of goods (in 1000 tons) regionally loaded in 1990 divided by the population of this region in 1990.

ROAD is the length of highways in a region measured in km in 1990 divided by the area of this region in square km.

LABOUR COSTS is constructed by dividing the regional value (in ECU) of wages and salaries in a specific industry in 1989 by the number of wage earners in this region and industry in 1989.

PRODUCTIVITY is defined as the regional value added (in ECU) in a specific industry in 1989 divided by the number of wage earners in this region and industry in 1989.

LABOUR COSTS and PRODUCTIVITY are constructed from EUROSTAT, 1993, *Structure et activité de l'industrie, données régionales 1988–1989*, Théme 4, Séries C, Luxembourg.

The variables constructed at the NACE 2-digit industry level are aggregated to the national level in the analysis presented in section IV of this chapter.

### Notes

1   See Thiran and Yamawaki (1996) for a detailed analysis of descriptive statistics.
2   The NUTS (Nomenclature of Territorial Units for Statistics) classification is the official regional classification defined and used by Eurostat.
3   Measuring the extent of direct investment by the number of employees could overestimate the importance of labour-intensive industry relative to capital-intensive industry. Sales figures are not available for a large number of companies in the Toyo Keizai directories.

4   The total counts of US subsidiaries are 3528, while the total counts of Japanese subsidiaries are 433.
5   When Spain is included in the Japanese data, it is ranked fourth with 8 per cent of total Japanese investment.
6   An additional explanation to the pattern observed for the US MNEs is the affinity of host and source countries particularly in terms of common language. While the Netherlands and Belgium are not English-speaking countries, the English language is more widely used in these countries than in other non-English-speaking countries in the EU. For the previous studies on the effects of common language on the location decision, see Dunning (1993), Caves (1996) and Veugelers (1991).
7   The analysis by Yamawaki, Thiran, and Barbarito (1996) presents regressions that determine the location choice of the Japanese MNEs. A comparable regression analysis of the location choice of US MNEs is forthcoming by the present authors.
8   For a detailed survey of the literature, see Caves (1996) and Dunning (1993).
9   There exists a literature which examines the location determinants of foreign direct investment flows in the European Common Market by using aggregate time-series data. Among others, Culem (1988) found that aggregate economic growth is a determinant of locations for US FDI flows in the European Common Market. Morsink and Molle (1991) found evidence that exchange rate variability influenced the destination of FDI flows. For a comparison of investment flows from the United States and Japan into the EC, see Buigues and Jacquemin (1994) and Neven and Siotis (1996).
10  For more detailed accounts of each of these hypotheses, see Yamawaki, Thiran and Barbarito (1996).
11  For the definition and construction of these variables, see the appendix of this chapter.
12  The selection of these six EU states was dictated by the availability of data for these states.
13  The number of observations in this analysis are 44 regions, and the variables do not vary across industries.
14  TRANSPORT is a composite index of AIR, ROAD and SEA.
15  Labour costs are assumed to be positively correlated with the level of human capital and skill.
16  For some evidence that one motivation for the Japanese firm to invest abroad is to source foreign technology, see Kogut and Chang (1991) and Neven and Siotis (1996).
17  All the Spanish regions are found in the south-west cell in figure 7.1.
18  Among the variables used in the principal components analysis, only PATENTS and TAXES are constructed at the country level. All other variables are constructed at the regional level.

## References

Audretsch, D.B. and M.P. Feldman (1996), 'R&D Spillovers and the Geography of Innovation and Production', *American Economic Review*, pp. 630–40.
Bughin, J. and S. Vannini (1995) 'Strategic Direct Investment under Unionised Oligopoly', *International Journal of Industrial Organization*, pp. 127–45.
Buigues, P. and A. Jacquemin (1994) 'Foreign Direct Investment and Exports to

the European Community', in M. Mason and D. Encarnation (eds), *Does Ownership Matter?*: *Japanese Multinationals in Europe*, Oxford: Oxford University Press.

Cantwell, J. (1989) *Technical Innovations in Multinational Corporations*, Oxford: Basil Blackwell.

Caves, R.E. (1996) *Multinational Enterprise and Economic Analysis*, second edn, Cambridge: Cambridge University Press.

Coughlin, C.C., J.V. Terza, and V. Arromdee (1991) 'State Characteristics and the Location of Foreign Direct Investment within the United States', *The Review of Economics and Statistics*, pp. 675–83.

Culem, C.G. (1988) 'The Location of Foreign Direct Investment Activity, Country Characteristics and Experience Effects', *European Economic Review*, pp. 885–904.

Davidson, W. (1980) 'The Location of Foreign Direct Investment Activity, Country Characteristics and Experience Effects', *Journal of International Business Studies*, pp. 9–22.

Dunning, J.H. (1980) 'Towards an Eclectic Theory of International Production: Some Empirical Tests', *Journal of International Business Studies*, pp. 9–31.

——— (1993) *Multinational Enterprises and the Global Economy*, Reading, Mass.: Addison-Wesley.

Friedman, J., D.A. Gerlowski, and J. Silberman (1992) 'What Attracts Foreign Multinational Corporations? Evidence from Branch Plant Location in the United States', *Journal of Regional Science*, pp. 403–18.

Glickman, N.J. and D.P. Woodward (1988) 'The Location of Foreign Direct Investment in the United States: Patterns and Determinants', *International Regional Science Review*, pp. 137–54.

Head, K.R., J. Ries, and D. Swenson (1995) 'Agglomeration Benefits and Location Choice: Evidence from Japanese Manufacturing Investment in the United States', *Journal of International Economics*, pp. 223–47.

Kogut, B., and S.-J. Chang (1991) 'Technological Capabilities and Japanese Foreign Direct Investment in the United States', *Review of Economics and Statistics*, pp. 401–13.

Kravis, I.B. and R.E. Lipsey (1982) 'The Location of Overseas Production and Production for Exports by US Multinational Firms', *Journal of International Economics*, pp. 201–23.

Krugman, P. (1991) *Geography and Trade*, Cambridge, Mass.: MIT Press.

Morsink, R.L.A. and W.T.M. Molle (1991) 'Direct Investment and European Integration'. Paper presented at the conference 'Direct Investment in Europe', Université catholique de Louvain, March.

Neven D., and G. Siotis (1996) 'Technology Sourcing and FDI in the EC: An Empirical Evaluation', *International Journal of Industrial Organization*, pp. 543–60.

Swedenborg, B. (1979) *The Multinational Operations of Swedish Firms: An Analysis of Determinants and Effects*, Stockholm: The Industrial Institute for Economic and Social Research.

Thiran, J.-M. and H. Yamawaki (1996) 'Patterns of Japanese Manufacturing Employment in the European Regions', forthcoming in J. Darby (ed.), *Japan and European Periphery*, London: Macmillan.

Veugelers, R. (1991) 'Locational Determinants and Ranking of Host Countries: An Empirical Assessment', *Kyklos*, pp. 363–82.

Yamawaki, H. (1993) 'Location Decisions of Japanese Multinational Firms in

European Manufacturing Industries', in K. Hughes (ed.), *European Competitiveness*, Cambridge: Cambridge University Press.
—— (1994) 'Entry Patterns of Japanese Multinationals in US and European Manufacturing', in M. Mason and D. Encarnation (eds), *Does Ownership Matter?: Japanese Multinationals in Europe*, Oxford: Oxford University Press.
Yamawaki, H., J.-M. Thiran, and L. Barbarito (1996) 'Regional and Country Determinants of Location Decisions: Japanese Multinationals in European Manufacturing', mimeo, Anderson Graduate School of Management, UCLA, August.

# 8

# Foreign Direct Investment, Cross-border Mergers and Competition Policy in the European Union

## Leo Sleuwaegen

## I Foreign Direct Investment in the European Union and European Investment Abroad

Foreign direct investment (FDI) in the European Union (EU) has been growing very strongly over the past ten years. The real upsurge in FDI started in 1987, the year in which, together with the signing of the European Single Act, the 1992 Single Market Project was also launched. This coincidence does not imply that all investment between EU Member States is entirely due to the 1992 Project. The strong growth in foreign direct investment has been a worldwide phenomenon. However, the scale and timing of direct investment flows going to EU Member States do suggest that the Single Market Programme has given a major impetus to cross-border investments within the EU. Figure 8.1 shows the evolution after 1982 of foreign direct investment between EU Member States (FDI intra-EU) and of direct investment into the EU originating from other regions of the world (FDI inward) for the twelve EU Members, before Sweden, Finland and Austria joined the EU in 1995, and compares the evolution in direct investments made by European firms in other regions of the world (FDI outward). The growth in outward bound FDI is less marked and the time pattern more continuous than the patterns found for intra- and inward EU investment, i.e., investments within the EU originating from countries outside the EU.

Table 8.1 details the geographical structure of FDI for the period

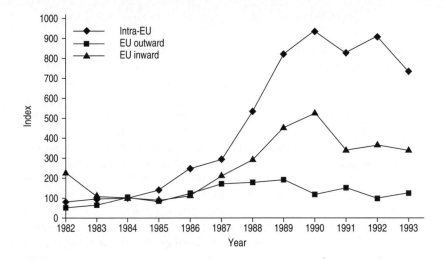

**Figure 8.1** Foreign direct investment, 1984=100
Source: Eurostat, European Union direct investment 1984–93

**Table 8.1a** Intra-EU direct investment (cumulative total 1991–3)

| Country | Outward DI (country of origin) % | Inward DI (country of destination) % |
|---|---|---|
| Belgium-Luxembourg | 12.99 | 17.14 |
| Denmark | 1.65 | 1.23 |
| Germany | 26.05 | 10.66 |
| Greece | 0.01 | 0.93 |
| Spain | 2.12 | 13.81 |
| France | 21.12 | 16.44 |
| Ireland | 1.21 | 7.37 |
| Italy | 7.35 | 5.51 |
| Netherlands | 14.45 | 11.97 |
| Portugal | 0.81 | 2.97 |
| United Kingdom | 12.25 | 11.97 |
| EUR 12 | 100 = 104152 million ecus | 100 = 104468 million ecus |

Source: Eurostat. European Union direct investment 1984–93.

**Table 8.1b** Inward and outward FDI in Europe (1991–3)

| Region | Outward DI (country of origin) % | Inward DI (country of destination) % |
|---|---|---|
| United States | 39.07 | 40.42 |
| Japan | 0.60 | 8.00 |
| EFTA | 13.91 | 22.56 |
| OPEC | 4.69 | 2.41 |
| ACP | 1.81 | 0.75 |
| EX-COMECON | 1.97 | 0.31 |
| Extra EUR 12 | 100 = 66350 million ecus | 100 = 64513 million ecus |

Source: Eurostat. European Union direct investment 1984–93.

1991–3. The most active countries for intra-EU direct investment are Germany and France in terms of firms investing in other EU Member States and France, Belgium and Spain in terms of receiving investment from firms based in other EU countries. The high percentages for Belgium and the Netherlands reflect the open character of these economies, geographically situated in the centre of the EU. FDI flows from and to countries other than EU Member States represent about 60 per cent of intra-EU flows. The main foreign investors in the EU are the US, EFTA and Japan. The US dominates with about 40 per cent of all incoming investment. The EFTA contribution totals 14 per cent, with Switzerland as major investing partner. The US and EFTA countries are also the main targets for investments made by EU firms in other countries. The US receives about 40 per cent of all outward investment, while EFTA countries receive 14 per cent with Sweden (prior to joining the EU in 1995) and Switzerland as the main single receivers.

The sectoral structure of FDI reveals the important role of the service sector in which deregulation and harmonization in the EU and other regions in the world are opening up many protected markets to international competition. Services accounted for about 70 per cent of

**Table 8.2** Direct investments: sectoral breakdown (in percentages) for 1991–3

|  | Intra-EU | Outward EU | Inward EU |
|---|---|---|---|
| **Sectors** | | | |
| Energy | 2.1 | 5.7 | 1.4 |
| Agriculture | 5.5 | 5.6 | 4.4 |
| Metallics | 0.5 | 2.1 | −2.5 |
| Machinery | 0.5 | 2.4 | 1.3 |
| Transport equipment | 2.7 | 5.2 | 6.9 |
| Electrical, electronics | 3.9 | 3.6 | 2.5 |
| Chemical industries | 3.8 | 3.4 | 4.6 |
| Other manufacturing | 7.5 | 9.9 | 12.3 |
| Total manufacturing | 24.4 | 32.4 | 29.6 |
| Building and construction | 1 | 1.7 | 0.3 |
| Finance and banking | 23 | 28.6 | 27.4 |
| Insurance | 8.3 | −1.2 | −2.5 |
| Trade, hotels and catering | 5.5 | 6.6 | 12.6 |
| Transport and communication | 1.4 | 2 | 2.1 |
| Real estate | 4.7 | 2.6 | 5.3 |
| Other commercial services | 28 | 17.6 | 21.5 |
| Total commercial services | 70.8 | 56.2 | 66.4 |
| Unallocated | 1.6 | 4.1 | 2.3 |
| **Total** | **100** | **100** | **100** |

Source: Eurostat, European Union direct investment, 1984–93.

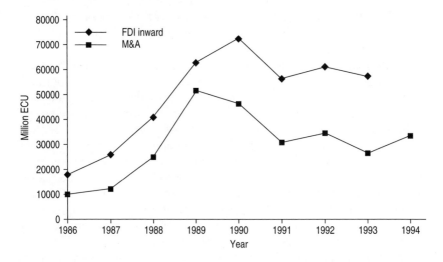

**Figure 8.2**   FDI and value of cross-border mergers and acquisitions

Source: European Economy, Supplement A, no. 3 (1995), based on Amdata.

intra-EU and inward direct investment. Finance, banking and insurance represent the main share followed by other commercial services, including accounting, consulting and related business services.

The recent developments in FDI are characterized by another important phenomenon: the major role played by cross-border mergers and acquisitions. Figure 8.2 shows the evolution of the aggregated value of cross-border merger deals – only for those deals for which the value is known, excluding smaller deals – and contrasts it with the evolution of FDI in the EU. The striking correspondence in patterns of FDI and the value of cross-border mergers and acquisitions, suggests that mergers have been playing a dominant role in recent FDI flows. The observed cyclicality of FDI seems to be due entirely to the cyclicality of mergers and acquisitions.

Because of their importance and significance for European competition policy, section II examines in greater depth recent trends in scale, scope and motives for European mergers and acquisitions. Section III of the chapter relates these trends to changes in the competitive environment, the structure and conduct of European firms. Section IV examines the extent to which competition policy, particularly the new merger control system, helps to guide the restructuring process in the desired direction.

## II Recent Trends in Cross-border Mergers and Acquisitions in the European Union

It is extremely difficult to obtain detailed figures of the number and value of mergers and acquisitions in the EU. The most reliable and comprehensive time-series material consists of the statistics that are published annually by the European Commission (Supplement A, European Economy). Over the period 1990–4 more than 70 per cent of all mergers and acquisitions in the EU involved firms located in the same Member State. These national operations doubled between 1987 and 1989 and diminished slightly thereafter to levels above 3,000 deals per year. National mergers can be a powerful weapon to stave off takeovers of firms by foreign groups, while providing an effective way to consolidate resources from which substantial scale economies and market leverage may arise. Cross-border mergers within the EU gained strong ground after 1987. The number of these Community-wide operations quadrupled after 1988 but fell back substantially after 1990. However, the level in 1994 (913 deals) remains close to three times the number of mergers in 1987.

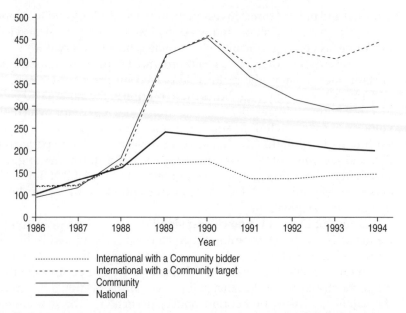

**Figure 8.3** Number of national, Community and international M&A operations (index: average 1986–88=100)

Source: European Economy, supplement A, no. 3 (1995), based on Amdata.

The changes in the number of Community cross-border mergers reflect very well the ongoing Europeanization of industries as a result of market integration as well as the strong sensitivity of mergers to business cycle conditions in Europe. International acquisitions with European firms as targets show an equally spectacular growth after 1987 and, with only a short interruption in 1991, continue to stay at high levels. The number of such deals has risen to more than half of Community cross-border mergers and about 10 per cent of all deals involving a European firm as target over the period 1990–4. International acquisitions with a Community target reached a maximum of 693 deals in 1994. The changes in the number of international operations where the bidder is a European firm are less marked. After increasing slightly until 1989, the number of transactions remained stable around the 1990–2 average annual level of 300 deals.

## Sectoral differences in cross-border mergers

The merger wave in Europe emerged earlier and more strongly in manufacturing than in services. However, service sectors have gained in relative importance in recent years. Among the ten most targeted sectors during the period 1991–4, the business services sector, including the activities of holding companies, ranks first. Distribution ranks second. Both these sectors, as well as banking and finance, are strongly affected by recent liberalization measures. The merger-active industries in manufacturing include mainly engineering industries and the food and chemical industries. Indeed, econometric research has pointed out

**Table 8.3** The ten most targeted sectors in cross-border M&A during the periods 1986–90 and 1991–4

| NACE | Description | 1986–90 (average) | 1991–94 (average) |
|------|-------------|-------------------|-------------------|
| 83 | Business services | 96 | 141 |
| 61 | Distribution – wholesale | 88 | 146 |
| 32 | Mechanical engineering | 68 | 116 |
| 25 | Chemical industry | 67 | 105 |
| 47 | Paper manufacture and production | 59 | 68 |
| 34 | Electrical and electronic engineering | 61 | 90 |
| 42 | Sugar and sugar by-products | 39 | 46 |
| 31 | Manufacture of metal articles | 22 | 37 |
| 81 | Banking and finance | 36 | 50 |
| 35 | Manufacture of motor vehicles and parts | 21 | 27 |

Source: European Economy (1996), based on Amdata.

that mergers in Europe occur more often in industries that are sensitive to the 1992 programme and in which new technologies and scale economies are important (Sleuwaegen and Van Den Houte 1992). Mergers and acquisitions in manufacturing have also occurred more frequently in downstream industries, i.e., closer to the final consumer (EC 1994, p. 30).

## Differences between Member States

British and French firms are the most active bidders in cross-border operations. Firms from Mediterranean countries are less well represented in table 8.4. Merger activity in these countries is well below what could be expected from their economic significance, revealed by the column labeled GDP in the table which lists the Gross Domestic Product of each Member State as a percentage of EU-wide GDP. This may be partially due to smaller transactions that are unrecorded. A shortage of resources in these countries may be a more general explanation. Spain has become an important target country for cross-border mergers in recent years. The high percentage for Germany as target country reflects the takeover of firms from the former East Germany after privatization started in 1990. The observed differences across EU Member States in the occurrence of mergers and acquisitions also reflect fundamental differences in the way capital markets function and corporate control is exercised.

Several observers, particularly Frank and Mayer (1990), have pointed

**Table 8.4** Breakdown by member state of cross-border M&A and GDP (1991–4)

| | 1991–93 Target | 1994 Bidder | GDP | Target | Bidder | GDP |
|---|---|---|---|---|---|---|
| Belgium | 5.5 | 3.4 | 3.2 | 4.0 | 2.9 | 3.4 |
| Denmark | 3.8 | 5.9 | 2.1 | 5.3 | 4.7 | 2.2 |
| Germany | 29.8 | 17.3 | 26.3 | 29.5 | 18.4 | 27.7 |
| Greece | 0.6 | 0.1 | 1.4 | 0.3 | 0.1 | 1.4 |
| Spain | 9.2 | 1.6 | 8.1 | 9.0 | 0.9 | 7.3 |
| France | 14.6 | 22.5 | 19.4 | 15.2 | 18.3 | 20.0 |
| Ireland | 1.0 | 3.0 | 0.7 | 0.9 | 4.7 | 0.8 |
| Italy | 7.0 | 6.2 | 17.3 | 7.6 | 2.7 | 15.5 |
| Luxembourg | 0.6 | 1.5 | 0.2 | 1.0 | 1.6 | 0.2 |
| The Netherlands | 8.3 | 10.1 | 4.7 | 7.2 | 11.5 | 5.0 |
| Portugal | 1.2 | 0.1 | 1.2 | 0.5 | 0.3 | 1.2 |
| United Kingdom | 18.5 | 28.4 | 15.4 | 19.4 | 34.0 | 15.4 |
| TOTAL | 100.0 | 100.0 | 100.0 | 100.0 | 100.0 | 100.0 |

Source: European Economy, Supplement A, no. 3 (1995), based on Amdata and DG-II.

out the major differences between EU Member States in terms of the frequency of hostile takeovers and management changes. In the UK, in particular, these practices appear to be important. Many restrictions regarding share swaps or the acquisition of a controlling stake in a firm ensure that there are far fewer hostile takeovers in countries such as France and Germany. It has been argued that in Member States in which firms are less exposed to takeover pressures and where groups of share-holders are able actively to monitor management, long-term interests can prevail over short-term interests. In addition, these 'shielded' firms can invest in mainly high-risk and dynamic projects and sectors, while hostile takeovers seem to be especially important in the case of firms and economies which focus on traditional and more mature sectors. According to this school of thought, there is no causal connection between an increase in growth and the apparently concomitant decrease in profitability, on the one hand, and management inefficiency, on the other hand. Rather, it would reflect a fundamental choice of firms, and the countries in which they are based, with regard to the preference for long-term, as opposed to short-term results, when choosing projects. In any case, it has been established by De Jong (1990) that the period 1979–88 showed significant differences in average profitability and growth of leading firms in the various EU Member States. He finds that in those countries with an open market for corporate control, i.e., a capital market with few restrictions on takeovers, average profitability is higher while the growth in turnover of the leading firms is limited. Further research is necessary to find out to what extent the observed differences can be attributed to different objectives and/or management inefficiency.

Such research should not overlook the fact that the threat of a (hostile) takeover can be a major factor in preventing or countering ineffective management. In an open and unified market, this factor will even gain in importance. A firm whose value is not maximized by management can become an attractive takeover prey for investors who think that a change in management will result in maximum efficiency. Therefore, takeover and other capital market restrictions may have a highly disturbing effect and determine the direction, the desirability and the consequences of industrial restructuring in Europe. Being aware of this problem, EU authorities are continuing to work towards harmonizing corporate law, including the regulations on the assignment of shares and the acquisition of controlling stakes in firms within the European Union. It should be clear that anti-trust policy, including the recent EU Merger Regulation, is not a substitute for the lack of harmonization in the 'market for corporate control', as, at this stage, anti-trust cannot prevent or prohibit inefficient firms from taking over efficient ones.

**Table 8.5**  The ten most active third countries for M&As concerning an EC firm, 1990–2 (average per year)

| | Third country as bidder | | | | Third country as target | | |
|---|---|---|---|---|---|---|---|
| | 1986–90 | 1991–3 | 1994 | | 1986–90 | 1991–3 | 1994 |
| USA | 118 | 245 | 336 | USA | 342 | 181 | 207 |
| Switzerland | 65 | 99 | 87 | Switzerland | 15 | 30 | 31 |
| Sweden | 68 | 61 | 41 | Sweden | 11 | 38 | 21 |
| Canada | 10 | 18 | 32 | Czech Republic* | 0 | 17 | 21 |
| Japan | 24 | 48 | 27 | Canada | 28 | 22 | 18 |
| Finland | 29 | 27 | 21 | Norway | 7 | 20 | 17 |
| Austria | 5 | 25 | 21 | Australia | 35 | 17 | 16 |
| Norway | 11 | 12 | 20 | Poland | 1 | 14 | 15 |
| Australia | 16 | 15 | 13 | Finland | 4 | 14 | 14 |
| Hong Kong | 3 | 12 | 7 | Austria | 6 | 17 | 14 |

* (86–93: Czechoslovakia)
Source: EC (1994) p. 29, based on Amdata.

Within the class of international mergers and acquisitions, US firms have been the most active third country purchasers of European firms since 1991 with about 1071 operations in the period 1991–4. Switzerland takes second place with about 384 purchases of EU firms over the same period. Table 8.5 provides a more detailed breakdown by country for the period 1986–94.

The US is also the most important target country for mergers and takeovers by European firms (about 569 operations over the period 1992–4). Growing interest in Eastern European countries is also striking.

## Motives for Mergers and Acquisitions

Observations based on public statements about the motives behind mergers and acquisitions, as collected by the European Commission and published annually up to year 1992, seem to reflect very well the changing sectoral structure and the widening geographical scope of these transactions (see table 8.6). The rising importance of strengthening market position as motive is noteworthy and comes at the expense of the rationalization and synergy motive, which had been stated most in the period up to 1988. Also the desire to expand operations has become a major motive behind mergers and acquisitions in Europe. Diversification plays a subordinate role in mergers, which contrasts with the merger wave in the 1960s. The revealed motives suggest that merger activities are clearly part of the strategic adjustment strategies with respect to the single market. The growing focus on a strong market position as the principal motive behind mergers and acquisitions also suggests that the future may hold major problems in terms of compe-

**Table 8.6** Firm motives for mergers and acquisitions as a percentage of all motives

|  | 1985–6 | 1986–7 | 1987–8 | 1988–9 | 1989–90 | 1990–1 | 1991–2 |
|---|---|---|---|---|---|---|---|
| Expansion | 17.1 | 22.1 | 19.6 | 31.3 | 26.9 | 27.7 | 32.4 |
| Diversification | 17.6 | 5.8 | 8.3 | 7.1 | 3.0 | 2.8 | 2.1 |
| Strengthening market position | 10.6 | 11.5 | 25.4 | 42.2 | 45.3 | 48.2 | 44.4 |
| Rationalization and synergy | 46.5 | 42.0 | 34.4 | 14.4 | 17.7 | 13.3 | 16.2 |
| R&D | 2.4 | 5.3 | 0.7 | 0.0 | 0.6 | 0.0 | 0.0 |
| Other | 5.9 | 13.3 | 11.6 | 4.9 | 6.4 | 8.0 | 5.0 |
| All | 100 | 100 | 100 | 100 | 100 | 100 | 100 |

Source: Annual Reports on Competition Policy and EC (1994), based on Dome.

tition and market power abuse, as well as intended gains in efficiency, by new large European corporate groups. To cope with these developments EU authorities are developing new tools to clamp down on anti-competitive practices including the creation of dominant market positions (see section IV). However, the major difficulty anti-trust authorities are facing concerns the distinction between short term and long term consequences of the newly implemented competitive strategies of European firms. As suggested by the changing motives for mergers, and further elaborated in the next section, corporate strategies respond strongly to market and environmental conditions, which have been changing strongly since the start of the Single Market Programme.

## III    FDI, Competition and Corporate Strategies

Foreign direct investment is the result of internationalization strategies of firms who are seeking to benefit from co-ordinating and sharing activities located in different countries. New technologies, especially in information and communication, and more favourable trade and investment policies have greatly stimulated the development of global corporate strategies. Co-operation among countries in different regions of the world provides an additional impetus to this internationalization process. The formation of the Single Market in Europe is undoubtedly the most far-reaching initiative in this respect. It creates a very favourable environment for firms which sell their products throughout the EU and locate their activities within the borders of the EU. The creation of a more homogeneous environment with a more favourable treatment of insiders through the use of common regulations, standards, fiscal measures, subsidies and related investment incentives, has been theorized to lead to production diversion and

creation effects which could account for a large inflow of direct investment into the EU and cross-border flows between Member States
(see in particular Baldwin, Forslid and Haaland 1995). However, as
shown, one should not overlook that a major part of direct investment
concerns mergers and acquisitions which do not necessarily lead to
production relocation. Mergers and acquisitions are motivated by a
wide set of factors, which can be conveniently grouped into two
categories, efficiency and competition motives, because of the effect
of European unification on both. European market integration
thoroughly influences competition through changing all major competitive forces, i.e., rivalry, supplier and buyer power, the availability
of substitutes and potential market entrants. The elimination of borders widens the relevant geographical market for those firms which are
looking for new suppliers of intermediate products and customers of
final products. At the same time the relevant competitive arena in
which firms compete widens and invites more vigorous competition
from hitherto unknown rivals. However, the short-run effects may differ substantially from the more durable long term effects, as it has been
observed for other regions in the world where market deregulation
and integration have been taking place.

## Short-term Consequences

### More intense and broad competition
The disappearance of the traditional market borders for hitherto
protected firms intensifies rivalry between market participants
resulting in a substantial broadening of competition within the markets
of the European Union (EU). Many firms which previously operated in
nationally protected sectors are suddenly faced with new European
competitors. This process is reinforced by the fact that, in many sectors,
firms are trying to improve their competitive position by capitalizing on
advantages of scale, and by better spreading and using their production
and distribution capacities on a European scale. Firms are also increasingly geared towards improving product properties in order to widen
their export markets. However, since all market participants are simultaneously attempting to exploit the benefits of cost savings and product
improvement, this will invariably lead to excess capacity in those sectors
where demand has not kept pace. This, in turn, necessitates in-depth
restructuring in a more long term perspective. Increasing competition
also results in a further harmonization of sales conditions. After the
abolition of the borders, price arbitration by buyers obviously increases
as they are able to obtain goods and services from suppliers all over the
EU. Consequently, they are able to compare the prices and quality in

the various European markets and buy from the suppliers and producers who offer the best terms.

The lifting of non-tariff barriers also facilitates spillovers from one market to another. An important type of spillover bears on the product and the sales instruments themselves. For instance, European firms which have developed a strong brand name may benefit from demand spillovers; a recognizable brand name, combined with strong sales and after-sales service in one Member State may reinforce consumer preferences for the product in another Member State.

*Cross-border entry*
The lifting of non-tariff barriers and freedom of establishment makes it easier for firms already active in a Member State to enter the market of another Member State. The costs connected with entering the market of another Member State have become substantially lower for established European firms. This gives rise to major market cross-entries within the EU with multi-market contacts among the same firms meeting each other in these different markets (van Witteloosteuijn and van Wegberg 1991). This applies not only to established firms, but also to smaller or newer firms which are no longer interested in entering a national market, but wish to launch themselves on the Single European Market. The competitive pressure caused by firms entering the market is often reinforced by the behaviour of firms based outside the EU which fear that the completion of an internal market will inexorably lead to an increase in protectionism and discrimination against non-EU firms. As a result, they choose to invest in new production and assembly units in the EU or, alternatively, buy existing firms. As a short-term defensive reaction, established firms anticipating this entry have responded by trying to consolidate their position on national markets through merging with domestic competitors.

## Long-term Adjustments

*Competition and efficiency gains*
For the purpose of long-term planning, firms concentrate not only on the first couple of years following market integration. Predictions of future developments are equally important as the competitive environment will change radically in the first years and will only stabilize after fundamental changes have been made. For most firms, a long-term view also means that, over the course of time, changes will occur in their strategic actions and tactics. The elements that are crucial for survival in the early market integration years differ from the elements that ensure the long-term success of the firm. For instance, firms that successfully

enter a new market may be inclined to differentiate their products after a few years in order to move to a more profitable market segment. In response to rising competition and new entries, established firms will aim to achieve drastic rationalization by adopting more efficient R&D, production, distribution and marketing organizations. The new market environment in Europe offers companies many ways to improve their operations. In addition to the direct efficiency gains from removing all kinds of technical and administrative barriers to cross-border trade and investment, the more important efficiency gains derive from economies of scale and scope and from an improved environment for realizing product and process innovations. Within this process, the restructuring and concentration of production facilities and distribution centres enable firms to benefit from large scale economies. For instance, the deregulation of international transport has lowered transportation costs in Europe and has created many opportunities for firms specializing in logistics to set up European networks through which additional economies can be realized. As a consequence, companies are increasingly outsourcing these services and concentrating their activities in these regions where external economies interact best with internal economies of scale. In relation to innovative efforts, the adoption of liberal regulatory codes and the introduction of European-wide standards have sharply reduced the cost of commercializing new innovative products and processes on a European scale. At the same time the various programmes through which the Commission of the European Union stimulates inter-firm co-operation across national borders aims at the reduction of wasteful duplication of R&D efforts and the broadening of the scale at which such efforts need to be undertaken. The search for more efficient pan-European operations gives rise to major industrial restructuring programmes in the shape of mergers and co-operative agreements between firms. Once these adjustments have taken place, it seems logical for successful firms to attempt to consolidate their market position. This again results in new mergers and co-operative ventures between firms.

*The creation of strategic entry barriers*
Long-term changes in the competitive environment, after a few years of market integration, also stimulate established firms to put up strategic barriers in order to hamper further entry by newcomers. In doing so, they may, for example, exploit first-mover advantages, create strong brand preferences, and build privileged relations with customers and/or suppliers to give themselves control of raw materials or distribution channels on a European level. In this context, Joel Bleeke (1990) argues that European firms can learn quite a lot from US firms and their

experience with deregulation. Although there are differences between the European and the US situations, it is useful to take a look at the US development following the disappearance of various regulatory restrictions. Indeed, on the whole, the same competitive dynamics emerged in each industry which was deregulated in the USA. In all these industries, there were great numbers of new entrants following deregulation. Unfortunately, many met with an untimely end. Temporary excess capacity and broader competition not only caused victims among the new competitors; large existing firms were forced to cease operations because of these elements. After deregulation the most attractive market segments became the least attractive, and vice versa, because all market participants began concentrating on the same markets. At the same time, a large gap in profitability appeared between the best and worst performing firms in the sector. Only a handful of firms were able to continue to offer their original range of products. Most firms were, mostly due to financial reasons, forced to narrow their range of products and concentrate on core activities in order to survive. Within this process, there were great numbers of mergers and acquisitions, with mainly weaker firms being taken over in a first wave, whereas the strongest merged in a second wave. In all of the industries studied, the first years following the deregulation were marked by restructuring with flexibility being a necessary condition for survival. After a period of some five years, the weakest firms had been driven out of the market. This phase also witnessed the emergence of new oligopolies which threatened to become as powerful as the oligopolies that had been destroyed by deregulation. Therefore, new regulatory schemes and anti-trust laws were aimed at exerting sufficient pressure to prevent competition-restrictive practices from prevailing.

In the light of these experiences, it is imperative that the EU authorities, too, remain vigilant and ensure compliance with the competition legislation (especially Article 85, which monitors collusive agreements and Article 86, which monitors abuse of market power). The recent Merger Regulation which bears on European-wide concentrations should also become a major tool to prevent the creation of new anti-competitive oligopolies.

## IV   European Competition Policy: The EC Merger Regulation

Economic restructuring in Europe calls for an effective and vigilant competition policy at the EU level. From the original EEC Treaty, Articles 85 and 86 provide the major input to the regulatory framework. Article 85 prohibits agreements and concerted actions affecting trade between Member States that have as object or effect the restriction of competition within the EC. Article 85(3) provides for the possibility of exempting agreements from the prohibition of Article 85(1) on the basis of their overall effect on economic welfare. For certain types of restrictive agreements 'block-exemptions' are granted, as, for instance, in the case of co-operative research and development projects. Article 86 prohibits a firm or groups of firms from abusing their dominant position, affecting the trade among Member States. While articles 85 and 86 could, under specific circumstances, be applied to mergers or acquisitions, their coverage is not adequate to deal effectively with large-scale restructuring. On 21 December 1989, the Council adopted a new legal instrument, the Merger Regulation, which came into effect on 21 September 1990. The Merger Regulation gives the European Commission the exclusive responsibility for controlling concentrations of a Community dimension, including mergers and concentrative joint ventures (i.e., joint ventures which operate as autonomously functioning economic entities). A concentration is considered as having a Community (EU) dimension if all of the following conditions are met:

- the aggregate world-wide turnover of all the undertakings concerned is more than ECU 5,000 million;
- the Community-wide turnover of each of at least two of the undertakings concerned is more than ECU 250 million; unless
- the undertakings concerned do not all achieve more than two-thirds of their Community-wide turnover within one and the same Member State.

The Commission must assess whether the concentration 'raises serious doubts as to the compatibility with the common market'. In the affirmative case, the Commission prohibits concentrations which would create or strengthen a firm's dominant position such that effective competition in the common market would be significantly impeded. In assessing an anti-competitive position the factors that are taken into account include: market structure, actual or potential competition from inside or outside the Community, the market position of the undertakings concerned and their economic and financial power, the opportunities available to suppliers and buyers, barriers to entry, supply and demand trends, the consumer interest and the development of technical and economic progress, provided that it is advantageous to consumers and does not form an obstacle to competition. Within one month after notification, the Commission can conclude that the concentration does not fall within the scope of the Merger Regulation, or decide to clear the concentration, or to initiate proceedings which can take up to another four months. The final decision may be an unconditional approval of the concentration, or an approval conditional on specific commitments by the parties so as to prevent the creation and abuse of a dominant position. If the final decision is negative, the Commission may require the separation of the assets or the undertakings for which a concentration has already been implemented. If an undertaking does not comply with the decision, the Commission may impose fines of up to 10 per cent of the aggregate takeover of the undertakings concerned.

In the first three years following the implementation of the Merger Regulation there were about 60 notifications per year but there was a sharp rise to 95 in 1994 and a further increase to 110 in 1995. Of all 387 concentrations controlled up to the end of 1995, 34 were found not to fall within the scope of the Regulation, 324 were cleared without further investigation and 27 were further investigated. Four concentrations were prohibited. For the majority (65%) of the other cases which were subject to further investigation, the approval was conditional upon certain commitments; this was also true for 22 of the 387 cases cleared within the first month. A large proportion (49%) of the notifications involved joint ventures. Of all notified cases, about three quarters consisted of cross-border transactions. The majority of cases involved firms active in the manufacturing sector. In 36 per cent of the cases, at least one of the parties was based outside the EU. In about 20 per cent of the notified cases German firms were involved. They were followed by French and British firms (16 per cent and 15 per cent, respectively).

The limited number of notifications and the large percentage of cross-border cases are primarily a consequence of the thresholds laid down in the Regulation. The very limited application of the Merger Regulation becomes clear when the actual number of notifications of pure merger operations, excluding joint ventures, is considered given the actual data on merger operations. Table 8.7 shows, for the period 1991–3, the number of mergers and acquisitions classified following different size categories, corresponding to the aggregate turnover of the merging firms (rows) and the turnover of the smallest firm taking part in the merger. Following the actual thresholds of the Merger Regulation (and provided that most mergers involved two firms) only the cases in the upper left cell fall under the Regulation. An overwhelming number of cases escape EU merger control because one of the merging firms had a turnover lower than ECU 250 million. This is mainly a problem for the cross-border transactions, which could entail strong anti-competitive effects on a EC scale. The situation is especially troublesome as it has been observed that the asymmetric, and thus, uncontrolled horizontal concentrations occurred more than four times more frequently in

**Table 8.7**   The number of mergers from 1991 to March 1993 falling within the scope of different thresholds[1]

| Aggregate turnover | Individual turnover >250 | Individual turnover >174 | Individual turnover >100 | Individual turnover >75 | Individual turnover >0 |
|---|---|---|---|---|---|
| | Part A: Cross-border and non-cross-border | | | | |
| >5000 | 86 | 108 | 152 | 184 | 635 |
| >4000 | 95 | 118 | 171 | 205 | 694 |
| >3000 | 109 | 136 | 199 | 237 | 792 |
| >2000 | 122 | 157 | 232 | 281 | 952 |
| >1000 | 141 | 187 | 287 | 353 | 1243 |
| | Part B: Cross-border | | | | |
| >5000 | 32 | 47 | 75 | 92 | 341 |
| >4000 | 34 | 49 | 85 | 102 | 375 |
| >3000 | 38 | 55 | 99 | 119 | 441 |
| >2000 | 46 | 66 | 117 | 147 | 532 |
| >1000 | 57 | 85 | 148 | 187 | 694 |

[1] All M&A deals where at least one Community firm was involved and full control was obtained.
Source: EC (1994) p. 40, based on Amdata.

sectors with high barriers to entry than in sectors with low barriers to entry (EC 1994, p. 38).

This asymmetry could mean that smaller fringe firms (in smaller Member States) are systematically bought up by larger firms without any effective Community control. As has been strongly argued in this chapter, the disappearance of small competitors and the creation of strategic entry barriers by the larger EC companies may especially lead to durable anti-competitive behaviour. Moreover, the observed change in the motives for mergers and acquisitions points to the same effect. Therefore, the Commission is currently discussing with Member States a proposal to lower thresholds to an aggregate turnover of ECU 2 billion and individual turnover of ECU 100 million in those cases where the merger in question would have to be notified to several national authorities. Such a proposal should be considered as an indispensable step towards mitigating this problem. Especially in sectors with substantial economies of scale and sunk costs, including telecommunications and energy industries, the domination of the sector by one or a few collusive firms could endanger efficient market outcomes. It is also essential that the initial screening in the first stage of the European merger control process does not focus solely on actual market shares of the relevant market, but also on the extent and nature of possible entry barriers that the proposed concentrations could entail.

Besides the threshold problem, the EC merger control has been criticized as lacking transparent procedures and objective judgements by experts independent from political pressure at the EU or Member State level (see Neven, Nuttall and Seabright 1993). The lack of transparency is especially troublesome for complex cases which involve large conglomerate firms or the exercise of joint dominance by a group of firms in the industry, The lack of transparency gives rise to growing judicial disputes, especially in the cases where joint dominance arguments seem to have played a role in the decisions taken by the Commission. In this connection Eleanor Morgan (1995) observes an evolution, starting with the Nestlé-Perrier case in 1992, in the way in which the Commission is increasingly interpreting the regulation to ban mergers which would facilitate collusive behaviour among oligopolists. However, this joint dominance approach remains cautious as the question of whether the Merger Regulation only applies to single-firm dominance, with one firm dominating the market as a result of the merger, or to joint dominance where the merger would facilitate anti-competitive behaviour by a group of firms is still under judicial review [since the decision in the case of Kali und Salz (a subsidiary of the chemicals firm BASF which formed a joint venture with the Treuhandanstalt) was appealed by a third party allegedly suffering from the conditions imposed in that case]. The lack of guidelines or clear principles that define dominance and the relevant market on which it is exercised constitute a major problem within this particular context.

An increasing number of mergers, acquisitions and joint ventures also involve firms based outside the European Union, or have a scope that widely exceeds the EU. The Merger Regulation explicitly takes this international dimension into account. In controlling whether a merger or concentrative joint venture leads to the creation of a dominant position the regulation stipulates that the Commission must take into account the actual and potential competition from firms located both within and outside the Community. Jacquemin (1993) observes in this connection that the first merger that was actually blocked by the Commission involved the acquisition of a Canadian subsidiary of Boeing, de Haviland, by two European firms – Aérospatiale of France and Alenia of Italy. Through their new venture the merger would have given the two European firms 50 per cent of the world market and 67 per cent of the EU market for 20–70 seat commuter aircraft. The potential strong position on the world market, the relevant geographic market for this product, was crucial in the decision of the Commission to block the proposed merger. The Merger Regulation also applies to concentrations between firms which have their headquarters outside the EU. As soon as the firms involved in the merger or joint venture meet the size and geographical criteria defining a concentration with a Community dimension (see above), the concentration must be reported and becomes the subject of control by the Commission. Examples of non-European mergers controlled by the Commission include the joint venture between Mitsubishi of Japan and Union Carbide of the US, the takeover of MCA by Matsushita and the recent merger between the two Swiss chemical companies, Sandoz and Ciba-Geigy.

The Merger Regulation also contains extra-territorial provisions in seeking to protect EU firms from discriminatory anti-trust treatments by non-EU states and in obtaining reciprocity in terms of policies dealing with concentrations of firms. More specifically, Article 24 of the Regulation provides for the role of the Commission as investigator of possible discriminatory or unequal treatments and in preparing and conducting negotiations, following the approval of the Council, to obtain reciprocity in the way concentrations of EU firms are dealt with in other countries; in other words, to obtain the same treatment for firms in non-member countries as what is offered to foreign firms in the EU. Jacquemin notes in this connection that, 'Given that the Regulation states that effective competition is the only reference for accepting or prohibiting a merger in the EC, Article 24 implies that the use of alternative criteria (of an industrial policy type) by a foreign country for blocking an acquisition by an EC firm would lead to international negotiation' (Jacquemin 1993, p. 96). So far, this proposition has not been developed in practice.

The extra-territorial provisions and applications of competition policies are giving rise to growing international conflicts concerning jurisdiction. International differences in competition, industrial and trade policies, which often closely interact, also put firms in very unequal positions in world markets and distort effective and fair competition. The problem is aggravated by the fact that there seems to be no consensus on what effective and fair competition really is (see Amsden and Singh 1994). So far, disputes concerning unfair competition have mostly been settled through bilateral negotiations. However, the resulting bilateral deals that emerge are no guarantee that competitive behaviour will emerge and might result in strong negative consequences for third countries which wish to trade with one of the countries engaged in the bilateral deal (e.g., the US–Japan deal in the field of semi-conductors (EC, 1994). The reciprocity or co-operative bilateral deals may also facilitate or help to sustain collusive behaviour of firms across national borders, similar to the arguments proposed in the theory on multi-market collusion and mutual forbearance (Feinberg 1985). In light of these arguments it is no surprise that differences in competition policies and their enforcement are becoming central in the discussions with respect to the removal of trade barriers at a global level.

A growing number of observers agree that, instead of bilateral agreements, competition policy should become harmonized and enforced at a global level. Distinguished industrial economists, including Alexis Jacquemin (1993) and Frederic Scherer (1994) have suggested the development of international competition rules and enforcement mechanisms at the level of the GATT in particular within the structure of the newly created World Trade Organisation. The growing concern by the WTO for competition issues and the increasing support it gets from both the academic and political worlds to develop a coherent global competition policy in accordance with new international trade arrangements seems to suggest that such an approach could materialize in a not too distant future.

# V  Conclusion

The rapid growth in FDI in Europe is mainly due to the massive number of cross-border mergers, acquisitions and joint ventures within the EU and across Triad regions. The great importance of cross-border mergers at a European scale and the changing motives for these operation with a strong emphasis on strengthening market position in the most recent period have become a major point of concern for anti-trust authorities. International differences in terms of regulation and practices related to merger and (hostile) takeovers not only influence the outcomes, but also seem to play a considerable role in the takeover frequency observed in the various countries. On this level, there is still too little European and global harmonization. The recently implemented EU Merger Regulation and control system can only partly remedy this problem. The system is designed to guide European-wide corporate restructuring in the desired direction by prohibiting mergers and joint ventures which could lead to the creation of a dominant market position with serious anti-competitive consequences. The new system undoubtedly constitutes a step in the right direction. However, the very restrictive criteria under which the regulation is applied seriously hamper its significance. Moreover, in order to avoid trade friction and unproductive policy measures, a vigilant and coherent competition policy is necessary, not only at the EU level, but also at the global level. As trade barriers come down between trade blocs, competitive conditions need to be harmonized as well. This essentially means that competition policy should be designed and enforced at a global level. Import-restricting policies or bilateral agreements are not good substitutes for the lack of a global anti-trust policy. The outcome of such partial policies may instead help to build power concentrations of firms on a European scale, with the danger that the intended efficiency gains from European integration will not transpire, but rather that existing inefficiencies will appear on an even larger scale than before.

### References

Amsden, A.H. and A. Singh (1994) 'The Optimal Degree of Competition and Dynamic Efficiency in Japan and Korea', *European Economic Review*, vol. 38, 941–51.

Baldwin, R.E., R. Forslid, and J. Haaland (1995) 'Investment Creation and Investment Diversion: Simulation Analysis of the Single Market Programme', Centre for Economic Policy Research, Discussion Paper Series, no. 1308.

Bleeke, J. (1990) 'Strategic Choices for Newly Opening Markets', *Harvard Business Review*, 158–65.

Commission Européenne (1994) 'Une Politique de Compétitivité Industrielle pour l'Union Européenne', Communication de la Commission au Conseil et au Parlement et au Comité Economique et Social et au Comité des Régions, Bruxelles, le 14 septembre 1994.

De Jong, H.W. (1990) 'Mergers and Competition Policies: Some General Remarks,' in P.H. Admiraal (ed.), *Merger & Competition Policy in the European Community*, Oxford: Basil Blackwell.

E(uropean) C(ommission) (1994) 'Competition and Integration, Community Merger Control Policy', *European Economy*, no. 57.

*European Economy* (1995) Supplement A, Economic Trends, Mergers and Acquisitions, no. 3.

Feinberg, R.M. (1985) 'Sales at risk: a Test of the Mutual Forbearance Theory of Conglomerate Behaviour', *Journal of Business*, vol. 58, pp. 225–41.

Feinberg, R.M. and B.T. Hirsch (1989) 'Industry Rent Seeking and the Filing of Unfair Complaints', *International Journal of Industrial Organization*, vol. 7, pp. 325–40.

Franks, J. and C. Mayer (1990) 'Capital Markets and Corporate Control: a Study of France, Germany and the UK', chapter 7 in Centre for Business Strategy, *Continental Mergers Are Different, Strategy and Policy for 1992*, London: London Business School.

Jacquemin, A.P. (1990) 'Mergers and European Policy', in P.H. Admiraal (ed.), *Merger & Competition Policy in the European Community*, Oxford: Basil Blackwell.

Jacquemin, A. (1993) 'The International Dimension of European Competition Policy', *Journal of Common Market Studies*, vol. 31, pp. 91–101.

Martin, S. (1993) *Advanced Industrial Economics*, Oxford: Blackwell.

Morgan, E.J. (1995) 'The Treatment of Oligopoly under the European Merger Control Regulation'. Paper presented at the 22nd Annual EARIE Conference, Juan les Pins, September.

Neven, D., R. Nuttall and P. Seabright (1993) 'Mergers in Daylight, the Economics and Politics of European Merger Control', London: CEPR.

Scherer, F. (1994) 'Competition Policy for an Integrated World Economy', Brookings Institution, Washington, USA.

Sleuwaegen, L. and P. Van Den Houte (1990) 'Economic Restructuring in the European Community: the Role of Mergers and Strategic Alliances', Working Paper No. 9026, K.U. Leuven.

Sleuwaegen, L. and H. Yamawaki (1988) 'The Formation of the European Common Market and Changes in Market Structure and Performance',

*European Economic Review*, vol. 32, 1451–75.
van Witteloosteuijn, A. and M. van Wegberg (1991) 'Multimarket Competition and European Integration', in A. Rugman and A. Verbeke (eds), *Research in Global Strategic Management, Global Competition and the European Community*, vol. 2, Greenwich: JAI Press.

# 9

# Liberalization in Services Trade and the Strategy of European Multinationals

## Patrick A. Messerlin

In the mid-1980s, the EC realized that the often celebrated 'common market' was only covering the manufacturing sector which, at this time, amounted to only 25–35 per cent of the GDP of the EC Member states (today's range is 20–30%). Service sectors were almost untouched by the Treaty of Rome, though by far they represented the bulk of the EC Member state economies with a share of 60–65 (today 60–70) per cent of their GDPs (or 50–55 per cent if the coverage is limited to non-public services). In 1985, the EC embarked on an effort for liberalizing the service sectors by launching the '1992 Programme'. The EC conversion to the idea of service liberalization induced the GATT Ministerial Meeting of Punta-del-Este to put the service issue on the agenda of the Uruguay Round, leading to the General Agreement on Trade in Services (GATS). Since then, almost all regional agreements (NAFTA, APEC, the CER and ASEAN) include provisions aiming at liberalizing services.

Despite these repeated successes in negotiating agreements on services, the general current mood about the impact of such agreements is rather disenchanted. In the EC, soft enforcement and counter-measures – from public subsidies to new discriminatory regulations or to private actions restricting competition – have aimed at limiting the effects of the 1992 Programme. In the WTO context, negotiations on a couple of key sectors (banking and basic telecommunications) have not been fruitful. The agreement on banking is very limited and the agreement on telecommunications is still pending (there were ongoing negotiations until mid-February). None of these interim agreements has received the signature of the US – the world's largest services market.

This chapter argues that the main reason for these disappointments lies in the fact that services liberalization may require a much larger dose of 'unilateralism' than trade liberalization in goods. The 1992 Programme and the GATS rely on the crucial assumption that services liberalization can be imposed from 'outside', from the pressures of negotiations with other countries. Peer pressures and mercantilist deals were (and still are, as illustrated by the key role of information technology goods in the WTO Singapore Ministerial Conference of December 1996) the dominant approach in the GATT liberalization of trade in goods. That is despite the fact that economists have a long analytical tradition showing that such an approach, though convenient from a political point of view, misses the most important aspect of liberalization: it is the best *domestic* choice between consumers' gains and costs from inefficient domestic firms. The whole experience of 'hijacking' a mercantilist approach à la GATT in order to open domestic markets has not – so far – been adapted to the case of services.

The chapter is organized as follows. Section I presents the EC 1992 Programme, and draws some major lessons from the EC regional approach. Section II provides information on the behaviour of European multinationals in two key sectors – banking and air transport. Section III reviews the GATS present situation. Section IV explains why a much more important dose of 'unilateralism' is likely to be necessary for liberalizing services.

## I   The EC Regional Agreements: the 'Single Market'

This section begins by reviewing the major steps of the EC 1992 Programme, now often called the Single Market Programme (SMP). This change of appellation is interesting. It cannot be related to the fact that the EC and the EC Member states were late in writing the new legal provisions required by services liberalization. Indeed in services, the EC did not have to stop the official clock for having been able to adopt these provisions (called Directives in the EC legal jargon). And EC Member states (at least, the most important ones) have introduced at a decent speed all the adopted Directives into their domestic legal systems. The change of appellation captures a more profound point: it implicitly recognizes that the time required by services liberalization is much longer than initially expected, and that perhaps more common regulations are necessary or that new approaches have to be investigated for speeding up the liberalization process.

## The Programme achieved in 1992

There are roughly 55 key directives concerning the service sectors in the SMP (out of a total of 300 measures). They deal with all the market service sectors, from banking to telecommunications and from air transport to advertising or audiovisuals. Most of these measures were included in the 1985 Commission's proposals and were adopted between 1991 and 1993, because of the long process of elaboration, negotiation, ratification and implementation involving the Commission and the Member states. Table 9.1 documents the recent adoption of these measures. It provides the year of adoption by the twelve EC Member states of key Directives for the two sectors examined in more detail in this chapter (banking and air transport). The average year for the whole EC ranges from 1992 (banking) to 1995 (airlines). But there are still some provisions to be implemented (such as intra-Member state flights in 1997). That the SMP has only a couple of years of existence in most of

**Table 9.1**   The EC single market programme: timing of implementation

| Selected Measures | Whole EC-12 | EC-12 excl. Britain | Britain |
|---|---|---|---|
| **Banking** | | | |
| 1. Key SMP Directives | | | |
| Second banking directive | 1992 | 1992 | 1993 |
| Own funds directive | 1992 | 1992 | 1992 |
| Solvency ratio directive | 1992 | 1992 | 1992 |
| 2. Other Key Measures | | | |
| Capital flow liberalization[a] | 1985 | 1986 | 1979 |
| Interest rate deregulation[a] | 1988 | 1989 | 1979 |
| **Transport** | | | |
| 1. Key SMP Directives | | | |
| International flights: 1st Package | 1988 | 1988 | 1988 |
| International flights: 2nd Package | 1990 | 1990 | 1990 |
| Intra-EC flights: 3rd Package | 1993 | 1993 | 1993 |
| Intra-Member state: 3rd Package | 1997 | 1997 | 1997 |
| Slot airport directive | 1995 | 1995 | 1995 |
| 2. Other Key Measures | | | |
| Price liberalization (before 1990)[b] | no | no | yes |
| Privatization of the flag carrier[c] | 2 | 1 | 1987 |

Sources: EC Commission. Various.
[a] Average year for the first and second columns
[b] Number of Member states allowing price liberalization.
[c] Number of Member states for the first & second columns.

the cases is a crucial point to be kept in mind when assessing the SMP impact on the EC multinationals.

The initial focus of the SMP was to ensure the right of establishment of EC firms in other Member state markets more than to dismantle discriminatory regulations (Sapir 1991). This focus was due to both EC legal constraints and economic thinking. Being based on the Treaty of Rome, the SMP made systematic reference to the Treaty's 'four freedoms' (free circulation of goods, services, capital and labour), with a focus on the two last freedoms. Moreover, the late 1980s were dominated by the idea that services were intrinsically different from goods because it was impossible to 'stock' them. It was assumed that competition between service providers would necessarily require a heavy commercial presence of these providers in each concerned market. This initial focus on establishment, to the detriment of cross-border trade, is still (in 1997) very present.[1] But, the increasingly omnipresent role of telecommunications – as a technology allowing one to 'stock' services over time and to trade them on long distance – is eroding this dominant focus on commercial presence.

The recent implementation of the SMP may explain its small impact today (section II provides some evidence supporting this point). However, one could argue that firms could have anticipated the SMP, and then observe that there have not been such anticipatory moves.

Why such a lack of reaction? A first explanation is simply that the major incumbents in each domestic market (for instance, flag carriers or telephone monopolies) have not been able correctly to realize their progressively emerging backwardness *vis-à-vis* competitors immersed in a more open environment. They may have simply underestimated the dynamics of markets – becoming only progressively laggards.[2] In the early years of service liberalization, certain regulated firms may well have been better equipped than the firms immersed in competitive markets. That was possible because these regulated firms were at the end of a catching-up process (such as France Telecom in the early 1980s). Their more recent equipment was hiding their lack of dynamic and appropriate economic incentives. For instance, it took a long time (as shown by the 'Minitel' experience) for the France Telecom management to understand that 'mimicking' the market is, in the long run, less efficient than playing the market.

Another reason for the lack of anticipation of the SMP is that the competitive domestic fringe in closed and highly regulated markets was unable to play a strong role. Most of these firms were tiny and easily threatened by the large incumbents, as best illustrated by the absence of strong charter carriers in Continental Europe (despite the emergence of strong tourist operators, which quickly understood that it would be too costly for them to become direct competitors).

Table 9.1 tries to catch a glimpse of this lack of anticipation by giving the years of introduction of crucial market mechanisms necessary for a rapid full implementation of the SMP. In banking, the two crucial market mechanisms were the interest rate and capital flow liberalizations. On average, these instruments were introduced in the late 1980s, less than five years before the SMP – except in Britain (and in Germany for capital flows). In air transport, charter carriers (which operate in a competitive environment) represent a substantial proportion of the domestic markets only in Britain. Airfare liberalization and privatization of the flag carriers are contemporary with the SMP in almost all the EC Member states – again if one excepts Britain.

A last explanation is that EC firms may have quickly realized the incomplete nature of the SMP. Table 9.2 presents the main deficiencies in the current SMP pinpointed by the recent review of the SMP by the Commission. Road transport is the only sector without serious holes in the SMP.

## *An essential feature*

An essential feature of the EC process of services liberalization is that it was not triggered by the Member states, nor by the Commission, but by the EC Court of Justice (ECJ). Acting as the active guardian of the letter and spirit of the Treaty of Rome, the ECJ opened the door to the 'mutual recognition' process in extending to services a landmark ruling on goods – the 1978 so-called Cassis de Dijon ruling. This ruling states that a product lawfully produced and sold in one Member state must be admitted in all Member states for sale: in other words, the production conditions imposed by one EC Member state have to be 'recognized' as legitimate by the other Member states. Since then, the ECJ has adopted other rulings in the same vein, including in services (air transport and insurance), showing that the ECJ's focus was the EC consumer gains (and presenting the ECJ as the EC institution which is the least influenced by a mercantilist approach of liberalization).

Why were all the EC governments so reluctant to liberalize services (and indeed why are they still often reluctant to make progress on this road, as documented in section II)? There are two reasons which deserve attention.

The most oft mentioned reason is the nature of protection in services. Regulation-based protection in services differs from tariffs because it raises rivals' costs in a very different way than tariffs. The substance of this difference is often described in terms of transparency. Though it is

**Table 9.2** Effectiveness of single-market measures in removing barriers to the free provision of services

| | Cross-border service restrictions | Restrictions on establishment | Restrictions on factor flows | Barriers — Regulatory/technical barriers[1] | Fiscal issues | Others |
|---|---|---|---|---|---|---|
| Banking | ✓✓ Discriminatory conditions for cross-border sale of services <br> ✓ Restrictions on marketing and service content | ✓✓ Discriminatory conditions for licences | ✓✓ Capital controls | ⊗ Prudential requirements <br> ✓ Conditions for sales | ⊗ Tax on savings <br> ⊗ Investment tax <br> ⊗ Death duties | — |
| Insurance | ✓✓ Discriminatory conditions for cross-border sale of services <br> ✓✓ Restrictions on marketing and service content | ✓✓ Discriminatory condition for licences | ✓✓ Capital controls | ✓ Consumer protection <br> Conditions for sales | ⊗ Taxation of reserves <br> ⊗ Taxation of premiums | ⊗ Contract law |
| Road freight transport | ✓✓ Bilateral quota restrictions on access to other EC markets <br> ✓✓ Price restrictions | ✓✓ Discriminatory licensing conditions | ✓ Cabotage restrictions <br> ✓✓ Recognition of diplomas | ✓✓ Weights and dimensions <br> ✓ Road safety rules <br> ✓ Speed limits <br> ✓ Resting hours | ✓✓ Excise duties | ✓✓ Border formalities for goods |
| Air transport | ✓✓ Bilateral restrictions on free access to other EC markets <br> ✓ Price restrictions <br> ⊗ Slots allocation | ✓✓ Exclusive rights for licensing of air carriers <br> ⊗ Ownership rules in third country bilaterals | ✓ Cabotage restrictions <br> ✓✓ Designation and capacity restrictions | ✓✓ Conditions for sales <br> ✓✓ Security and safety rules <br> ⊗ Airport charges | ✓ VAT | ✓ Border formalities for passengers <br> ✓✓ Access to computer reservation systems <br> State aid, unfair practices |
| Telecoms liberalized services | ✓ Discriminatory conditions for access to network | ✓✓ Exclusive rights on: mobile, data and satellite services | ✓✓ Exclusive rights to sell equipment | ✓ Technical conditions for use of networks | — | ⊗ Fair access to networks |
| TV broadcasting services | ✓ Restrictions on cross-frontier broadcasting <br> ✓ Rental and lending rights <br> ✓ Term of copyright protection <br> ✓ Copyright applicable to satellite and cable | ⊗ National licensing rules for broadcasters <br> ⊗ Media ownership restrictions | — | ✓ Technical conditions for use of networks | — | — |
| Distribution (fast moving consumer goods) | No restrictions | No restrictions | ✓ Restrictions on free movement of goods | | ✓ VAT | ✓✓ Border formalities for goods <br> ✓ Technical barriers on products |
| Advertising | ⊗ Types of products and media <br> ⊗ Comparative advertising | No restrictions | ✓ Restrictions on media | ✓ Misleading advertising <br> Content restrictions | — | — |

✓✓ Barrier effectively removed; ✓ Barrier partially removed; ⊗ Remaining barrier; — not relevant

[1] These types of barriers tend to increase the cost of supplying services internationally and could be considered equivalent to technical barriers in manufacturing.

certainly true that regulation-based protection is much less transparent than tariffs, that does not mean that transparency is the most crucial point. From a dynamic perspective on service liberalization (or protection), it seems much more important to recognize that regulation-based protection does not provide revenues to the government, but incomes to domestic interests. The key point is not transparency *per se*, but income (or rent) transfers. Protectionist regulations oblige foreign service providers to operate as domestic firms, that is, to pay domestic labour costs, domestic interest rate charges, domestic inputs, and to co-operate with domestic bureaucrats for enforcing domestic rules. In sum, regulation-based protection has the key feature of import quotas (not even of VERs): they grant incomes or rents to domestic factors of production. As a result, when domestic incumbents obtain regulation-based protection, they do not only raise the costs of their foreign competitors (as they would have done by getting tariffs). They also enlarge the domestic constituency of interests vested in maintaining the *statu quo*, including the foreign entrants which have to absorb noticeable fixed costs and thus tend to be less interested in a further opening of the borders. In sum, at any point of time, the domestic constituency of pro-liberalization interests remains small – making it difficult for governments not motivated by consumers' interests to start, develop and implement services liberalization.

All the EC Member states illustrate what has just been described, including the British government (which has shown the deepest and most continuous commitment to a certain degree of services liberalization). In Britain, successive governments were not only convinced by economic arguments, but they were also determined to reduce as much as possible the vested interests associated with public firms running services monopolies. When this second motive disappeared (after privatization), regulatory reforms tended to slow down substantially, as is well observed by many economists who were at the origin of the services liberalization (Beesley 1996).

This first reason for explaining the difficulties of Member states in fully implementing the SMP is, by nature, permanent. There is another reason, more circumstantial, but which has played (and still plays) an essential role in some Member states. During the past forty years, some EC governments have invested heavily in services which, today, pertain to market services and should be liberalized. For reasons that the economic analysis of the capture of public firms can explain, these governments are likely to have 'over-invested'. As a result, they may be more inclined to resist service liberalization than governments which have invested less, simply because they will lose more: they protect the public service providers in order to maintain (artificially) the 'public rate of profit' as high as possible. This consequence is not the only one to be considered. In such a situation of existing large excess capacities, service liberalization may imply a brutal shift from the existing monopoly situations to full-fledged competition. For instance, if in the past, the railways or electricity monopolies had been able to receive funds for building telecom lines much above their needs (in the case of the French railways company, SNCF is said to use only 10 per cent of the capacity of its 7000 km telecom network), a rapid liberalization would have meant that the railway or electricity monopoly could have become (almost immediately) large competitors of the telecom public monopoly – with all the 'destructive' capacities associated with the special features of competition between public firms. In sum, there is an intrinsic 'instability' in a wide system of over-funded public firms which may inhibit governments from promoting a rapid shift to service liberalization.

## II   The Strategy of European Multinationals

It would be very difficult to design a taxonomy of the strategies that the major European multinationals operating in the services area have adopted since the start of the SMP. It would be even more difficult to make a clear distinction between the strategies that have been influenced by the SMP, and those that have reacted to more general factors, such as technological progress, economic growth and business cycles. By nature, regulatory reforms such as the SMP do not come from nowhere: they are introduced because the business environment is changing rapidly, as best illustrated by the stupendous technological progress in telecommunications (echoed by the not less rapid and deep changes in US regulations). The recent series of studies done for the European Commission (1996a) in order to review the 1992 Programme have shown the importance of such difficulties.

In light of the above provisos, this section has two much more modest objectives – focusing on price and investment behaviour. First, can one observe breaking points in price patterns which could clearly echo the implementation of certain SMP phases? Second, can one observe changes in investment patterns which could clearly correspond to the implementation of SMP provisions? Negative answers would suggest at most a marginal influence of the SMP. This preliminary conclusion would be reinforced if meanwhile there is evidence of counter measures taken by EC Member states in order to limit the SMP's impact on domestic incumbents.

In order to examine these two points, two services sectors have been selected – air transport and banking. We shall examine the price and investment behaviour, respectively. Because SMP legal provisions are much more advanced in these two sectors (in contrast with telecommunications where crucial SMP measures will emerge in 1998 only), the chance to observe reactions to the SMP are higher. EC air transport is a two-tier sector, with a portion dominated by (state) monopolies (scheduled flights operated by flag carriers) and a portion (the charters operating non-scheduled flights) exposed to competition at the world and EC level for two to three decades. By contrast, banking is a regulated sector with few oligopolies under increasing technological stress; it is an industry inclined to focus on commercial presence.

The choice of two sectors may introduce a bias in the assessment of the SMP presented in the chapter. However, the series of studies done for the European Commission (1996b) also suggest limited gains in productivity and efficiency in other sectors (telecommunications), and 'the extent to which the observed changes are linked to the SMP is very uncertain'. Large gains in productivity and efficiency have been observed only in liberalized telecommunication services. However, it is hard to estimate (even in cellular telephony with the adoption of the GSM standard) to what extent the SMP has contributed to the promotion of rapid technological change, which is the main source of these gains.

Lastly, the view taken here is not contradicted by the perceptions that service firms expressed about the SMP in an Eurostat survey. On average, 22.5 per cent of the opinions are positive concerning the impact of the SMP, compared with 74 per cent of 'neutral' opinions (no or minor impact of the SMP), and 3.5 per cent of negative opinions. If there is any lesson to be drawn from such a survey, it is that the SMP is still a marginal force.

*Price behaviour: air transport*

When discussing the SMP's impact on air transport, there are three aspects to be taken into account.[3] First, EC chartered flights have always been subject to competition forces within some strong limits (in particular those imposed by airport slot regulations). Consequently, air transport liberalization concerns directly only flag carriers. Second, EC flag carriers have a very different mix of domestic (intra-EC Member state), intra-EC (between EC Member states) and international (extra-EC) flights. The share of domestic and intra-EC flights ranges from 80 per cent of the airline revenues (SAS) to less than 30 per cent (KLM), and the share of domestic flights ranges from 40 per cent of the airline revenues (Iberia) to almost nothing (KLM). As a result, EC flag carriers are, by definition, very diversely affected by the various EC Directives listed in table 9.1, depending on their revenue mix, and the focus and timing of the Directives. Lastly, rules for extra-EC flights are still governed by EC member state policies, hence they are out of the reach of the EC Directives and mostly influenced by global factors of the air transport markets (including the evolution of the content of bilateral air agreements).

A first indicator of the impact of the pro-competition SMP could be marked changes in the trends of the average global airfare which is a mix of full and discount airfares. Table 9.3 shows the evolution between 1985 and 1995 of the average discount airfare charged in the EC air markets, as well as the evolution of the share of passengers having bought such discount airfares. Despite the fact that until 1993, most airfares required governmental acceptance, discount airfares (in percentage of full airfares) decline steadily after 1989, with a clear step in 1992, until 1995 when the evolution reversed. During the same period, the share of passengers buying discount airfares has increased, with the same significant step in 1992 and the same reversal in 1995. Were the full economy airfare stable, the average global (discount and full) airfare would have declined by almost 15 per cent (from index 74.6 to index 64). However, column 4 shows an estimate of the evolution of the average full (economy) airfare: based on this estimate, the average global (discount plus full) airfare would have declined by only 5 per cent between 1985 and 1995. In this case, the price discrimination between discount and full airfares is more marked (almost 21%).

These evolutions of EC airfares are modest by any standard. They seem even more modest when compared to the US evolution. This impression is reinforced by two facts. First, the market shares of the major EC and non-EC airlines in EC markets have remained relatively stable during most of the period, suggesting stable EC incumbents and market structures. Second, EC regulatory reforms have been implemented during the downturn in air transport related to the Gulf War and to the slow growth in the major continental European economies. As these factors could only have amplified price decreases, one cannot exclude the possibility that they could be responsible for the observed 1992 step in price decline.

In sum, the observed evolutions suggest a very modest impact of the SMP *per se*. Two opposite reasons could explain these limited results.

First, as shown by table 9.1, key impediments to increased competition between European airlines for the period examined did remain until 1995: the Slot Airport Directive was scheduled to be implemented in 1995, and the Third Package on 'domestic' (intra-Member state) flights only in 1997. Even if the Slot Directive is said to be too modest

**Table 9.3** Airlines: evolution of market shares, airfares and subsidies, 1985–94

| Years | Discount fares[a] | 'Discount' passengers[b] | Total fare revenue[c] | Full fare[d] | Total fare revenue[e] | Market share US airlines[f] | Subsidies[g] |
|---|---|---|---|---|---|---|---|
| 1985 | 58.0 | 60.5 | 74.6 | 100.0 | 74.6 | 47.2 | n.a |
| 1986 | 56.5 | 61.0 | 73.5 | 98.5 | 72.9 | 43.0 | n.a |
| 1987 | 57.0 | 61.5 | 73.6 | 97.0 | 72.4 | 46.6 | n.a |
| 1988 | 57.0 | 62.0 | 73.3 | 95.6 | 71.7 | 49.2 | n.a |
| 1989 | 57.0 | 62.0 | 73.3 | 99.4 | 73.1 | 46.9 | n.a |
| 1990 | 54.0 | 63.0 | 71.0 | 103.4 | 72.3 | 46.3 | n.a |
| 1991 | 54.0 | 64.0 | 70.6 | 107.5 | 73.3 | n.a | 1.2 |
| 1992 | 51.0 | 67.0 | 67.2 | 110.7 | 70.7 | n.a | 14.7 |
| 1993 | 48.6 | 70.1 | 64.0 | 114.0 | 68.2 | n.a | 5.1 |
| 1994 | 48.3 | 71.7 | 62.9 | 117.5 | 67.9 | n.a | 26.9 |
| 1995 | 49.2 | 70.9 | 64.0 | 121.0 | 70.1 | n.a | 5.4 |

Sources: Association of European Airlines. Doganis.
[a] Average discount fare, as a percentage of full fare.
[b] Percentage of passengers flying with discount fares
[c] Weighted average (discount and full fares) if full fare is set to 1.
[d] Estimated evolution of the full (economy) fare.
[e] Weighted average (discount & full fares) if full fare is from column d.
[f] Shares of the EC air market.
[g] Declared state aids, in percentages of the operating revenue of the flag carrier.
n.a.: not available.

(as argued by air transport experts), this first reason would lead to an optimistic perspective: it is simply too early to observe an impact of the SMP in the few past years, and one could still expect a substantial impact in the future. Two events of late 1996 would add support to this view. British Airways is close to increasing substantially its market share in the French air market: adding the new airline AOM to its too small subsidiary TAT could make BA a major operator in Orly Airport. Another illustration of coming changes is the start-up of new European airlines: a dozen airlines have been recently created in Europe. But these new firms operate three aircraft on average (and lessons have to be drawn from the US experience).

However, the second reason leads to a much less optimistic tone. The few last years of emerging liberalization have witnessed the immediate emergence of protectionist counter-measures eroding or eliminating the SMP impact, despite the absence of strong competitive pressures. Denying access to airport slots is a powerful protectionist instrument, as illustrated by the refusal of the French government to grant slots to TAT (the British Airways French subsidiary) at Orly Airport in 1994 (and the 'twin' decision for the AOM application to Heathrow). But, table 9.3 shows that the most worrisome protectionist measure is subsidies to flag carriers.[4] Subsidies have been granted to all the EC-12 flag carriers, except British Airways and Luxair. More importantly, they are rapidly increasing and huge: since 1992, the average rate of subsidisation is 13 per cent of the average annual operating revenues of the firms concerned.

The subsidy problem is compounded by the typical solution adopted by the European Commission for handling this issue. Under EC law, state aids cannot be granted without the authorization of the Commission (acting under the provisions on competition policy of the Treaty of Rome). In airline subsidies, the Commission was torn between political pressures and its desire to protect other EC airlines from the fact that subsidies were giving 'unfair' advantages to the subsidised firms. The compromise of the Commission was to accept the subsidies, but to submit the subsidised airlines to restrictions such as no fleet expansion, no possibility of acquiring other airlines, no possibility to price aggressively, etc. Such a compromise has two effects. It imposes limits on the competitive nature of all the markets on which the subsidised airline is operating or which are substitutes or complementary to these markets. For instance, limiting seat capacities of the subsidised airline is intrinsically a 'monopolistic' device (it limits the supply) which ultimately 'facilitates the collusion' between subsidised and non-subsidised airlines.[5] The second effect of the Commission's compromise is to run the risk of transforming subsidised airlines into permanent lame-ducks, by making more difficult their restructuring (and giving good excuses for new subsidies). There are two alternatives to the Commission's approach which are probably better. The first would have been to trade drastic reductions in the state aids envisaged by the Member state in exchange for the freedom of the carrier to follow its desired strategy without constraints related to the state aid. The second alternative would have been to balance the (somewhat reduced) state aid envisaged by the Member state with a disinvestiture plan (that would have made public subsidies closer to what would have occurred in the private sector in similar circumstances) coupled with a total degree of freedom of action for the subsidised (but reduced) carrier.

The fact that the SMP is likely to have had a small impact should also be reflected in EC carrier strategies, which present the three following components.

First, the EC dimension of their strategies seems marginal and essentially based on a defensive attitude. EC carriers sitting on a large domestic market try to protect this market by buying small or regional airlines operating in this market, as best illustrated by Air France (buying UTA and the domestic monopoly Air Inter) or by Lufthansa (buying stakes in Lauda Air or Luxair). Eventually (if they are profitable enough), EC flag carriers try to sneak into other large EC markets, as illustrated by British Airways (with TAT in France and Deutsche BA in Germany). That EC domestic markets are consolidated allows flag carriers to behave still as the market leader *vis-à-vis* the new entrants, and to use instruments more favourable to them than price changes (such as flight frequency and connections) for fighting competitors. For instance, Air France-Air Inter reacted to the entry of AOM on the Paris–Nice route by increasing the frequency of its flights but with smaller aircraft, so that the total number of seats per day has decreased and the price changed as little as possible. On their side, entrants tend not to compete on prices but on service quality, so that they really emerge as significant alternatives only in specific circumstances (for instance, because of repeated strikes in flag carriers).

Second, EC flag carriers focus their attention on world markets. However, large pan-European alliances for achieving this objective have failed for two reasons: such alliances imply the choice of a US (and Asian) ally (and the choice of one European hub) to the detriment of the other airlines (and their hubs). The best example of a pan-European alliance was Alcazar (KLM, SAS, Swissair and Austrian) which disappeared when SAS joined Lufthansa, because it lacked US connections (and an undisputed central hub). Indeed, when competing between themselves, a crucial source of advantage for EC carriers is their links with a US carrier: an EC carrier well connected with a US airline can play

**Table 9.4** Emerging mega-alliances in air transport, 1996

| | Participants | | | | Features | | | |
|---|---|---|---|---|---|---|---|---|
| | US carriers | EC carriers | Asian carriers | Other carriers | sales $b. | passengers million | airplane fleet | labour force '000s |
| 1.[a] | American US Air | Brit. Airways | Quantas | Canadian | 44.1 | 195.3 | 1706 | 252.0 |
| 2. | United Atlan. Coast Air Wisconsin | Lufthansa Lauda Air Luxair SAS Brit. Midland | Thai Airways | Air Canada S. Africa Air Varig | 46.3 | 188.7 | 1522 | 243.0 |
| 3. | Delta | Austrian Sabena Swissair | Singapore | Comair Atl. Southeast Skywest | 27.2 | 126.5 | 1004 | 122.6 |
| 4. | Northwest Express | KLM Martinair Air UK | | Kenya Mesaba Aviation | 16.7 | 70.5 | 654 | 79.8 |

5. Large US and EC companies left outside mega-alliances emerging in 1996
Continental    Air France
Pan Am    Alitalia
TWA    Iberia
    TAP

Source: Airline Business, reported by International Herald Tribune, 2 September 1996.
[a] Under investigation by the US, EC and British competition authorities.

a leader role *vis-à-vis* certain other EC carriers. If one focuses on transatlantic links, table 9.4 shows that there are four emerging mega-alliances which have left only Air France and Alitalia, among the major EC flag carriers, without strong US connections.[6]

The last component is the implicit alliance between a flag carrier and a national hub: British Airways and Heathrow, Air France and Roissy-CDG, KLM and Amsterdam, etc. There are two (at least) ways to look at EC hubs. On the one hand, they can be seen as competing by their capacity to be 'fed' European travellers. That can be obtained in many ways, including co-ordination between flag carriers and other means of transport (such as railways, as best illustrated by the direct connections between Roissy-CDG Airport and the European network of rapid trains, TGVs). On the other hand, European hubs are also competing by their capacity to be fed *non*-European travellers.[7] In particular, they compete between themselves to be 'the' European counterparts of hubs of non-EC carriers (for instance, Amsterdam is the counterpart of Detroit). That is why the 'airport' component of the US 'open skies' programme is so important: it is a powerful force contributing to the emergence of a few 'European' hubs connected to a few world networks. That there are only half-a-dozen major US airlines implies that there can be only half-a-dozen major European hubs – hence half-a-dozen European airlines.[8]

## Investment behaviour: the banking sector

As all the key directives in this domain have been adopted in 1992 (see table 9.1), banking is the sector which has had the longest time to react to the SMP provisions. Indeed, as shown in table 9.5, EC banking has been subject to noticeable structural changes. The total number of banks has substantially declined (by 10–20%), except in Belgium (where it has increased) and in Britain and Netherlands (where it has been stable). Table 9.5 shows that if foreign banks have increased their market shares of EC total assets, they are still marginal in large EC Member states, even in Britain, with a penetration rate of less than 3 per cent.

Table 9.6 looks at the number of deals (the only available information, since the magnitude of deals is rarely divulged) in the world banking sector during the last ten years. At first glance, it suggests that the European banks do not behave very differently from US banks: during the last ten years, almost 83 per cent of the deals concluded by EC banks have been 'internal', either in their own EC Member state or within the EC. The corresponding figures are almost 90 per cent for the US banks (81 per cent for the banks of the 'rest of the world', i.e., the world excluding the EC, US and Japan). But, a more careful analysis

**Table 9.5** The EC banking sector, 1985–94

| | Number of banks 94/85 | Share of foreign banks[a] | | Assets[b] | Assets[b] |
| --- | --- | --- | --- | --- | --- |
| | | 94/85 | 1994 | 1985 | 1994 |
| Belgium | 109.2 | 136.6 | 8.2 | 2.7 | 3.1 |
| Britain | 96.9 | 107.7 | 2.9 | 2.1 | 2.3 |
| France | 82.4 | 105.2 | 0.6 | 1.9 | 2.2 |
| Germany | 81.7 | 250.0 | 0.1 | 1.8 | 2.1 |
| Italy | 91.0 | 116.7 | 0.3 | 1.0 | 1.2 |
| Netherlands | 97.2 | n.a. | n.a. | 1.3 | 2.3 |
| Spain | 86.8 | n.a. | n.a. | 1.4 | 1.7 |

Sources: Central Banks.
[a] In percentage of total assets.
[b] In percentage of GDP.
n.a.: not available.

shows that a large share of EC internal deals are related to British banks: almost 60 per cent of these EC deals have involved British banks (410 out of 710 deals); the US deals in the EC have been located in Britain in almost 80 per cent of the cases; and the deals from the banks of the rest of the world have involved British banks in half of the cases. Because of this atypical British case, it is useful to look at intra-EC deals (excluding intra-Member state deals). In this case, table 9.6 shows a different breakdown, with a much larger share of deals located in the US and rest of the world markets.[9]

All these figures do not suggest a strong impact from the SMP: they seem much more related to the British banking and financial policy. Available trade data confirm this point. According to Eurostat estimates of international trade in services, the intra-EC trade (exports and imports) of banking services reaches indexes of 3.75 and 7.5 in 1991 and 1993 respectively, whereas the corresponding indexes for the extra-EC banking trade are 3 and 6, respectively. That intra-EC as well as extra-EC trade has doubled between 1991 and 1993 in the immediate aftermath of the SMP does not suggest *prima facie* a strong impact of the SMP.

Again, this limited SMP impact can be explained by the fact that the EC Directives are relatively recent and – implicitly – that financial firms did not really anticipate any impact of the SMP. That can be the sign that crucial forces are at work at another level – at the world level (the EC level is already too small). This interpretation would be supported by recent mergers which have clearly the world as the relevant market in mind (as, for instance, the merger between the two French insurers,

**Table 9.6**  Number of deals in banking and finance, 1985–95

| making deals in . . . | Buyers in | | | | Domestic and Intra-EC M&As | | |
|---|---|---|---|---|---|---|---|
| | EC12 | USA | Japan | Rest of world | Domestic | Intra-EC | Dom./Total |
| Belgium | 21 | | | 1 | 10 | 11 | 47.6 |
| Britain | 410 | 15 | | 18 | 380 | 30 | 92.7 |
| France | 107 | 4 | | 5 | 77 | 30 | 72.0 |
| Germany | 31 | | 1 | 3 | 22 | 9 | 71.0 |
| Italy | 35 | | | 2 | 22 | 13 | 62.9 |
| Netherlands | 14 | | | 1 | 7 | 7 | 50.0 |
| Spain | 42 | | | 1 | 26 | 16 | 61.9 |
| Other ECMS | 50 | | | 5 | 36 | 14 | 72.0 |
| EC12 | 710 | 19 | 1 | 36 | 580 | 130 | 81.7 |
| USA | 57 | 353 | 13 | 28 | — | 57 | — |
| Japan | 0 | 1 | 12 | 0 | — | 0 | — |
| Rest of world | 91 | 20 | 6 | 270 | — | 91 | — |
| Non-Internal | 148 | 40 | 20 | 64 | — | 148 | — |
| World | 858 | 393 | 32 | 334 | 580 | 278 | — |
| Shares (as percentage of world deals) of deals in country: | | | | | | | |
| EC12 | 82.8 | 4.8 | 3.1 | 10.8 | — | 46.8 | — |
| USA | 6.6 | 89.8 | 40.6 | 8.4 | — | 20.5 | — |
| Japan | 0.0 | 0.3 | 37.5 | 0.0 | — | 0.0 | — |
| Rest of world | 10.6 | 5.1 | 18.8 | 80.8 | — | 32.7 | — |
| Number of deals in the EC11 (EC12, excluding Britain) | | | | | | | |
| EC11 | 300 | 4 | 1 | 18 | 200 | 100 | 66.7 |

Source: Acquisitions and Mergers Annual Reports.

UAP and AXA) and which, in turn, could destabilize European banking. And, in the same vein as the mega-alliances in air transport, there are the credit-card networks (ATMs) which also raise difficult problems in terms of possible anti-competitive practices (Federal Reserve Bank of St Louis 1995).

But the absence of expectations about the SMP's impact can also be a sign that EC banks were confident of facing a slow liberalization and / or of slowing it down, if necessary. A first reason is that large banks of most of the EC Member states are almost certain to be supported at any cost by their government. That has been shown with the huge subsidies that the French government agreed to pour into Crédit Lyonnais (the largest European bank in terms of total assets in 1993): at least 45 billion French francs, or 650,000 francs per employee (US $9 billion, or US $130,000 per employee) according to the minimal estimate of the Commission reviewing the state aid granted to the bank.[10] Table 9.7 gives some support to this last possibility, by glancing through a few intra-EC barriers in banking services enforced in 1994. By all means, these barriers are substantial. Detailed studies confirm the permanence and the effectiveness of such barriers (Steil 1995).

## III   Service Liberalization in the WTO Context

After a brief summary of the well-known principles of the General Agreement on Trade in Services (GATS), section III reviews the more recent developments in service liberalization in the WTO context, particularly in banking and telecommunications.

### The GATS framework

The GATS is often presented as a 'GATT for services'. This parallel is misleading. In sharp contrast to the GATT, the GATS is a pure framework agreement with almost no operative content. That flows from the fact that, though it uses the same general concepts as the GATT (unconditional MFN, national treatment, binding concession, transparency and reciprocity), the GATS immerses them in a very different perspective: the real impact of all these concepts depends almost entirely on the commitments which can qualify them in a crucial way. As a result, the core of the service liberalization is embodied in the sectoral negotiations about detailed commitments. This difference between GATT and GATS is particularly essential for the two most crucial concepts – unconditional MFN and national treatment. For instance, the GATT unconditional MFN has an impact, whatever the detailed commitments about tariffs are, because it is a concept which cannot be qualified

**Table 9.7**   Remaining regulatory barriers in the EC banking sector: a selected list

| | |
|---|---|
| Belgium | Discriminatory guarantee system from central government |
| Britain | Growing dissatisfaction with self-regulation in the London market |
| Denmark | Bans of many marketing techniques (telephone sales, etc.) |
| France | Ban of interest-bearing cheques and cash-deposit accounts<br>Discriminatory regulations about SICAVs (collective investment schemes)<br>Restrictions about foreign direct investment in French banks and firms<br>Government debt markets limited to local operators<br>Ban of comparative advertising<br>Delays imposed on foreign investment exchanges to locate trading terminals in France |
| Germany | Stringent data protection laws inhibiting sales of services cross-border in Germany<br>Restrictions on marketing techniques (Unfair Trading Act)<br>Requirement for foreign fund managers to have a link with German unit trust managers<br>Variations in legal standing of contracts, conduct of business and investor protection |
| Ireland | none |
| Italy | Restrictions on provision of payment instrument services by non-residents<br>Access to a wide range of activities limited to institutions linked to the Italian Securities Board (ISB)<br>SIMs must be incorporated in Italy and managed separately<br>Marketing techniques limited to SIMs and under the control of ISB<br>SIMs' agents personally responsible for deals |
| Luxembourg | Strict secrecy and confidentiality rules |
| Spain | Limit on the number of branches for new banks during their first years<br>No "off-the-page selling"<br>Delays imposed on foreign investment exchanges to locate trading terminals in France<br>Foreign professional qualifications not always accepted by the Spanish authorities |

Source: British Invisibles European Committee, 1994.

(limited or expanded) by multilateral negotiations on tariffs in such or such goods.

That is not the case in the GATS. A GATS member can declare exceptions from unconditional MFN for entire sectors or for specified sectoral measures. As a result, service liberalization can be easily country-specific. This possibility gives to 'detailed' reciprocity (reciprocity on a sector by sector, or on a measure by measure basis) a central role in service liberalization in the WTO context. That is in sharp contrast to the GATT strict unconditional MFN which has obliged each country to think of its trade policy in terms of 'global' reciprocity – *aggregating* all manufacturing sectors and measures in *one* package. However, this essential difference between GATT and GATS may narrow in the future. Exceptions to unconditional MFN will normally be subject to changes over time: they are to be reviewed after five years, and they should not exceed ten years – in principle. It is thus possible that the GATS could evolve towards the GATT structure after the year 2005 (or with very limited 'zones' of conditional MFN for narrowly defined services).

GATS national treatment (the fact that border-cleared imported services and domestic services should be treated equally) is also a conditional obligation: it is granted only after the relevant sector has been scheduled in the country's commitments. However, this restricted scope in terms of service sectors concerned by national treatment is counter-balanced by a wider coverage in terms of barriers. That is the consequence of the (rather confusing) provision about 'market access' of GATS Article XVI (which has no counterpart in the GATT). This provision requires that, in the sectors scheduled, foreign services and service providers should be treated 'no less favourably' than domestic counterparts. Because it is so vaguely written, this condition covers a wide range of issues. In particular, it could include issues related to competition broadly speaking – be they regulatory reforms or competition policy *per se*. The coverage of national treatment in terms of barriers is enlarged by the notion of market access, more especially as (contrary to the GATT) the GATS covers the whole range of international transactions: not only cross-border trade (like the GATT), but also labour and capital flows associated with commercial presence.

## Sectoral commitments

In sum, service liberalization in the WTO context is heavily biased towards a country/sector-specific approach. The sectoral specificity is particularly worrisome because it is well known that such specificity tends to reduce the set of possible deals, by eliminating beneficial cross-sectoral trade-offs. It is a paradox that the Uruguay Round has produced a narrowly sectoral approach to service liberalization, whereas it has expanded cross-sectoral possibilities of compensation or retaliation between goods, services and intellectual property rights.

The decisive role of scheduled commitments for designing the real dimension of unconditional MFN and national treatment would have required a clear technique for defining these commitments. This requirement would have pledged for commitment schedules based on negative lists (that is, on lists of measures or sectors excluded from commitments, all the other measures or sectors being considered as part of the commitments). Unfortunately, it has been decided that the GATS schedules in services will be based on positive lists. That is an unsatisfactory approach because it makes almost impossible, except for the sector experts, a reasonably correct and clear appreciation of the concessions received. As concessions received are much publicized, this technique is a recipe for limited progress in liberalization.

## *The consequence: a strong tendency to sectoral reciprocity*

Most of the fears raised by the GATS framework have proven to be correct with the negotiations held since the end of the Uruguay Round in the three sectors where initial commitments were suspended during the Uruguay Round: financial sectors (banking), telecommunications and maritime transport. During the Uruguay Round, MFN exceptions were taken in these three sectors by the US (and a few other countries) in order to induce other countries to improve their initial offers (banking and telecommunications) or as a response to domestic vested interests hostile to market opening (maritime transport). Indeed, the hostile US attitude on maritime transport has meant that negotiations have been postponed until the year 2000.

### *Banking*
The banking negotiations (which excluded certain segments for prudential reasons) ended in July 1995, with results so limited that the WTO members decided to leave open the possibility for further negotiations in November–December 1997. In other words, the existing July 1995 agreement is an 'interim' agreement.

Under this interim agreement, the US invoked an MFN exception for the entire sector – that is, it was decided to open the US markets on a reciprocal basis. The reason for US attitude was the poor (from the US point of view) offers of the trading partners, and the resulting 'imbalance' between the openness of the US financial markets and the closed nature of the partners' markets. Trading partners which triggered the US reaction were never mentioned officially, except Indonesia (unofficial names include Brazil, Chile, Korea, India, Malaysia and the Philippines).

The consequences of the fact that the US walked out of the negotiations are difficult to assess. On the one hand, it is a major blow to the world-wide dimension of the WTO: one of the world's largest financial powers did not participate in the first WTO agreement in this sector. That was reinforced by the fact that two-thirds of the concerned WTO membership (47 countries) did not offer any improvement of their initial commitments. On the other hand, the US used its conditional MFN approach to grant MFN status to the EC and to Japan – implying that a very large proportion of the financial markets was covered by the interim agreement.

*Basic telecommunications*

These negotiations, initially due to conclude on 30 April 1996, were suspended, after the withdrawal of the US offer. Meanwhile, standstill commitments are to apply. Negotiations are due to resume in January 1997 for completion by mid-February of the same year – the initial schedule for enforcing the agreement (January 1998) being still reachable.

Although the US declared that it considered 24 out of the 34 offers available as unacceptable, its attitude was essentially related to one crucial issue. Outgoing calls from the US based on satellite telephony are cheap: that allows non-US phone monopolies to charge high prices to connect overseas phone calls and to increase their rents. As a result, the US wanted to grant applications to operate services out of the US only to the foreign phone companies which could not use domestic market power. During the negotiations attached to the First WTO Ministerial Conference (held in Singapore, in December 1996), some progress was made. The EC improved its offer, essentially by including Spain in it (initially, Spain enjoyed a slower pace of liberalization in the SMP). The same is expected from a few other countries.

# IV    What Lessons?

This section draws two general lessons from the last decade of EC and WTO negotiations in services and the few years of EC implementation. These lessons concern the instruments of service liberalization and the role of competition policy in the WTO context.

*Instruments: second thoughts?*

As mentioned above, the SMP is built on the concept of 'mutual recognition' as elaborated by the European Court of Justice. Does the experience of the last years suggest lessons about the most appropriate instruments for service liberalization?

There are four major options for eliminating the protectionist aspect of regulations and opening markets: no regulation at all, unconditional mutual recognition of the existing regulations, conditional mutual recognition of these regulations, or full harmonization. The option of no regulation is the only one which is not always possible since regulations have other goals than to protect the producers. Unconditional mutual recognition means that for the service considered, a country recognizes the regulations of its trading partner being as valid as its own regulations. Under conditional mutual recognition, a country shall adopt a common core of minimal provisions (minimal harmonization *ex ante* and / or *ex post*) before benefiting from the recognition of the rest of its own regulations by its trading partners (and vice versa).

These four options can be ranked by decreasing order of trust and by increasing order of legislative work load. Under the no regulation option, the country trusts the regulations existing in its trading partners as much as its own (or it distrusts the foreign regulations as much as its own). Harmonization implies the absence of any noticeable trust. Conditional and unconditional mutual recognition correspond to intermediate situations – conditional being closer to harmonization, unconditional to no regulation. Countries tend to choose the option which they believe offers the best trade-off between demanded trust and legislative cost. If the four options are ordered on a horizontal axis (from no regulation to harmonization) as in figure 9.1, trust can be illustrated by a declining demand-type curve, and the legislative work load by an increasing cost-type curve. Other things being constant, the best option (equilibrium) is illustrated by the intersection point of the marginal curves of these two aspects.

Figure 9.1 allows us to sketch the EC history (and it would be interesting to check whether it fits the APEC major programme of mutual recognition agreements).[11] At the beginning of the EC, the equilibrium point A corresponded to full harmonization: demanded trust was high, and the legislative costs imposed by the unanimity voting system of the Community of the early days were also high. The crucial Cassis de Dijon ruling of the Court of Justice shifted down the level of trust required within the EC: taken literally, it would have shifted the equilibrium strongly leftwards to point B – towards unconditional mutual recognition. But, this move was limited by two forces which left the equilibrium point more in the direction of harmonization, at the point C corresponding to conditional mutual recognition (the favoured instrument of the SMP). First, the SMP was initiated in 1985, that is, the year of the adoption of the Single European Act establishing a majority-based voting system in the EC – hence shifting down the cost curve. Second, the full application of the Cassis de Dijon ruling threatened the rents associated with closed service sectors. Governments showed their readiness to protect their domestic vested interests by adopting new regulations in order to raise new barriers and by 'co-operating' with (often public) incumbents – in other words, all actions which shifted the trust curve up again .

Since the early 1990s, it has become increasingly clear that the adoption of conditional mutual recognition has not solved the costs associated with the *enforcement* of the new regulations. The impact of this last factor may push the equilibrium in two opposite directions.[12] First, it can shift upward *both* the trust demand and the legislative (now including enforcement) costs: hence it can shift back the equilibrium towards harmonization (point A). Second, it can induce Member states

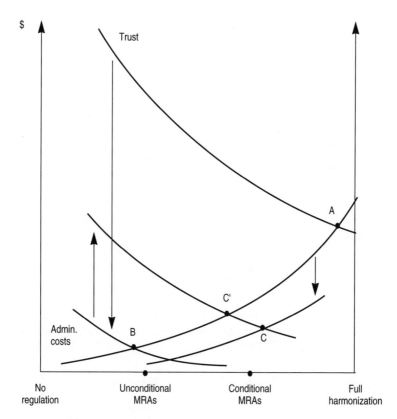

**Figure 9.1**  Trust, regulation and administrative costs in the European Community

which trust each other to conclude agreements limited to themselves – shifting back these countries to the point C of unconditional mutual recognition. Such moves, which generate sub-regional (often bilateral) agreements, have been observed recently, such as in the 'standards' area (Neven 1996).[13]

If correct, this sketch of the EC history suggests two observations for the WTO. First, the harmonization point is unlikely to be reached for many services in the WTO context because the WTO includes more countries that are more different than the EC – two factors which tend to increase initial distrust and high administrative costs.

Second, the fact that unconditional mutual recognition may be the best instrument of service liberalization in the future has important consequences. It suggests that the geographical scope of WTO agreements having some substance may well be limited for a long time: regional or *ad hoc* plurilateral agreements could be the main support of service liberalization within the WTO for a long time to come.

In fact, such a variable geometry within the WTO is not very surprising. It reflects the idea that trade liberalization in services is not a 'natural' idea. It requires governments sufficiently interested in good governance to bet on 'unilateralism', as was the case for trade in goods during the nineteenth century (with some premium attached to such efforts to 'be the first'). Ideally, such a variable geometry could include efforts aiming at favouring the multilateralization of the plurilateral agreements. For instance, there could be *ex ante* conditions stating that any country which has not some well-defined type of protection (some types of rules or kinds of institutions judged as particularly protective) can be automatically accepted as a member of the existing agreement.

Such an approach is particularly well fitted for allowing developing countries to be involved as soon as possible in a liberalization deal for a given service. Developing countries would be included in such a deal as long as they do not use specific instruments for protecting this service sector at home. A return to the more traditional mercantilist approach of requesting specific market access commitments would be postponed until the time when the developing country concerned would have a sector of noticeable size in the service under discussion. This approach is consistent with the 'progressive liberalization' concept of the GATS, and it is more economically sound.

*Competition law in the WTO and service liberalization*[14]

Over the past few years, there have been many advocates of competition provisions at the WTO level. Certain motivations for such provisions are related to problems encountered in the product area (such as anti-dumping), but other motivations are related to services. Indeed, the dominant role of the European Court of Justice in EC service liberalization has shown how powerful competition institutions and rules can be when dealing with service liberalization – both for launching the process and for monitoring its evolution. As seen above, such types of issues are raised nowadays by the mega-alliances in air transport or banking (credit-card networks).

Among the many competition issues, one problem dominates all the others: the risk of confusion between regulatory reforms and competition policy which could easily generate obstacles to market liberalization, rather than facilitate it. This point deserves some attention.

Service liberalization requires the definition of new rules favouring the emergence *and* the survival of new competitors. These new rules brought by 'regulatory reforms' are different, by nature, from competition rules for three reasons: they are sector-specific, often generating *ad hoc* competition bodies and rules; they are transitory and should last only during the transition period necessary for shifting from the 'state planned' situation to full competition; and they can be extremely intrusive, limiting competition from incumbents in order to protect entrants. In the long run, these regulatory reforms should be dismantled, and replaced by the perennial and horizontal approach of competition law, with its general procedures and rules. Confusing regulatory reforms and competition law will weaken both competition policy and WTO: sectoral competition regulations and bodies will be detrimental to the unifying role of central competition law and authorities; and they will be inconsistent with the implicit WTO approach of non-discrimination between economic activities.

The April 1996 WTO Draft for telecommunications illustrates these issues.[15] The Draft refers to the notion of a 'major' supplier which does not correspond to any concept of competition policy (monopolizing or dominant firm). It defines it as a supplier with the 'ability to materially affect the terms of participation (having regard to price and supply)' in the market for telecommunication services as a result of 'control over essential facilities' or 'use of its position in the market'. This lax definition can be easily used as a basis for protectionist decisions. Moreover, the Draft sketches 'competitive safeguards' (a nicely ambiguous expression) against anti-competitive practices which could include engaging 'in anti-competitive cross-subsidisation' (without any reference to some critical level of subsidisation, nor to injury and causal relationships), 'using information obtained from competitors with anti-competitive results' (without defining 'results') and 'not making available to other suppliers on a timely basis technical information about essential facilities and commercially relevant information' (without defining 'timely'). Far from being competition rules, most of these points are traditional elements of market access (subsidies, non-discriminatory access to information, etc.) immersed in the notion of 'fair' competition, rather than 'free' competition. These ambiguities may be the price to be paid for a transitory step towards freer markets. But then, the transitory situation of regulatory reforms should be clearly distinguished from the targeted final situation of free competition.

### Notes

I would like to thank S. Chirathivat, R. Langhammer and all the participants to the Japan–Europe Symposium for their very helpful comments and suggestions. All remaining errors are mine.

1   That is best illustrated by the audiovisual sector. If there are a substantial number of EC broadcasters which have invested in other Member states, none has really tried to create cross-border activities (except, purely pan-European satellite-broadcasters, most of them being US based, either fully such as CNN, or partly, such as the Murdoch-Fox group).

2   Independently from the fact that the often wide differences between the environments of incumbent firms in regulated and in competitive markets did indeed make the proper comparisons more difficult.

3   What follows focuses on passenger transport. Air cargo is not an essential aspect of European airlines – contrary to what happens in Asia. During the 1980s, the average growth rate of air cargo in Europe has been half of the rate in Asia-Pacific, and 15 per cent smaller than the rate in North America. That mirrors the fact that European surface transport is very competitive (and favoured by short distances and state subsidies).

4   For instance, the state aids granted to Air France represent 11 per cent of Air France revenues, or almost half a million French francs ($100,000) per employee. This chapter discusses only public subsidies disbursed by governments. But, there are more hidden subsidies. For instance, the AOM airline has received more cash (as a percentage of revenues) from Crédit Lyonnais (a nationalized bank close to bankruptcy) than Air France from the French government. On the other hand, European airlines have been taxed through the obligation to buy Airbus aircraft at higher prices than market-driven prices.

5   The non-subsidised firm, knowing the constraints imposed on the subsidised firm, can act strategically on the routes under constraints, hence on related routes. For instance, it needs to reduce prices or increase quantities only to the extent necessary to undercut slightly the subsidised airline. It can then focus on other routes, in order to get more competitive advantages.

6   However, the evolution of the BA–US Air case makes it hard to know the real future of these emerging mega-alliances.

7   As usual, competition can take many aspects. For instance, Heathrow may benefit from the fact that because Britain has not signed the Schengen

Convention, travellers from the US to Frankfurt via Heathrow do not have to clear customs at Heathrow, but at Frankfurt. Travellers from the US to Frankfurt via Paris have to clear customs at Paris (and not at Frankfurt). Taking into account the time of arrival (very early morning), regular travellers from the US probably prefer Heathrow.

8   The evolution of the British–US negotiations on Heathrow will be extremely interesting from this point of view: they will reveal the level of competition British and US governments are eager to give up for building mega-carriers.

9   This result reduces by half the gap between the EC and Japan. However, Japan remains an atypical country, with a huge share (almost 41%) of deals in the US market.

10   It seems that this estimate will be effectively reached in 1997.

11   APEC has launched such a programme according to a predetermined timetable for the following sectors: foodstuffs, toys, telecommunications equipment, electrical and electronic goods.

12   This conclusion is very similar to the conclusion reached by Neven (1996).

13   R. Langhammer has kindly provided me information gathered by R. Vaubel. According to Vaubel, there has not been any mutual recognition according to Article 100b of the Treaty of Rome (that is, unconditional mutual recognition at the EC level).

14   This subsection draws heavily on Messerlin (1996).

15   What follows is based on the summary of the draft published by *Inside US Trade* (26 April 1996). Similar conclusions are reached by Hoekman, Low and Mavroidis (1996).

## References

Beesley, M.E. (ed.) (1996) *Regulating Utilities: A Time for Change?* Institute of Economic Affairs, Readings 44.

Dermine, Jean (1996) 'International Trade in Banking', in Claude E. Barfield (ed.), *International Financial Markets: Harmonization versus Competition*, American Enterprise Institute.

European Commission (DG-XV) (1996a) *The Single Market and Tomorrow's Europe*, European Office of Official Publications, Luxembourg.

European Commission (DG-II) (1996b) 'The Review of the 1992 Single Market Programme', forthcoming in *European Economy*.

Federal Reserve Bank of St. Louis (1995), *Antitrust Issues and Payment Systems Networks*, vol. 77, no. 6, November–December.

Hoekman, Bernard, Patrick Low, and Petros Mavroidis (1996) Antitrust Disciplines and Market Access Negotiations: Lessons from the Telecommunications Sector, mimeo, World Bank and World Trade Organization.

Messerlin, Patrick A. (1996) 'Competition Law and Antidumping Regulations: An Exercise in Transition', in Jeffrey J. Schott (ed.), *The World Trading System: Challenges Ahead*, The Institute for International Economics, Washington.

Neven, Damien J. (1992), 'Regulatory Reform in the European Community', *American Economic Review*, vol. 82, no. 2, May, pp. 98–103.

—— (1996) Regulatory Reform and the Internal Market, mimeo, OECD.

Sapir, André (1991) From Fragmentation to Restructuring of Service Markets in the European Community, mimeo, European Commission.

Snape, Richard H. and Malcolm Bosworth (1996) Advancing Services Negotiations, mimeo, The Institute for International Economics.

Steil, Benn (1995) *Illusions of Liberalisation: Securities Regulation in Japan and the EC*, The Royal Institute of International Affairs and Japan Institute of International Affairs.

# Index